THE LURE OF
FANTASY ISLAM

THE LURE OF FANTASY ISLAM

Exposing the Myths and Myth Makers

Stephen M. Kirby Ph.D.

ISBN-10: 1546316973

ISBN-13: 978-1546316978

CreateSpace
Charleston, South Carolina

The Canon of Islam

Islam does not, like Christianity, have a clergy. There is no temporal or even spiritual institute that holds it together or unifies it. So how has it held together—and indeed, flourished—for the last fourteen centuries approximately, when its scholars and temporal policymakers keep changing and dying out over time? How has it remained so homogeneous that the Islam of 1900 CE was doctrinally exactly the same as the Islam of 700 CE? Where have its internal checks and balances come from?

The answer is that Islam has a traditional canon: a collection of sacred texts which everyone has agreed are authoritative and definitive, and which 'fix' the principles of belief, practice, law, theology and doctrine throughout the ages. All that Muslim scholars (called ulema and muftis or sheikhs and imams) have left to do is to interpret these texts and work out their practical applications and details (and the principles of interpretation and elaboration are themselves 'fixed' by these texts), so that in Islam a person is only considered learned to the extent that he can demonstrate his knowledge of these texts. This does not mean that Islam is a religion of limitations for these texts are a vast ocean and their principles can be inwardly worked out almost infinitely in practice. It does mean, however, that Islam is 'fixed' and has certain limits beyond which it will not go.

The Muslim 500 – The World's 500 Most Influential Muslims 2016, The Royal Islamic Strategic Studies Centre (Amman, Jordan), p. 23

Islamic Modernism

Islamic modernism is a reform movement started by politically-minded urbanites with scant knowledge of traditional Islam. These people had witnessed and studied Western technology and socio-political ideas, and realized that the Islamic world was being left behind technologically by the West and had become too weak to stand up to it. They blamed this weakness on what they saw as 'traditional Islam,' which they thought held them back and was not 'progressive' enough. They thus called for a complete overhaul of Islam, including—or rather in particular—Islamic law (sharia) and doctrine (aqida). Islamic modernism remains popularly an object of derision and ridicule, and is scorned by traditional Muslims and fundamentalists alike.

The Muslim 500 – The World's 500 Most Influential Muslims 2016, The Royal Islamic Strategic Studies Centre (Amman, Jordan), p. 31

Innovation is Heresy

Muhammad said: *The most truthful speech is Allah's Speech, and the best guidance is the guidance of Muhammad. The worst matters are the newly invented (in religion), every newly invented matter is an innovation, and every innovation is a heresy, and every heresy is in the Fire.*

Tafsir Ibn Kathir, Vol. 2, p. 588

Muhammad bin Jarir reported that Ibn 'Abbas said that the Prophet said, 'Whoever explains the Qur'an with his opinion or with what he has no knowledge of, then let him assume his seat in the Fire.'

Tafsir Ibn Kathir, Vol. 1, pp. 32-33

It was narrated from Ibn 'Abbas that the Messenger of Allah said: "Whoever denies a Verse of the Qur'an, it is permissible to strike his neck (i.e. execute him)..."

Sunan Ibn Majah, Vol. 3, No. 2539, p. 455

Table of Contents

Introduction

Fantasy Islam: A game in which an audience of non-Muslims wish with all their hearts that Islam was a "Religion of Peace," and a Muslim strives to fulfill that wish by presenting a personal version of Islam that has little foundation in Islamic Doctrine.

Fantasy Islam is perhaps the largest obstacle to the understanding of Islam. The Islam I am talking about is the religion commanded by Allah, as found in the verses of the Koran, and taught by Allah's prophet Muhammad, as found in authoritative biographies, histories, and reports (*hadiths*) about the teachings of Muhammad. This is supplemented by the writings of authoritative Muslim scholars that are based on the Koran and the teachings of Muhammad.

On the other hand, there are Muslims who feel that they can come up with their own versions of Islam, usually in an attempt to "modernize" that religion, or make it more compatible with their own personal beliefs. They decide on their own which verses of the Koran and teachings of Muhammad should have doctrinal authority, simply ignoring conflicting verses and teachings. And they often make up their own history of Islam, and their own interpretations of Koran verses, even if these personal versions have no basis in history or Islamic Doctrine. Nevertheless, they are given credibility because they are Muslims. This is *Fantasy Islam*.

Over a number of years I have written numerous articles with the *Fantasy Islam* theme. Some of the articles also addressed non-Muslims, so I coined the term *Fantasy Islam (Kafir Edition)*:

> *Fantasy Islam (Kafir Edition): A game in which an audience of non-Muslims wish with all their hearts that Islam was a "Religion of Peace," and a Kafir (non-Muslim) strives to fulfill that wish by presenting a version of Islam that has little foundation in Islamic Doctrine.*

This book is an anthology of those *Fantasy Islam* themed and related articles.

Fantasy Islam is an obstacle to understanding Islam because there is such a contrast between the two "versions" of Islam. As you will see in these articles, *Fantasy Islam* is very appealing to non-Muslims, but has virtually no support in the larger Muslim community (*ummah*), even in the United States. This lack of support from other Muslims should be a wake-up call for those non-Muslims who have succumbed to the lure of *Fantasy Islam*.

These articles are as they were submitted to the respective publications. Due to space limitations for articles, the footnotes for many of these articles were originally abbreviated; the format of the footnotes has now been adapted to the book format. Hyperlinks in the articles have been changed to footnotes.

Stephen M. Kirby
May 1, 2017

Fantasy Islam

Fantasy Islam: A game in which an audience of non-Muslims wish with all their hearts that Islam was a "Religion of Peace," and a Muslim strives to fulfill that wish by presenting a personal version of Islam that has little foundation in Islamic Doctrine.

Stephen M. Kirby

1

The Lure of Fantasy Islam[1]

Fantasy sports such as football and baseball have become increasingly popular on the internet. For those not familiar with fantasy sports, the emphasis is on fantasy. The simple explanation is that you pretend to be the owner of a team, join a pretend league which has other pretend teams, and then man your team with actual professional players from that particular sport. In this fantasy world you can pick players from any team to be a member of your own team.

When it comes to Islam, there is a similar world that has been created. In this world there are two teams involved, of differing sizes and membership, and interacting at different times and places. The large team consists of a group of non-Muslims who know little if anything about Islam, generally wish with all of their hearts that it is a "Religion of Peace," seem to prefer any presentation that will support that wish, and frown on anyone who expresses skepticism about that wish during the presentation, or afterwards. The small team usually consists of one Muslim making a presentation that largely fulfills the wish of the large team. The accuracy of the presentation is not questioned because the presenter has already established his credentials simply by being a Muslim.

In this world of Fantasy Islam, the presenter is able to create his own version of Islam, react with patronizing sympathy or condescending dismissiveness toward any non-Muslim who questions his version, and

---

[1] This article first appeared in *FrontPage Mag* on July 8, 2015: http://www.frontpagemag.com/fpm/259380/lure-fantasy-islam-dr-stephen-m-kirby.

knows that the majority of his audience will support him in maintaining the comfort of this fantasy.

Since the make-up of the large team changes regularly and this team is the more passive of the two, let's look at two of the individuals who have appeared on the small team:

Dr. M. Zuhdi Jasser, MD

Dr. M. Zuhdi Jasser is the Muslim Founder and President of the American Islamic Forum for Democracy (AIFD). He is well-known as a proponent of reforming and modernizing Islam, and for years has been a guest on countless television and radio programs. Unfortunately, for years Jasser has also played Fantasy Islam.

Mickelson in the Morning

We can go back to October 11, 2010 when Jasser was on a major Iowa radio station with host Jan Mickelson here. During the interview,[2] Jasser said he didn't believe that Muhammad had really spoken what was in the *hadith* about killing a Jew hiding behind every stone (Time: 17:58). Here is that *hadith*:

> *Narrated Abu Hurairah: Allah's Messenger said, "The Hour will not be established until you fight against the Jews, and the stone behind which a Jew will be hiding will say, 'O Muslim! There is a Jew hiding behind me, so kill him.'"*[3]

---

[2]   http://mickelson.libsyn.com/monday-october-11-2010

[3]   Muhammad bin Ismail bin Al-Mughirah al-Bukhari, *Sahih Al-Bukhari*, trans. Muhammad Muhsin Khan (Riyadh, Kingdom of Saudi Arabia: Darussalam, 1997), Vol. 4, Book 56, No. 2926, p. 113.

The collection of *hadiths* by Al-Bukhari has been considered by Muslim scholars to be the most authoritative collect of *hadiths* since the 9th Century. Jasser simply has no doctrinal basis for dismissing Al-Bukhari.

Later in the same program, Jasser talked about the Verse of the Sword in the Koran (Time: 24:09 and 26:20). He said that this verse only referred to a specific battle against a specific tribe and applied only to 623 AD; it no longer had any relevance today. Here is that verse:

> *Then when the Sacred Months have passed, then kill the Mushrikun wherever you find them, and capture them and besiege them, and lie in wait for them in every ambush. But if they repent [by rejecting Shirk (polytheism) and accept Islamic Monotheism] and perform As-Salat (the prayers), and give Zakat (obligatory charity), then leave their way free. Verily, Allah is Oft-Forgiving, Most Merciful.*
>
> Chapter 9, Verse 5

Where did he come up with 623 AD? 9:5 was among the verses from Chapter 9 that were revealed in early 631 AD. And these verses were not related to a specific battle or to a specific tribe, but rather directed toward all non-Muslims.[4]

There is no basis in Islamic doctrine for Jasser's assertion that 9:5 has no relevance today. His assertion ignores the facts that Muslims believe the

---

[4]   Muhammad ibn Ishaq, *The Life of Muhammad (Sirat Rasul Allah)*, trans. Alfred Guillaume (Karachi, Pakistan: Oxford University Press, 2007), pp. 617-619; Abu Ja'far Muhammad b. Jarir al-Tabari, *The History of al-Tabari: The Last Years of the Prophet*, trans. and annotated Ismail K. Poonawala (Albany, New York: State University of New York Press, 1990), Vol. IX, pp. 77-79; and Abu al-Fida' 'Imad Ad-Din Isma'il bin 'Umar bin Kathir al-Qurashi Al-Busrawi, *Tafsir Ibn Kathir* (Abridged), abr. Shaykh Safiur-Rahman al-Mubarakpuri, trans. Jalal Abualrub, et al. (Riyadh, Kingdom of Saudi Arabia: Darussalam, 2000), Vol. 4, pp. 370-376.

Koran consists of the eternal words of Allah, and Chapter 9 of the Koran was the last chapter to be "revealed" to Muhammad. Consequently, the commands found in Chapter 9 are the final, eternal words of Allah on the matters addressed in that Chapter.

Abraham's Tent

Over the years Jasser has continued playing Fantasy Islam. He was interviewed on a segment of the *Abraham's Tent* radio program, which was aired on September 29, 2014.[5] In this interview he made his standard assertion that 5:51 of the Koran, which commands Muslims not to be friends with Jews and Christians, had been intentionally misinterpreted (Time: 25:38). Here is that verse:

> *O you who believe! Take not the Jews and the Christians as Auliya' (friends, protectors, helpers), they are but Auliya' of each other. And if any amongst you takes them as Auliya', then surely, he is one of them. Verily, Allah guides not those people who are the Zalimun (polytheists and wrongdoers and unjust).*

Jasser claimed that *Auliya'* really meant "legal representatives." He said this verse simply meant that when it came to picking such a representative, Muslims should pick someone who understands the legalisms in Islam, meaning a Muslim, and not somebody of another faith. It had nothing to do with prohibiting Muslims from being friends with Jews and Christians.

Once again Jasser is flying in the face of Islamic doctrine. As I pointed out in an earlier article,[6] in 5:51 Allah commands Muslims not to be friends with Jews and Christians. And, as I also pointed out in that article,

---

[5]   http://www.abrahamstentradio.com/archives/AT092914.mp3

[6]   Stephen M. Kirby, "Don't Take Jews and Christians as Friends?" *FrontPage Mag*, May 10, 2015: http://www.frontpagemag.com/2015/dr-stephen-m-kirby/dont-take-jews-and-christians-as-friends/.

this understanding is supported by five modern translations of the Koran; the messages of additional verses of the Koran; five authoritative Koran commentaries, written at different times between circa 900-1995 AD; and the teachings of Muhammad.

Jasser also expressed the basis for his Fantasy Islam: "Every Muslim has the right to interpret their faith." (Time: 29:11). This too flies in the face of Islamic doctrine, e.g.:

> *Muhammad bin Jarir reported that Ibn 'Abbas said that the Prophet said, 'Whoever explains the Qur'an with his opinion or with what he has no knowledge of, then let him assume his seat in the Fire.'[7]*

In this interview Jasser suggested that 5:38 of the Koran, which commands amputation for theft, was "metaphorical" and "not literal" (Time 54:25). Here is that verse:

> *And (as for) the male thief and the female thief, cut off (from the wrist joint) their (right) hands as a recompense for that which they committed, a punishment by way of example from Allah. And Allah is All-Powerful, All-Wise.*

Not only is this verse not a metaphor, it is explicit in commanding the amputation of hands for theft. In addition, Muhammad, who is the example of conduct for Muslims, ordered the hands of many thieves to be cut off; he even said he would cut off the hand of his favorite daughter if she committed theft.[8]

---

[7]   *Tafsir Ibn Kathir*, Vol. 1, pp. 32-33.

[8]   *Sahih Al-Bukhari*, Vol. 5, Book 64, No. 4304, pp. 361-361.

6

A Battle for the Soul of Islam

In 2013 the paperback edition of Jasser's widely acclaimed book *A Battle for the Soul of Islam* was published. After reading only the eleventh chapter, "How the Qur'an is Misinterpreted," I decided not to read the rest of the book.

Jasser's version of Fantasy Islam is best epitomized in this eleventh chapter with the following statement he wrote on p. 252:

> *Nowhere in the Qur'an does God tell Muslims that they must repeat and thus emulate the Prophet Muhammad's role and actions as a military or governmental leader.*

This statement is immediately repudiated by 33:21 of the Koran:

> *Indeed in the Messenger of Allah (Muhammad) you have a good example to follow for him who hopes for (the Meeting with) Allah and the Last Day, and remembers Allah much.*

There are no limitations here on the circumstances in which Muhammad is to be considered a good example. In fact, this verse was actually "revealed" as a result of Muhammad's military leadership and the example he set for his Muslim warriors during the Battle of the Trench in 627.[9]

Since 33:21 is a verse that counters Jasser's Fantasy Islam, he has apparently decided to deny it, which means he has apparently also decided to ignore this warning from his prophet Muhammad:

---

[9]   *Tafsir Ibn Kathir*, Vol. 7, p. 658; Jalalu'd-Din al-Mahalli and Jalalu'd-Din as-Suyuti, *Tafsir Al-Jalalayn*, trans. Aisha Bewley (London: Dar Al Taqwa Ltd., 2007), p. 900; *Tafsir Ibn 'Abbas*, trans. Mokrane Guezzou (Louisville, KY: Fons Vitae, 2008), p. 546; and Salahuddin Yusuf, *Tafsir Ahsanul-Bayan*, trans. Mohammad Kamal Myshkat (Riyadh, Kingdom of Saudi Arabia: Darussalam, 2010), Vol. 4, p. 374.

*It was narrated from Ibn 'Abbas that the Messenger of
Allah said: "Whoever denies a Verse of the Qur'an, it is
permissible to strike his neck (i.e. execute him)..."[10]*

Dr. Syed Mohiuddin

Dr. Syed Mohiuddin is President of the American Muslim Institute (AMI),
the Muslim group involved in building a new mosque as part of the Tri-
Faith Initiative in Omaha, Nebraska. I recently attended a presentation he
made at St. Pius X Catholic Church in Omaha. The presentation was titled
The True Nature of Islam. Here is how Mohiuddin presented "the true
nature" of Islam.

When asked about the treatment of women, Mohiuddin assured the
audience that the Koran repeatedly stated that men and women were equal,
without, however, mentioning any supporting verses. In reality, the Koran
says that it takes the testimony of two women to equal that of one man
(2:282); a woman is to receive only half the inheritance of a man (4:12); a
Muslim woman can only marry a Muslim man (2:221), while Muslim men
can marry Jews and Christians (5:5) and have up to four wives (4:3).

Mohiuddin was wise not to mention things that Muhammad said about
women, e.g.:

*It is not wise for anyone of you to lash his wife like a
slave, for he might sleep with her the same evening.[11]*

*Treat women well, for they are [like] domestic animals
with you and do not possess anything for themselves.[12]*

---

[10]   Muhammad bin Yazeed ibn Majah al-Qazwini, *Sunan Ibn Majah*, trans.
Nasiruddin al-Khattab (Riyadh, Kingdom of Saudi Arabia: Darussalam, 2007),
Vol. 3, No. 2539, p. 455.

[11]   *Sahih Al-Bukhari*, Vol. 6, Book 65, No. 4942, p. 392.

[12]   *The History of al-Tabari: The Last Years of the Prophet*, p. 113.

8

Mohiuddin was asked why, if Islam says we are all brothers and sisters, do we see beheading of Christians on the beaches of Libya? He replied that Islam,

> *if practiced appropriately and correctly, would never, never allow that... And the true Muslims in true Islamic countries would never allow that to happen.*

In reality, there are two verses in the Koran (8:12 and 47:4) and numerous *hadiths* that allow Muslims to behead people, even captive non-combatants.

Mohiuddin said there were "major differences" in how the Koran was interpreted. And he said there were instances when people added their own thoughts to provide an incorrect interpretation. He gave an example from *Al-Fatihah*, the first chapter of the Koran, in which he said the translator had included in parenthesis the words "Jews" and "Christians" to explain "those who go astray" (1:7). For some reason, much of the audience laughed when he said this.

In reality, Muhammad himself said that the Christians had gone astray,[13] and it was also an accepted belief among later Muslim scholars that the Jews too had gone astray.[14] But in Mohiuddin's version of Islam, this was a bad translation.

I asked Mohiuddin to explain the Doctrine of Abrogation. His first response was to confuse it with apostasy. To prompt him a bit, I pointed out that abrogation meant that when there was a conflict between the meanings of two verses, the verse "revealed" later would supersede the earlier verse (meaning that the belligerent Medinan verses found in Chapter 9 supersede the peaceful Meccan verses elsewhere in the Koran).

---

[13]   *Tafsir Ibn Kathir*, Vol. 4, p. 410; and Abu 'Abdullah Muhammad ibn Ahmad al-Ansari al-Qurtubi, *Tafsir Al-Qurtubi: Classical Commentary of the Holy Qur'an*, trans. Aisha Bewley (London: Dar Al Taqwa Ltd., 2003), Vol. 1, p. 127.

[14]   *Tafsir Ibn Kathir*, Vol. 1, p. 87.

I asked him to comment on this principle. After some general, and not necessarily germane remarks, he concluded by saying that the message "was the first one which supersedes the other one."

The Doctrine of Abrogation is fundamental to understanding the messages of the Koran. How can one talk about the "true nature of Islam" without understanding the Doctrine of Abrogation?

When asked about 5:51, which prohibits Muslims from being friends with Jews and Christians, Mohiuddin said this verse only referred to a specific tribe of people during a specific time of war. He said this verse had to be specific to a time and tribe because of the other verses in the Koran that "repeatedly emphasized the importance of" Jews and Christians. He did not mention any supporting Koran verses.

So let's consider some supporting Koran verses that emphasize Jews and Christians: Allah is angry with the Jews, and the Christians are misguided because they believe that Jesus is the son of God (1:7); Jews are among the worst enemies of Islam (5:82); Muslims are commanded to fight Jews and Christians until the Jews and Christians pay protection money with willing submission and feel themselves subdued (9:29); Allah curses the Jews and the Christians (9:30); and Jews and Christians are among the worst of creatures and "will abide in the fire of Hell" (98:6).

These verses show us that Jews and Christians are certainly important to Islam, but not in the positive way implied by Mohiuddin.

In hindsight, Mohiuddin's presentation should have been titled *Dr. Mohiuddin's Personal Impressions of Islam*, or more simply, *Fantasy Islam*. After the presentation, the audience of 60-70 people walked out misinformed, but also feeling comforted about Islam; the latter which, from the apparent attitude of the hosts and much of the audience, appeared to be the main purpose of the event.

Conclusion

For many years non-Muslims in the West have been fed a steady diet of how Islam is a "Religion of Peace" and is similar, and even related to, Judaism and Christianity. At the same time we have seen an increasing number of acts of violence done in the name of Islam.

For those willing to learn and investigate, the irrefutable conclusion is that most, if not all, of the violent acts committed by the *jihadists* are truly supported by Islamic doctrine, just as the *jihadists* themselves claim. But this conclusion can create a cognitive dissonance between what we have heard about Islam and what we see actually being done in the name of Islam and supported by Islamic doctrine. This dissonance can create stress. The antidote to this stress for many is to turn to Fantasy Islam, where Islam is what any peaceful-sounding Muslim wants it to be, and the *jihadists* are the hijacking outliers.

But this is only a temporary resolution. Just because you continue to ignore the reality of Islam, doesn't mean that the reality of Islam will continue to ignore you. The Christians in the Middle East and Africa are the canaries in the coal mine.

The Fantasy Islam of
Mike Mohamed Ghouse[15]

As I pointed out in an earlier article,[16] *Fantasy Islam* is a popular game among many non-Muslims and so-called "moderate" or "reformist" Muslims. Mike Mohamed Ghouse appears to be such a Muslim.

Ghouse was born Mohamed Ghouse in India (He adopted the name Mike later). He was raised as a Muslim until he became an atheist in the late 1960's; he returned to Islam in the late 1990's and lives in the United States. Ghouse is a frequent guest commentator on Fox News and syndicated talk radio programs, and he writes for major newspapers. Ghouse also plays *Fantasy Islam*.

Apostasy

In an article titled *Quraan on Apostasy*,[17] Ghouse makes the following claim about the punishment for apostasy:

---

[15]   This article first appeared in *FrontPage Mag* on September 3, 2015: http://www.frontpagemag.com/fpm/259994/fantasy-islam-mike-mohamed-ghouse-dr-stephen-m-kirby.

[16]   Kirby, "The Lure of Fantasy Islam."

[17]   Mike Ghouse, "Quraan on Apostasy," *Qur'aan Today*, August 9, 2009; accessed at: http://quraan-today.blogspot.com/2009/08/quraan-on-apostasy.html.

Unfortunately, it is a common belief that 'death' should be the punishment for apostasy. However, the Qur'aan mentions nothing of such punishment, so why should we impose such a cruel and inhumane form of punishment? Are we so insecure about our own religion that if anyone is to leave it we kill them?

But Ghouse is wrong, because in 4:89 of the Koran Allah commands Muslims to take hold of those apostates who have left Islam and "kill them wherever you find them."

And, for the sake of argument, even if it wasn't in the Koran, death for apostasy is still a part of Islam because that is what Muhammad commanded. Muhammad said that death was the penalty for a Muslim who left Islam.[18] And Muhammad even specified the nature of that death:

If someone changes his religion - then strike off his head![19]

So we see that this *cruel and inhumane form of punishment* for apostasy is well-grounded in Islamic doctrine.

Muslim-Americans "uphold" the U.S. Constitution

In an article titled *Muslims are an integral part of American Heritage,*[20] Ghouse made the following statement:

---

[18]　E.g., *Sahih Al-Bukhari*, Vol. 9, Book 87, No. 6878, p. 20, and Book 88, No. 6923, pp. 46-47; and Abu'l Hussain 'Asakir-ud-Din Muslim bin Hajjaj al-Qushayri al-Naisaburi, *Sahih Muslim*, trans. 'Abdul Hamid Siddiqi (New Delhi, India: Adam Publishers and Distributors, 2008), Vol. 5, No. 1676, pp. 118-119.

[19]　Malik ibn Anas ibn Malik ibn Abi 'Amir al-Asbahi, *Al-Muwatta of Imam Malik ibn Anas: The First Formulation of Islamic Law*, trans. Aisha Abdurrahman Bewley (Inverness, Scotland: Madinah Press, 2004), 36.18.15, in a section titled "Judgement on Abandonment of Islam."

As American Muslims we uphold, protect, defend and celebrate the values enshrined in the U.S. constitution.

Islamic doctrine, found in the verses of the Koran and the teachings of Muhammad (the *Sunnah*), is diametrically opposed to the U.S. Constitution. Consider just these three Amendments to our Constitution:

1st Amendment – Freedom of Religion and Speech: The penalty for a Muslim who wants to leave Islam is death (4:89 and *Sunnah*). Non-Muslims are given the option of fighting to the death, converting to Islam, or paying the jizyah (9:5, 9:29, and *Sunnah*). Once Allah and Muhammad have decided on a matter, Muslims are not allowed to disagree (33:36, 4:115), and criticism of Muhammad is cursed by Allah and punishable by death (33:57, and *Sunnah*).

8th Amendment – Cruel and Unusual Punishment is Prohibited: Islam commands the following punishments: Flogging (24:2), Stoning (*Sunnah*), Amputation for Theft (5:38 and *Sunnah*), Beheading (8:12, 47:4, and *Sunnah*), Crucifixion (5:33), and Cutting-off of Hands and Feet from Opposite Sides for waging war against Islam (5:33).

13th Amendment – Prohibition of Slavery: Slavery, and using captured non-Muslim women as sex slaves (*those whom your right hands possess*) is allowed in Islam (e.g., 2:221, 4:3, 4:24, 4:92, 23:6, 24:58, 33:50, and *Sunnah*).

So just by considering these three Amendments, we can see that if Muslim-Americans believe in Islamic Doctrine, they cannot *uphold, protect, defend and celebrate the values enshrined in the U.S. constitution.*

---

[20]   Mike Ghouse, "Happy 4th – Muslims are an Integral Part of American Heritage," *The Ghouse Diary*, July 3, 2015; accessed at: http://theghousediary.blogspot.com/2015/07/happy-4th-muslims-are-integral-part-of.html.

The "best way to understand" the Koran

What is the "best way" to understand the Koran? Ghouse wrote this simple explanation:[21]

> *The best way to understand Quran [sic] is to remember, "If it is not about justice, mercy and creating harmony", then the translation is wrong.*

The immediate response to Ghouse's statement is to look at the preceding section involving the three Amendments to our Constitution. There is little justice, mercy and harmony there.

But Ghouse also said that Marmaduke Pickthall's translation of the Koran, *The Meaning of the Glorious Koran*, was one of three translations he recommended.[22] So let's look for the justice, mercy and harmony in some of the verses from Pickthall's translation:[23]

> *Warfare is ordained for you, though it is hateful unto you; but it may happen that ye hate a thing which is good for you, and it may happen that ye love a thing which is bad for you. Allah knoweth, ye know not.*   (2:216)

> *...In truth the disbelievers [non-Muslims] are an open enemy to you.*   (4:101

---

[21]   Mike Ghouse, "Quran is Not for Muslims," *HuffPost*, January 17, 2015; accessed at: http://www.huffingtonpost.com/mike-ghouse/quran-is-not-for-muslims_b_6174940.html#es_share_ended.

[22]   Ibid.

[23]   *The Meaning of the Glorious Koran*, trans. Marmaduke Pickthall (1930; rpt. New York: Alfred A. Knopf, 1992).

*O ye who believe! Take not the Jews and the Christians
for friends. They are friends one to another. He among
you who taketh them for friends is (one) of them. Lo!
Allah guideth not wrongdoing folk.* (5:51)

*Then, when the sacred months have passed, slay the
idolaters wherever ye find them, and take them (captive),
and besiege them, and prepare for them each ambush.
But if they repent and establish worship and pay the poor-
due, then leave their way free. Lo! Allah is Forgiving,
Merciful.* (9:5)

O Prophet! Strive against the disbelievers [non-Muslims]
*and the hypocrites! Be harsh with them. Their ultimate
abode is hell, a hapless journey's-end.* (9:73)

Lo! those who disbelieve [in Islam], *among the People of
the Scripture* [Jews and Christians] *and the idolaters, will
abide in fire* [sic] *of hell. They are the worst of created
beings.* (98:6)

There is not a lot of justice, mercy and harmony in these verses from
Pickthall's translation, so according to Ghouse's standard, he appears to be
recommending a translation of the Koran that is "wrong".

Allah Loves Everybody

In an article titled *Quran is not for Muslims*,[24] Ghouse wrote that

---

24   Ghouse, "Quran is Not for Muslims."

God [Allah] *is not the God of Muslims and no where he claims that in Quran* [sic]*...God loves us all, and no one is deprived of his love...*

In reality we find that in the Koran Allah states that the only religion acceptable to him is Islam (e.g., 3:19 and 3:85). And Allah states that Islam is to be made superior over all other religions, even if the non-Muslims don't like it (e.g., 9:33, 48:28, and 61:9). Allah curses the Jews and Christians (9:30). He states that non-Muslims are among the worst of creatures who "will abide in the fire of Hell" (98:6), while Muslims are the best of creatures (3:110 and 98:7). Non-Muslims are "open enemies" to Muslims (4:101) and Jews are among the worst of those enemies (5:82). And Allah commands Muslims to be harsh toward non-Muslims (e.g., 8:57, 9:73, 9:123, and 48:29) and to kill those non-Muslims (9:5)

In spite of Ghouse's claim, and as I noted in more detail in a previous article,[25] Allah is only the god of Islam and the Muslims, and Allah has no love for non-Muslims.

The Ubiquitous 2:62

Chapter 2, Verse 62 of the Koran is commonly quoted by Muslim-Americans to indicate that Judaism and Christianity are respected in Islam and the adherents of those two faiths will be rewarded by Allah. Ghouse continues with this theme in an article titled *Quran is not for Muslims:*[26]

if you take care of his creation (neighbor), you need not worry; your rewards are with him. Just to make sure we understand this precisely, he says, whether you are a Jew

---

[25]   Stephen M. Kirby, "Do We All Believe in the Same God?" *FrontPage Mag*, December 22, 2014; accessible at: http://www.frontpagemag.com/2014/dr-stephen-m-kirby/do-we-all-believe-in-the-same-god.

[26]   Ghouse, "Quran is Not for Muslims."

*or a Christian and by corollary other, if you take care of
your neighbor, I will take care of you (2:62).*

Here is Chapter 2, Verse 62

*Verily, those who believe and those who are Jews and
Christians, and Sabians, whoever believes in Allah and
the Last Day and does righteous good deeds shall have
their reward with their Lord, on them shall be no fear, nor
shall they grieve.*

In spite of what Ghouse and other Muslim-Americans claim, this verse
only means that Jews and Christians would be rewarded for the good deeds
they did <u>before</u> the advent of Islam; after the advent of Islam, *righteous
good deeds* would be accepted by Allah only if they are done by Muslims.
And this verse was actually abrogated by 3:85 which stated that Islam is
the only acceptable religion to Allah, and non-Muslims will be "losers" in
the Hereafter.[27]

<u>Conclusion</u>

As is common in *Fantasy Islam*, Ghouse's personal version of Islam has
little, if any, support from Islamic Doctrine, and actually often runs
counter to that Doctrine. This appears to be of little concern for many in
his non-Muslim audience, because such personal versions relieve their
concerns about Islam and allow them to continue to consider the *jihadists*
as just a fringe group of "radicals" who have "hijacked" and "perverted"
the Religion of Peace. Ignorance, whether willful or not, can be a great
anesthesia. But anesthesia is only temporary and will not alter the world
going on around you, and to which you will eventually reawaken.

---

[27]   *Tafsir Ahsanul-Bayan*, Vol. 1, p. 72; *Tafsir Ibn Kathir*, Vol. 1, pp. 248-
249; and *Tafsir Al-Qurtubi*, p. 267.

The Fantasy Islam of Ingrid Mattson[28]

As I pointed out in an earlier article,[29] *Fantasy Islam* is a popular game among many non-Muslims and so-called "moderate" or "reformist" Muslims. Ingrid Mattson appears to be such a Muslim.

Ingrid Mattson was born in 1963 in Canada to Roman Catholic parents. In the mid-1980's she converted to Islam. In 2006 Mattson became the president of the Islamic Society of North America (ISNA). In 2011 she resigned as president of ISNA and in 2012 was appointed as the London and Windsor Community Chair in Islamic Studies at Huron University College at the University of Western Ontario in London, Canada.

The year 2013 saw the release of the Second Edition of Mattson's acclaimed book, *The Story of the Qur'an, Its History and Place in Muslim Life*.[30] In her book, Mattson plays *Fantasy Islam*.

The Peaceful Conquest of Mecca

On p. 68 Mattson wrote:

---

[28]   This article first appeared in *FrontPage Mag* on September 17, 2015: http://www.frontpagemag.com/fpm/260135/fantasy-islam-ingrid-mattson-dr-stephen-m-kirby.

[29]   Kirby, "The Lure of Fantasy Islam."

[30]   Ingrid Mattson, *The Story of the Qur'an, Its History and Place in Muslim Life* (West Sussex, UK: John Wiley and Sons, Ltd., 2013).

*Before the Muslims marched on Mecca, the Prophet
announced a general amnesty and the city was taken
peacefully...revenge killings were prohibited...*

It is strange that Mattson makes this claim, because the endnotes in this
particular chapter of her book frequently refer to specific pages in *The Life
of Muhammad (Sirat Rasul Allah)*, by Ibn Ishaq. She apparently
overlooked parts of Ibn Ishaq's book, because here is what we find that he
wrote about the Muslim conquest of Mecca:

1.   A Muslim force entered the lower part of Mecca and
met resistance. The Meccans lost 12-13 men and the
Muslims lost three in the ensuing battle – pp. 549-550.

2.   Muhammad had instructed his commanders when
they entered Mecca to only fight those who resisted them,
except for a select few individuals who were to be killed
regardless – p. 550.

3.   Ibn Ishaq listed some of those Muhammad had
ordered to be killed. There were nine total, including four
women. Four or five of these nine were captured and
killed. The others saved themselves by converting to
Islam before they could be killed – pp. 550-551.

4.   Shortly after the conquest of Mecca, Muhammad
said,
> *If anyone should say, The apostle killed men in
> Mecca, say God permitted His apostle to do so
> but He does not permit you.*   (p. 555)

In the *Bibliography* of her book, Mattson listed *The History of Prophets
and Kings*, the multi-volume history written by the 10th century Muslim
historian Abu Ja'far Muhammad b. Jarir al-Tabari. Al-Tabari mentioned

the following in Vol. VIII (*The History of al-Tabari: The Victory of Islam*):[31]

> 1.   Khalid's battle against the Meccan force and the killing of two Muslims and 12-13 of the Meccans – pp. 177-178.

> 2.   Muhammad ordered certain Meccans to be killed if they were captured, and some were subsequently killed – pp. 178-181.

For some reason Mattson ignored information provided by Ibn Ishaq and al-Tabari in order to create her own version of the Muslim conquest of Mecca. I'm sure that those killed during the Muslim conquest of Mecca would have preferred Mattson's version of events.

Apostasy

On pp. 233-234 Mattson discusses freedom of religion. She starts out by quoting the first sentence of 2:256 in the Koran: *There is no compulsion in religion.* Then she goes on to qualify that by pointing out that most Muslims

> *do not believe that freedom of religion entails the freedom to apostatize from Islam or to insult or belittle Islam.*

However, she states that some "contemporary scholars" ("certainly a minority at this time") believe that 2:256 is clear and includes the freedom to leave Islam. These "scholars" argue that the traditional justification for punishing apostates comes from the teachings of Muhammad (the *Sunnah*); but these "scholars" claim that these teachings have been

---

[31]   Abu Ja'far Muhammad b. Jarir al-Tabari, *The History of al-Tabari: The Victory of Islam*, Vol. VIII, trans. and annotated Michael Fishbein (Albany, New York: State University of New York Press, 1997).

"misinterpreted," and Muhammad never punished anyone for leaving Islam.

Mattson claimed that these scholarly arguments "are becoming more accepted by Muslim religious leaders." But it is difficult to see how these arguments could become more accepted by Muslims who know their religion, because Muhammad actually sought to punish those who left Islam.

Muhammad said that death was the penalty for a Muslim who left Islam.[32] And Muhammad even specified the nature of that death:

> *If someone changes his religion - then strike off his head!*[33]

At the conquest of Mecca there were two individuals that Muhammad ordered to be killed because they had left Islam:

> 1) 'Abdallah b. Khatal, who was discovered and killed while hiding inside the Ka'bah); and

> 2) 'Abdallah b. Sa'd b. Abi Sarh, who came to Muhammad seeking his protection. 'Abdallah lived only because the surrounding Muslim warriors did not kill him while Muhammad was "silent for a long time" before agreeing to that protection. Muhammad was later angry with those warriors, saying, "By God, I kept silent so that one of you might go up to him and cut off his head!"[34]

---

[32]   E.g., *Sahih Al-Bukhari*, Vol. 9, Book 87, No. 6878, p. 20, and Book 88, No. 6923, pp. 46-47; and *Sahih Muslim*, Vol. 5, No. 1676, pp. 118-119.

[33]   *Al-Muwatta of Imam Malik ibn Anas*, 36.18.15, in a section titled "Judgement on Abandonment of Islam."

[34]   *The History of al-Tabari: The Victory of Islam*, p. 179.

And even Allah commands those leaving Islam to be killed. In 4:89 of the Koran Allah commands Muslims to take hold of those apostates who have left Islam and "kill them wherever you find them."

But in spite of the commands of Allah in the Koran and the teachings and example of Muhammad, Mattson provided the following explanation on p. 234 for why more Muslims aren't joining the "contemporary scholars" in believing that one should be free to leave Islam:

> ...the history of Christian mission in the context of
> European colonialism, and aggressive Christian
> evangelizing in the context of American military
> occupation, leave many reluctant to adopt this position.

So according to Mattson, it is Christianity, not the Doctrines of Islam, which is preventing Muslims from enjoying the freedom of religion.

Wife-Beating

On pp. 237-241 Mattson takes on the claim that 4:34 of the Koran allows Muslim men to beat their wives. Here is that verse:

> Men are the protectors and maintainers of women,
> because Allah has made one of them to excel the other...As
> to those women on whose part you see ill conduct,
> admonish them (first), (next) refuse to share their beds,
> (and last) beat them (lightly, if it is useful)...

She devotes a bit of space to summarizing different understandings of the word "beat" in Arabic (*idribuhunna*) and new interpretations by Muslims "whose primary training is not in the traditional Islamic religious sciences." But her main argument against the claim that this verse allows Muslim men to beat their wives appears to be based on Muhammad's "dislike" of such action. To show Muhammad's "dislike," Mattson refers to some teachings of Muhammad (*hadiths*) mentioned in a 2003 article written by another person (a). In reality, Mattson should have gone directly to the authoritative *hadith* collections instead (b).

1a. <u>Mattson quoted:</u> *(It is shameful that) one of you beats his wife like someone beats a slave and then sleeps with her at the end of the day.*

1b. <u>*Sahih Al-Bukhari* (One of the "near canonical texts" – Mattson, p. 106), No. 4942:</u> *It is not wise for anyone of you to lash his wife like a slave, for he might sleep with her the same evening.*[35]

2a. <u>Mattson quoted:</u> *There are a number of hadith which show the Prophet disgusted by those who hit their wives, saying... "Do not beat the female servants of God," and "Some women visited my family complaining about their husbands (beating them); they are not the best of you."*

2b. <u>*Sunan Ibn Majah,* No. 1985:</u> *"The Prophet said: 'Do not beat the female slaves of Allah.' Then 'Umar came to the Prophet and said: 'O Messenger of Allah, the woman [sic] have become bold towards their husbands. So order the beating of them,' and they were beaten. Then many women went around to the family of Muhammad. The next day he said: "Last night seventy women came to the family of Muhammad, each woman complaining about her husband. You will not find that those are the best of you.'"*[36]

---

[35] *Sahih Al-Bukhari*, Vol. 6, Book 65, No. 4942, p. 392.

[36] *Sunan Ibn Majah*, Vol. 3, No. 1985, p. 134.

In Comparison No. 1 we see that what Muhammad actually said had nothing to do with shame; it seemed to have more to do with the potential for the beating to spoil the mood later on. In Comparison No. 2 we see that although Muhammad initially said not to beat the Muslim women, when 'Umar requested it be done because of the boldness of the women, Muhammad then ordered the women to be beaten. After the women complained, Muhammad only criticized the men for the extent of the beating they gave their wives, not that they had actually beaten them. After all, these men were simply following Muhammad's orders.

In determining whether or not Muhammad disliked the beating of wives, also consider the following:

1. Muhammad said "to beat them [wives] but not with severity."[37]

2. The authority to beat one's wives appeared to have been widely exercised in the early Muslim community, as Muhammad's young wife Aisha noted:

    > 'Aishah said that the lady (came), wearing a
    > green veil (and complained to her ('Aishah) of
    > her husband and showed her a green spot on her
    > skin caused by beating)...so when Allah's
    > Messenger came, 'Aishah said, "I have not seen
    > the women suffering as the believing [Muslim]
    > women. Look! Her skin is greener than her
    > clothes!"[38]

3. And Aisha herself was also a recipient. One time, when it was her turn among the wives to have Muhammad spend the night with her, she secretly followed Muhammad when he left her bed. Aisha said that when she later confessed to Muhammad that she

---

[37] *The Life of Muhammad (Sirat Rasul Allah)*, p. 651.

[38] *Sahih Al-Bukhari*, Vol. 7, Book 77, No. 5825, p. 392.

had followed him, "He struck me on the chest which caused me pain..."[39]

4. And because Muhammad was sad on one occasion, 'Umar, who became the second Caliph, used the story of slapping a woman to make Muhammad laugh. This led to the slapping of two of Muhammad's wives, Aisha and Hafsa, who happened to be present, with no reported objections from Muhammad.[40]

5. Muhammad said: "A man should not be asked why he beats his wife..."[41]

To claim that Muhammad disliked the hitting of women by Muslim men requires one to ignore the teachings and examples of Muhammad.

The Ubiquitous 2:62

Chapter 2, Verse 62 of the Koran is commonly quoted by Muslim-Americans to indicate that Judaism and Christianity are respected in Islam and the adherents of those two faiths will be rewarded by Allah. We find that on p. 66 Mattson wrote:

Although the Qur'an recognizes the enmity that developed between the Muslims and many of the Jews of Medina...the Qur'an still recognizes the validity of Judaism as a path to God:

Verily those who believe, and those who follow the Jewish faith and the Christians and the

---

[39]   *Sahih Muslim*, Vol. 3, No. 974R1, p. 72 (*Sahih Muslim* is one of the "near canonical texts" – Mattson, p. 106).

[40]   *Sahih Muslim*, Vol. 4, No. 1478, p. 408.

[41]   *Sunan Ibn Majah*, Vol. 3, No. 1986, p. 135.

Sabians – anyone who believes in God and the
Last Day and does good deeds – will have their
reward with their Lord and they will have no
fear, nor will they grieve.

(Baqara; 2:62...)

In spite of what Mattson and other Muslim-Americans claim, this verse only means that Jews and Christians would be rewarded for the good deeds they did <u>before</u> the advent of Islam; after the advent of Islam, *righteous good deeds* would be accepted by Allah only if they are done by Muslims. And this verse was actually abrogated by 3:85 which stated that Islam is the only acceptable religion to Allah, and non-Muslims will be "losers" in the Hereafter.[42]

It's interesting to note that on pp. 196 and 197 Mattson refers to the *Tafsir Al-Jalalayn* as, "One of the most influential classical *tafsirs*...," and "the 'unofficial Sunni Canon' of *tafsir*." Even with her high regards for this *tafsir*, she apparently did not bother to consult it before she explained the meaning of 2:62. This *tafsir* pointed out that to be rewarded, the good deeds had to accord with *Sharia Law*,[43] which undermines Mattson's claim that this verse *recognizes the validity of Judaism as the path to God.*

The Koran is Inclusive toward Christians

On p. 153 Mattson states:

> *It can be argued further that the Qur'an does more than offer guidelines for a legal policy of tolerance and that its attitude toward other faith communities in general and Christianity in particular is, in many ways, inclusive.*

---

[42]   *Tafsir Ahsanul-Bayan*, Vol. 1, p. 72; *Tafsir Ibn Kathir*, Vol. 1, pp. 248-249; and *Tafsir Al-Qurtubi*, p. 267.

[43]   *Tafsir Al-Jalalayn*, p. 23.

Mattson's statement is, in many ways, wrong. In the Koran we find that Allah states that the Christians are misguided in their beliefs (1:7). Allah states that Christians are among the worst of creatures who "will abide in the fire of Hell" (98:6). He forbids Muslims from being friends with Christians (5:51). Instead, Allah commands Muslims to fight Christians until those Christians pay the *jizyah* (protection tax), with willing submission and feeling themselves subdued (9:29). Allah states that Christianity is a false religion because Jesus was not crucified, but it only appeared so (4:157-158). Allah also states that those who believe that Jesus is the Son of God commit the one unforgiveable sin in Islam, *Shirk* (e.g., 4:48 and 4:116). In fact, Allah curses Christians specifically for this belief (9:30) and says that those who so believe will go to Hell (e.g., 3:151 and 5:72-73).

In spite of Mattson's claim, one does not find tolerance and inclusiveness toward Christians in the Koran.

Conclusion

In the *Preface* to the first edition of this book, Mattson noted that her book "reflects my personal perspective on the Qur'an." She wrote that she approached

> the Qur'an from the perspective of a Western academic
> who is also trying to live as a faithful Muslim. This is not
> the only perspective on the Qur'an, but it is one that,
> perhaps, has been underrepresented in the literature.

When it came to the Koran verses mentioned in the book, she wrote that

> the context provided for each citation is of my own
> choosing. But each of these verses can be found in other,
> often drastically different contexts throughout Muslim
> societies…I hope to replicate an aspect of the way in
> which Muslims can decontextualize and recontextualize
> verses they encounter throughout their lives.

So who needs the commands of Allah in the Koran, the teachings and examples of Muhammad, and over a thousand years of Islamic scholarship? Ingrid Mattson is a champion *Fantasy Islam* player.

4

The Fantasy Islam of Reza Aslan[44]

As I have mentioned before, *Fantasy Islam* is a popular game among many non-Muslims and so-called "moderate" or "reformist" Muslims. Reza Aslan appears to be such a Muslim.

Reza Aslan was born in Iran. In 1979, at the age of seven, he and his family fled the Iranian Revolution and came to the United States. At the age of 15 he converted to evangelical Christianity, but later returned to Islam. His website states that he is "an internationally acclaimed writer and scholar of religions." He is currently a Professor of Creative Writing at the University of California, Riverside.

In 2005 Aslan wrote a book titled *No god but God: The Origins, Evolution, and Future of Islam*. The updated edition came out in 2011. This article addresses that updated edition.[45]

It should be noted that in his book Aslan listed *The Life of Muhammad* and the multi-volume work *The History of al-Tabari*, as among the books he "consulted." These are classical works by Muslim scholars and major sources for information about Muhammad and Islam. Aslan even specifically mentions them as among those that have "catalogued" the story of Islam (p. xxiv). Unfortunately, although Aslan claims that he

---

[44] This appeared in *FrontPage Mag* on October 27, 2015: http://www.frontpagemag.com/fpm/260569/fantasy-islam-reza-aslan-dr-stephen-m-kirby.

[45] Reza Aslan, *No god but God*, (New York: Random House Trade Paperback Edition, 2011).

"consulted" them, we will see that he apparently overlooked conflicting information in these works in favor of playing *Fantasy Islam*.

Death Penalty for Apostasy is "Un-Quranic"

On p. 121 Aslan stated that the death penalty for apostasy was "un-Quranic," and he stated that nowhere in the Koran "is any earthly punishment prescribed for apostasy."

The only problem for Aslan is that in 4:89 of the Koran Allah commands Muslims to take hold of those apostates who have left Islam and "kill them wherever you find them." So the death penalty for apostasy from Islam is in the Koran.

In addition, Muhammad said that death was the penalty for a Muslim who left Islam.[46] And Muhammad even specified the nature of that death:

> *If someone changes his religion - then strike off his head!*[47]

No Foundation in the Koran for Stoning

On p. 71 Aslan wrote about the "misogynistic tendencies" of Umar, the second Caliph, and how Umar

> *instituted a series of severe penal ordinances aimed primarily at women. Chief among these was the stoning to death of adulterers, a punishment which has absolutely no foundation whatsoever in the Quran but which Umar*

---

[46]   E.g., *Sahih Al-Bukhari*, Vol. 9, Book 87, No. 6878, p. 20, and Book 88, No. 6923, pp. 46-47; and *Sahih Muslim*, Vol. 5, No. 1676, pp. 118-119.

[47]   *Al-Muwatta of Imam Malik ibn Anas*, 36.18.15, in a section titled "Judgement on Abandonment of Islam."

justified by claiming it had originally been part of the
Revelation and had somehow been left out of the
authorized text. Of course, Umar never explained how it
was possible for a verse such this "accidentally" to have
been left out of the Divine Revelation of God...

It is a common play in *Fantasy Islam* to claim that stoning is not a part of Islam because it is not in the Koran, so let's take a look at this claim.

In the first place, it is correct to state that the Koran says nothing about stoning. The original punishment for adultery in the Koran (4:15) focused on women and confining them to their houses until they died; but there was a key provision at the end of this verse: "...or Allah ordains for them some (other) way."

Muhammad later received a "revelation" from Allah explaining that "other way":

'Ubada b. As-Samit reported: Allah's Messenger (SAW)
saying: Receive (teaching) from me, receive (teaching)
from me. Allah has ordained a way for those (women).
When an unmarried male commits adultery with an
unmarried female (they should receive) one hundred
lashes and banishment for one year. And in case of
married male committing adultery with a married female,
they shall receive one hundred lashes and be stoned to
death.[48]

So now, instead of confinement, the punishment for adultery would be lashing and stoning. The punishment of lashing was codified in 24:2 of the Koran. Muhammad considered stoning as the appropriate penalty for adultery up to his death. He ordered many an adulterer to be stoned, as did his successors.

---

[48]   *Sahih Muslim*, Vol. 5, No. 1690, p. 131.

Umar did make the claim that the Verse of Stoning had been left out when the Koran was compiled.[49] But when the Koran was being compiled Umar had tried to get it included. However, the standard for including a "revelation" as a verse was that it had to be certified by two witnesses, and there appeared to be only one witness: Umar.

But in reality there was a second witness, Muhammad's favorite wife Aisha:

> It was narrated that 'Aishah said: "The Verse of stoning and of breastfeeding an adult ten times was revealed, and the paper was with me under my pillow. When the Messenger of Allah died, we were preoccupied with his death, and a tame sheep came in and ate it."[50]

Even though on p. 70 Aslan had written that "nearly one sixth of all 'reliable' hadith can be traced back to Muhammad's wife Aisha," the idea of using her as a witness apparently came up against 2:282 of the Koran. This verse requires the testimony of two women in order to equal that of one man in property matters. So even though both Umar and Aisha claimed there had been a stoning verse "revealed," we would still only have at best one and one-half witnesses, therefore falling short of the two witnesses required to include a verse in the Koran. It would appear that this is why there is no Verse of Stoning in the Koran. Nevertheless, it is still a part of Islam:

> Now the punishment of adultery has been fixed, which is stoning to death. That punishment also remained in force during the times of the Rightly-Guided caliphs (successors of the Messenger of Allah) and that remained the unanimous opinion of all the jurists and scholars afterwards... The law that prescribes stoning the adultery [sic] to death is supported by authentic hadeeths, and their narrators are numerous, and hence, scholars grade those

---

[49] E.g., *Sahih Al-Bukhari*, Vol. 8, Book 86, No. 6830, p. 431.

[50] *Sunan Ibn Majah*, Vol. 3, No. 1944, pp. 113-114.

hadeeths as mutawatir [frequently reported]. *A Muslim has, therefore, no choice except to acknowledge and accept it.*[51]

Muhammad's "Political Marriages"

Aslan pointed out that Muhammad had been married to nine different women over the course of ten years; he explained that most of these marriages had been political arrangements to forge links outside the Muslim community. Aslan mentioned two of those "marriages" on p. 64:

> *His marriage to Rayhana, a Jew, linked him with the Jewish tribe of Banu Qurayza, while his marriage to Mariyah, a Christian and a Copt, created a significant political alliance with the Christian ruler of Egypt.*

However, two of the works "consulted" by Aslan have this to say about these "marriages":

> **Rayhana:**   Rayhana was among the female captives taken when the Muslims conquered the Banu Qurayza tribe. Muhammad supervised the beheading of 600-900 of the captured Jewish males (combatants and non-combatants) and picked Rayhana for himself as his share of the plunder. Some of the women were sold to purchase horses and weapons, and others of the women were divided among the Muslim warriors.[52]

> **Mariyah:**   Muhammad sent a letter to Al-Muqawqis, the Christian ruler of Egypt, "inviting" him to Islam. Al-

---

[51]   *Tafsir Ahsanul-Bayan*, Vol. 3, p. 665.

[52]   *The Life of Muhammad (Sirat Rasul Allah)*, pp. 461-468; *The History of al-Tabari: The Last Years of the Prophet*, pp. 137 and 141; and *The History of al-Tabari: The Victory of Islam*, pp. xiii, and 27-39.

Muqawqis declined, but sent Muhammad either two or four slave girls. Two of these slave girls were Mariyah and her sister Sarin. Muhammad kept Mariyah as his slave concubine and gave Sirin to Hassan B. Thabit as a gift.[53]

With regard to the first "marriage," after Muhammad and the Muslims got finished there simply wasn't much left in terms of a Jewish tribe with which to be "linked." With regard to the second "marriage," the ruler of Egypt simply sent some slave girls over for Muhammad to do with as he pleased. There was no "significant political alliance."

No One Speaks for God

In the *Prologue* of his book, Aslan wrote (p. xxvi):

> *No one speaks for God – not even the prophets (who speak about God).*

Aslan has some major conflicts with Allah and Muhammad. For example, in the Koran we find Allah saying:

> *He who obeys the Messenger (Muhammad) has indeed obeyed Allah...* (4:80)

And Muhammad himself said:

> *Whoever obeys me, he obeys Allah, and whoever disobeys me, he disobeys Allah...*[54]

---

[53]   *The Life of Muhammad (Sirat Rasul Allah)*, pp. 499, 653, and 711, n. 129; *The History of al-Tabari: The Last Years of the Prophet*, pp. 137, 141 and 147; and *The History of al-Tabari: The Victory of Islam*, pp. xiii, 66, 100, and 131.

[54]   *Sahih Al-Bukhari*, Vol. 9, Book 93, No. 7137, p. 160.

To claim that no one speaks for God requires Aslan, a Muslim, to deny statements from Allah, the god of Islam, and Allah's Messenger, Muhammad.

Islam Has Never Had a Single Religious Authority

On p. 283 Aslan made an amazing claim:

> *Unlike Judaism and Christianity, however, Islam has never had a single religious authority…that is, a centralized religious authority that claims the right to speak for the entire Muslim community.*

One might expect to hear such a claim from a non-Muslim who knows little about Islam. But Aslan says he is a Muslim and his book is about Islam. To make such a claim, Aslan had to not only dismiss the Koran verse and *hadith* mentioned in the previous section, but he also had to dismiss Koran verses such as these:

Chapter 33, Verse 36

> *It is not for a believer, man or woman, when Allah and His Messenger, have decreed a matter that they should have any option in their decision. And whoever disobeys Allah and His Messenger, he had indeed strayed into a plain error.*

Chapter 59, Verse 7

> *…And whatsoever the Messenger (Muhammad) gives you, take it; and whatsoever he forbids you, abstain (from it). And fear Allah; verily, Allah is Severe in punishment.*

Chapter 4, Verse 115

*And whoever contradicts and opposes the Messenger
(Muhammad) after the right path has been shown clearly
to him, and follows other than the believers' way, We shall
keep him in the path he has chosen, and burn him in Hell -
what an evil destination!*

And Aslan also had to dismiss the following statement from his prophet
Muhammad:

> *Whoever obeys me will enter Paradise, and whoever
> disobeys me is the one who refuses (to enter it).*[55]

To deny the centralized, singular religious authority of Muhammad is to
deny Islam.

Muslims, Christians and Jews are One Big *Ummah*

On p. 101 Aslan wrote that Muhammad believed that although Muslims,
Christians and Jews each

> *comprised its own distinct religious community (its own
> individual Ummah), together they formed one united
> Ummah...Muhammad aligned his community with the
> Jews in Medina because he considered them, as well as
> the Christians, to be part of his Ummah.*

To be valid, this claim would have meant that Muhammad rejected both
the words of Allah in the Koran, and his own teachings:

In the Koran we find that Allah is angry with the Jews, and the Christians
are misguided because they believe that Jesus is the son of God (1:7).

---

[55]   *Sahih Al-Bukhari*, Vol. 9, Book 96, No. 7280, p. 235.

Muslims are commanded not to make friends with Jews and Christians (5:51), although Muslims can pretend to be friends if the situation so dictates (3:28). Jews are among the worst enemies of Islam (5:82). Muslims are commanded to fight Jews and Christians until the Jews and Christians pay protection money with willing submission and feel themselves subdued (9:29). Allah curses the Jews and the Christians (9:30). And Jews and Christians are among the worst of creatures and "will abide in the fire of Hell" (98:6).

Muhammad said:

> Jews and Christians are each worth only half of a Muslim.[56]

> *Do not greet the Jews and the Christians before they greet you and when you meet any one of them on the roads force him to go to the narrowest part of it.*[57]

> *The Hour will not be established until you fight against the Jews, and the stone behind which a Jew will be hiding will say, 'O Muslim! There is a Jew hiding behind me, so kill him.*[58]

> The Jews were grave robbers.[59]

> Jews and Christians will take the place of Muslims in Hell.[60]

---

[56] *Sunan Ibn Majah*, Vol. 3, No. 2644, p. 521.

[57] *Sahih Muslim*, Vol. 6, No. 2167, p. 439.

[58] *Sahih Al-Bukhari*, Vol. 4, Book 56, No. 2926, p. 113.

[59] *Sahih Al-Bukhari*, Vol. 4, Book 60, No. 3452, p. 413.

[60] *Sahih Muslim*, Vol. 8, No. 2767R1, p. 269.

*I will expel the Jews and Christians from the Arabian
Peninsula and will not leave any but Muslims.*[61]

Muhammad did not reject the Koran or his own teachings, but Aslan had
to in order to make the claim of there being one, big *Ummah*.

Muhammad and the Banu Qaynuqa

On p. 91 Aslan wrote that the Jewish Banu Qaynuqa tribe had broken their
oath of mutual protection with the Muslims and had therefore committed
treason; so, according to "Arab tradition," the men of the tribe were to be
killed, and the women and children were to be sold into slavery. But
Aslan wrote that everyone was shocked when Muhammad "rejected
traditional law" and simply exiled the tribe from Medina.

But some of the works "consulted" by Aslan tell a different story. In
reality, after the Banu Qaynuqa were defeated, Muhammad actually
wanted to kill his fettered captives, but he was persuaded otherwise by
'Adbullah b. Ubayy, who went to the point of grabbing Muhammad by the
collar to get him to exile the Banu Qaynuqa instead of killing them.
Muhammad finally had this to say about the Banu Qaynuqa: "Let them go;
may God curse them, and may he curse [b. Ubayy] with them."[62]

Conclusion

On p. 286 Aslan stated that Islam was a personal religion with "no
mediator between the believer and God," and "all people have the ability

---

[61]   *Sahih Muslim*, Vol. 5, No. 1767, p. 189.

[62]   Abu Ja'far Muhammad b. Jarir al-Tabari, *The History of al-Tabari: The
Foundation of the Community*, Vol. VII, trans. and annotated W. Montgomery
Watt and M. V. McDonald (Albany, New York: State University of New York
Press, 1987), p. 86; and *The Life of Muhammad (Sirat Rasul Allah)*, p. 363.

to discern God's will for themselves." He called this a "radical creed" that some have used

> to develop wholly new interpretations of Islam that foster pluralism, individualism, modernism, and democracy; others have used it to propound an equally new ideal of Islam that calls for intolerance , bigotry, militancy, and perpetual war. Which of these interpretations is "true Islam" is an unanswerable question, since the rejection of institutional authority means that all interpretations of Islam must be considered equally authoritative.

So according to Aslan, Islam is whatever anybody wants it to be, and on top of that it can still be called Islam! And so *Fantasy Islam* is played.

5

The Clarion Project's Advisory Board: Zuhdi Jasser[63]

The Clarion Project has an interesting website to visit.[64] Here is what Clarion says about itself:

> *Founded in 2006, Clarion Project (formerly Clarion Fund Inc) is an independently funded, non-profit organization dedicated to exposing the dangers of Islamist extremism while providing a platform for the voices of moderation and promoting grassroots activism.*

The Clarion Project has an Advisory Board consisting of three Muslims: Zuhdi Jasser, Raheel Raza, and Elham Manea. The Clarion site explains:

> *The purpose of The Clarion Project's Advisory Board is to advise management how to best achieve the organization's goals of educating the public about Islamic extremism and providing a platform for Muslim human rights activists.*

What kind of "education" will the Clarion Project's management be receiving from these three advisors? Let's start out with Zuhdi Jasser. According to the Clarion Project:

---

[63] This appeared in *Militant Islam Monitor* on February 5, 2017, with the title "The Clarion Project's Advisory Board Plays Fantasy Islam - Part 1: Zuhdi Jasser: Islam's Modernizing Prophet": http://www.militantislammonitor.org/article/id/7484.

[64] http://www.clarionproject.org/

*M. [Mohammed] Zuhdi Jasser, M.D. is the Founder and
President of the American Islamic Forum for Democracy
(AIFD). A devout Muslim, Dr. Jasser founded AIFD in
the wake of the 9/11 attacks on the United States as an
effort to provide an American Muslim voice advocating
for the preservation of the founding principles of the
United States Constitution, liberty and freedom, through
the separation of mosque and state.*

Jasser has been playing Fantasy Islam for many years. In 2015, in my first article about Fantasy Islam (*The Lure of Fantasy Islam*[65]) Jasser was one of the Muslims I looked at. In that article I showed that Jasser believed that Islam could pretty much be whatever the individual Muslim wanted it to be, in spite of the teachings of Jasser's prophet Muhammad. Jasser arbitrarily dismissed disconcerting teachings of Muhammad and decided that certain uncomfortable verses of the Koran applied only to the 7th Century or needed to be reinterpreted *a la* Jasser.

Jasser was also one of the "founding authors" of the Muslim Reform Movement, a small group of Muslim "reformers" I wrote about who also play Fantasy Islam and have to rely on the non-Muslim world to help them "reform" Islam.[66] But there is even more to Jasser's Fantasy Islam.

The Third Jihad

In 2008 we saw the release of the widely-acclaimed "documentary" titled *The Third Jihad: Radical Islam's Vision for America*. It was narrated by Zuhdi Jasser and distributed by the then-Clarion Fund; it was advertised as

---

[65]   Kirby, "The Lure of Fantasy Islam."

[66]   Stephen M. Kirby, "The Muslim Reform Movement Plays Fantasy Islam," *FrontPage Mag*, December 10, 2015; accessible at: http://www.frontpagemag.com/fpm/261067/muslim-reform-movement-plays-fantasy-islam-dr-stephen-m-kirby.

being the result of Jasser's investigation into Radical Islam. The documentary opened with this reassuring statement:

> *This is not a film about Islam. It is about the threat of radical Islam.*

The phrase "Radical Islam" was actually just one of the terms Jasser used to identify the "enemy." Throughout the documentary he also referred to "Islamists" and "Political Islam." However, the closest he came to defining any of these terms was when he talked about "Wahhabism, which is the radical Saudi brand of Islam" (28:25). This was in the context of a 2005 study done by the Center for Religious Freedom, and here is what Jasser had to say:

> *The study found that much of the official Saudi-supplied literature they found in American mosques contained texts and teachings that could be considered hate speech against non-Muslims. One such example reads "Never greet the Christian or Jew first." And then it goes on to say, hate them for their religion and oppose them in every way according to Islamic law.*

What Jasser failed to mention about "Never greet the Christian or Jew first" was that this was actually a command from his prophet Muhammad:

> *Abu Huraira reported that Allah's Messenger (may peace be upon him) had said: Do not greet the Jews and the Christians before they greet you and when you meet any one of them on the roads force him to go to the narrowest part of it.*[67]

In terms of "hate them for their religion," the Koran states that Jews are among the worst enemies of Muslims (5:82), Muslims are specifically commanded to fight Jews and Christians (9:29), and the adherents of those

---

[67]   *Sahih Muslim*, Vol. 6, No. 2167, p. 439.

two religions are not only cursed by Allah (9:30), but they are among the worst of creatures who are destined for Hell (98:6). And these just scratch the surface of the hate Islamic Doctrine expresses towards Jews and Christians.

Jasser then talked about the "hate speech" found in a textbook in a Saudi-funded Muslim school in Northern Virginia (30:00):

> *An example is from a twelfth grade Koranic interpretation that says it's permissible to kill an adulterer or a convert who left the faith.*

At the time of this narration by Jasser, the following statement was being shown on the screen:

> *[To shed] the blood of a Muslim man...shall not be permissible except in three cases: soul for soul; adultery; and he who renounces his faith and abandon* [sic] *the community.*

But again, Jasser failed to mention that this "hate speech" is actually supported by Islamic Doctrine. The death penalty for adultery was commanded by Muhammad (see below), and Muhammad ordered many an adulterer to be stoned to death.

In 4:89 of the Koran Allah commands Muslims to take hold of apostates who have left Islam and "kill them wherever you find them." Muhammad even said that such apostates were to be beheaded.[68]

With regard to the above statement about the "blood of a Muslim man" and allowing the killing of adulterers and apostates, this is actually a

---

[68]   *Al-Muwatta of Imam Malik ibn Anas*, 36.18.15.

statement from Muhammad that has been reported in numerous authoritative *hadith* collections.[69]

Jasser continued his criticism of Saudi influence by looking at college campuses (32:00):

> *Many of the Saudi-funded courses profess the noble aim of bridging the gap between Islam and Christianity. But this is absurd when one considers that there isn't even one church in all of Saudi Arabia, and that it's an offense for a non-Muslim to even set foot in Mecca, Islam's holiest city.*

Such actions by the Saudis should not be surprising, because before he died Muhammad prohibited Christianity from being allowed to remain on the Arabian Peninsula.[70] And in 9:28 of the Koran, Allah states that non-Muslims (including Christians) are "impure" and not allowed to be in Mecca.

In reality, *The Third Jihad* is about Islam.

Jasser and Saudi Arabia

In 2013 Jasser took a pilgrimage to Saudi Arabia. This was not the *Hajj*, but it was the less formal *Umrah*. Jasser travelled as a member of the U.S. Commission on International Religious Freedom (USCIRF), and had arrived before his delegation so he could visit Mecca. The article[71] about this trip reported an interesting claim by Jasser:

---

[69]   E.g., *Sahih Al-Bukhari*, Vol. 9, Book 87, No. 6878, p. 20; *Sahih Muslim*, Vol. 5, No. 1676, pp. 118-119; and *Sunan Ibn Majah*, Vol. 3, Nos. 2533-2535, pp. 451-453.

[70]   E.g., *Sahih Muslim*, Vol. 5, No. 1767, p. 189.

[71]   Stephen Lemons, "Muslim Phoenix Doctor Seeks to Save America and Islam from ISIS-Inspired Extremists," *Phoenix New Times*, December 9, 2015;

*Because of his criticism of Islam as practiced by Saudi
Arabia, Jasser doubts that he would have been able to
travel there, were it not on a diplomatic passport from the
USCIRF.*

As we are seeing in this article, and saw in *The Lure of Fantasy Islam*,[72]
the Islam Jasser criticizes is not "radical/political Islam" or "Islamism."
What Jasser is criticizing is the Islam found in the Koran, and taught and
practiced by Jasser's prophet Muhammad. Consequently, it would be a
good bet to say that the Saudis consider Jasser to be an apostate.

Following Muhammad's Example, Sometimes

Jasser's approach to Fantasy Islam is well illustrated in the following
statement he made in his book *A Battle for the Soul of Islam* (p. 253):

*My interpretation of the Qur'an has always included the
overriding idea that the Prophet Muhammad's example,
spiritually and morally, is for all times – but that his
political and military actions were an example that cannot
be taken out of the context of the times in which he lived
and its specific conflicts.*

As I had pointed out in *The Lure of Fantasy Islam*, [73] this statement is
immediately repudiated by 33:21 of the Koran:

*Indeed in the Messenger of Allah (Muhammad) you have a
good example to follow for him who hopes for (the*

---

accessed at: http://www.phoenixnewtimes.com/news/muslim-phoenix-doctor-
seeks-to-save-america-and-islam-from-isis-inspired-extremists-7881682.

[72]   Kirby, "The Lure of Fantasy Islam."

[73]   Ibid.

*Meeting with) Allah and the Last Day, and remembers
Allah much.*

There are no limitations here on the areas in which Muhammad is to be considered a good example. In fact, 33:21 was actually "revealed" as a result of Muhammad's military leadership and the example he set for his Muslim warriors during the Battle of the Trench in 627.[74]

But Jasser goes beyond ignoring 33:21. On p. 234 of his book, he asked

*what about the idea of reforming those aspects of shariah
law – such as stonings, blasphemy, apostasy, sexism – so
that it can more accurately reflect the present day?*

Sharia Law is Islamic Sacred Law based on the Koran and the teachings of Muhammad. So not only is Jasser talking about the need to reform (modernize) certain aspects of Islamic sacred law, but he is contradicting what he wrote on p. 253 (quoted above), in which he said Muhammad's spiritual and moral example was "for all times." Let's take a quick look at stoning and apostasy.

Muhammad spoke about stoning being "the order of God" and that he was the first to revive its practice for adulterers.[75] Stoning is obviously a moral matter.

Apostasy was a spiritual matter, having nothing to do with politics or the military, and, as pointed out above, both Allah and Muhammad said apostates should be killed.

So for Jasser, his prophet's spiritual and moral examples are "for all times," except when Jasser comes across some aspect of Islamic Sacred Law that he wants to modernize. A few years ago Jasser summed it up well:

---

[74]   E.g. *Tafsir Ibn Kathir*, Vol. 7, p. 658; and *Tafsir Al-Jalalayn*, p. 900.

[75]   *The Life of Muhammad (Sirat Rasul Allah)*, p. 267.

There is a dire need for moderates to reinterpret the Qur'an and Hadith and dismiss ideas or sira not commensurate with modernity...others may view this as heresy or marginal thought in Islam. I would disagree, but also admit that it is not predominant among the thought leaders of Sunni Islam.[76]

So Jasser strives to "reinterpret" the foundations of Islam using the nebulous concept of "modernity," and not the commands of Allah and the teachings of Muhammad, as the standard. This is truly Fantasy Islam.

In Part 2 we will look at the second Muslim on the Clarion Project's Advisory Board: Raheel Raza.

---

[76]   Jamie Glazov, "Symposium: The World's Most Wanted: A 'Moderate Islam,'" *FrontPage Mag*, May 26, 2010; accessed at: http://www.frontpagemag.com/fpm/61171/symposium-worlds-most-wanted-moderate-islam-jamie-glazov.

6

The Clarion Project's Advisory Board: Raheel Raza[77]

Raheel Raza is the second Muslim on the Clarion Project's Advisory Board. According to the Clarion Project:

> *Raheel Raza is president of The Council for Muslims Facing Tomorrow, author of the book Their Jihad – Not My Jihad, award winning journalist, public speaker, activist for human rights, featured in the award-winning documentary Honor Diaries…Raheel bridges the gap between East and West, promoting cultural and religious diversity…A fervent advocate for gender equality…*

Raheel Raza, along with Zuhdi Jasser, was one of the "founding authors" of the Muslim Reform Movement, a small group of Muslim "reformers" I wrote about who also play Fantasy Islam and who have to rely on the non-Muslim world to help them "reform" Islam.[78]   But Raza is a fervent player of Fantasy Islam in her own right.

---

[77]   This appeared in *Militant Islam Monitor* on February 6, 2017, with the title "The Clarion Project's Advisory Board Plays Fantasy Islam - Part 2: The 'Radical' Raheel Raza": http://www.militantislammonitor.org/article/id/7485.

[78]   Stephen M. Kirby, "The Muslim Reform Movement Plays Fantasy Islam," *FrontPage Mag*, December 10, 2015; accessible at: http://www.frontpagemag.com/fpm/261067/muslim-reform-movement-plays-fantasy-islam-dr-stephen-m-kirby.

In her book *Their Jihad – Not My Jihad*,[79] Raza wrote on p. 26 that the problem was:

> [T]*here are two Islams being practiced today – one, the Islam of Prophet Mohammad - the Islam of peace and love, of forgiveness and compassion, of tolerance and spirituality, women's rights and equality. The other Islam is the militant, extremist, fanatic cult of those who misappropriate religious teachings to justify murder, inflict destruction on human society in the name of Shari'a, subjugate and suppress minorities and women to promote injustice, and have a philosophy that fellow Muslims who don't subscribe to their brand of religiosity are heretics.*

In subsequent articles she referred to this "other Islam" as *Political Islam* or *Islamism*,[80] and *Radical Islam*.[81]

By the Numbers

Raza provided us some specific examples of what she meant by *Radical Islam* when she narrated the Clarion Project's short film *By the Numbers – The Untold Story of Muslim Opinions and Demographics*.[82] In this film

---

[79]   Accessible at: http://www.raheelraza.com/pdf/RaheelRaza.pdf.

[80]   Raheel Raza, "Islamism Simply Put: Islamic-Flavored Totalitarianism," *Clarion Project*, June 10, 2013; accessed at: http://www.clarionproject.org/blog/islamism-simply-put-it-islamic-flavored-totalitarianism.

[81]   "A Muslim Confronts Radical Islam," *JINSA*, June 16, 2011; accessed at: http://www.jinsa.org/events/regional-cabinet-meetings/new-york/muslim-confronts-radical-islam

[82]   This film can be viewed at: http://www.clarionproject.org/news/numbers-watch-clarions-new-short-film.

she stated that the "most important issue" of our time was "the rise of Radical Islam." The "Spheres of Radicalization" were discussed, with the outer circle being the largest and consisting of the "fundamentalists." Raza explained that these fundamentalists "hold beliefs and practices that no doubt will seem radical to you and me."

The first example she brought up was the support among many Muslims for the execution of apostates leaving Islam. She then asked:

> Do you know anyone who has left their faith? Do you think they should be executed? Do you think that that's a radical belief?

In reality, in 4:89 of the Koran Allah commands Muslims to take hold of apostates who have left Islam and "kill them wherever you find them." In addition, Muhammad said that death was the penalty for a Muslim who left Islam.[83] And Muhammad even specified the nature of that death:

> If someone changes his religion - then strike off his head![84]

Raza then talked about whippings and cutting off the hands of thieves, among other punishments. In terms of these punishments, she asked, "Do you think that's a radical belief?

The punishment of "a hundred stripes" for adulterers is found in 24:2 of the Koran, and Muhammad even commanded it, specifying 100 lashes for an unmarried male or female adulterer.[85] But Muhammad did suggest caution when it came to one's wife; he said:

---

[83]   E.g. *Sahih Al-Bukhari*, Vol. 9, Book 87, No. 6878, p. 20.

[84]   *Al-Muwatta of Imam Malik ibn Anas*, 36.18.15, in a section titled "Judgement on Abandonment of Islam."

[85]   *Sahih Muslim*, Vol. 5, No. 1690, p. 131.

*It is not wise for anyone of you to lash his wife like a
slave, for he might sleep with her the same evening.*[86]

And the command to cut off the hand of a thief is not only found in the
Koran (5:38), but Muhammad said it was "one of the legal punishments
prescribed by Allah",[87] and on numerous occasions he ordered it to be
done.

Raza then, with a tone of restrained wonder, talked about the support in the
Muslim world for stoning spouses if they are unfaithful.

This support should come as no surprise. Raza's own prophet Muhammad
ordered many an adulterer to be stoned to death. And Muhammad even
spoke proudly about it being "the order of God" and that he was the first to
revive its practice.[88] And, in an earlier, seeming act of prescience, Raza
herself had provided an explanation for this support:

*Muslims unanimously hold there is no greater example of
conduct for us than the Prophet Mohammad.*[89]

Even though these punishments are found in the Koran and the teachings
of Muhammad, Raza criticized "versions" of Islam which included such
"archaic laws." Although she did acknowledge that some Muslims would
consider folks like her to be "heretics." [90]

---

[86]   *Sahih Al-Bukhari*, Vol. 6, Book 65, No. 4942, p. 392.

[87]   *Sahih Al-Bukhari*, Vol. 5, Book 64, No. 4304, p. 361.

[88]   *The Life of Muhammad (Sirat Rasul Allah)*, p. 267.

[89]   *Their Jihad – Not My Jihad*, p. 38.

[90]   Raheel Raza, "'Boxed and Packaged Islam' Trying to Pass Itself Off as
Mainstream Islam," *Gatestone Institute*, October 17, 2014; accessed at:
https://www.gatestoneinstitute.org/4792/boxed-packaged-islam.

If Raza believes that matters actually supported by the Koran and Muhammad are "radical" Islam, and if some Muslims consider her a heretic, then we need to take a look at how Raza understands Islam.

Raheel Raza's Islam

Raza has written:

> ...*I am a believer and I do what I do because I want to take back the narrative from the jihadists and because the Islam I see today is not the Islam I grew up with. I am a staunch follower of the spiritual message of my faith...*[91]

So what is Islam to Raza? Here is how she summed it up:

> *If it's not moderate, progressive, enlightening, delightful or tolerant - then it's not Islam.*[92]

Here are some characteristics of Raza's Islam:

There is no compulsion in Islam: Raza wrote that

> *Tolerance is the cornerstone of Islam and has emerged out of the very nature and history of Islam.*[93]

For this she relies heavily on 2:256 in the Koran that starts off by saying, "There is no compulsion in religion." However, as I show in my latest book, *Islam's Militant Prophet: Muhammad and Forced Conversions to*

---

[91]   Raheel Raza, "Who is a 'Moderate Muslim'?" *Clarion Project*, August 15, 2016; accessed at: https://clarionproject.org/who-moderate-muslim/.

[92]   *Their Jihad – Not My Jihad*, p. 172.

[93]   *Their Jihad – Not My Jihad*, p. 30.

Islam,[94] the doctrinal authority of 2:256 lasted only from the time of its "revelation" in August 625 until it was abrogated by the actions of Muhammad in December 627. From December 627 until Muhammad's death in 632, Islam was spread across the Arabian Peninsula by Muhammad and Muslim armies offering most of the non-Muslim tribes the choice of Islam or the sword. And Muhammad's example has been followed over the centuries by Muslim rulers whenever the power relationship has allowed. The *very nature and history of Islam* refute Raza's claim about tolerance.

Individual Muslims have the right to personally interpret the Koran:

Raza is explicit about this:

> ...*Islam gives each one of us the freedom to logically research and interpret the Qur'an with reason and intellect.*[95]

However, this goes directly against the teachings of her prophet:

> *Muhammad bin Jarir reported that Ibn 'Abbas said that the Prophet said, 'Whoever explains the Qur'an with his opinion or with what he has no knowledge of, then let him assume his seat in the Fire.*[96]

Muhammad even said that it was disbelief (*Kufr*) to argue about the Koran based only on one's personal opinions.[97]

---

94   Stephen M. Kirby, *Islam's Militant Prophet: Muhammad and Forced Conversions to Islam* (Charleston, South Carolina: CreateSpace, 2016).

95   *Their Jihad – Not My Jihad*, p. 40.

96   *Tafsir Ibn Kathir*, Vol. 1, pp. 32-33.

97   Abu Dawud Sulaiman bin al-Ash'ath bin Ishaq, *Sunan Abu Dawud*, trans. Yaser Qadhi (Riyadh, Kingdom of Saudi Arabia: Darussalam, 2008), Vol. 5, No. 4603, p. 159.

Nevertheless, Raza has decided to ignore her own prophet, along with the established *Principles of Tafsir* (Koran Commentary):

> *The scholars have said: Whoever wishes to interpret the Qur'aan, he should first turn to the Qur'aan itself. This is because what has been narrated succinctly in one place might be expounded upon in another place, and what is summarized in one place might be explained in another…*
>
> *If he has done that, then he turns to the Sunnah* [teachings of Muhammad], *for it is the explainer of the Qur'aan, and a clarifier to it.*
>
> *If he does not find it (the tafseer) in the Sunnah, he turns to the statements of the Companions, for they are the most knowledgeable of it, since they witnessed the circumstances and situations the Qur'aan was revealed in…*[98]

Raza's approach to *tafsir* only has a single step: Come up with your own interpretation, just as long as it's moderate, progressive, enlightening, delightful, and tolerant.

Violence is prohibited in Islam: This claim can only be understood by remembering that Raza believes individual Muslims have the right to have their own personal version of Islam. This claim requires ignoring verses in the Koran that command violence against non-Muslims, e.g. 4:101, 8:57, 9:5, 9:14, 9:29, 9:73, 9:123, 48:16, and 48:29. It also requires ignoring the well-documented, violent example of Muhammad and his Muslim armies as they conquered the Arabian Peninsula in the name of Islam.

Deception is a little known concept: Here is what Raza wrote about "deception" (*taqqiya*):

---

[98]   Abu Ammaar Yasir Qadhi, *An Introduction to the Sciences of the Qur'aan* (Birmingham, UK: Al-Hidaayah Publishing, 1999), pp. 299-300.

I first heard the word taqqiya when I came to the West.
It's a little known concept (mostly in the Shia community)
which gives Muslims the freedom to lie about their faith
only if their lives are in danger.[99]

Here Raza's Fantasy Islam ignores two relevant verses in the Koran: 3:28, which allows Muslims to pretend to be friends with non-Muslims, and 16:106, which allows Muslims to publicly "renounce" Islam; both are allowed only if the Muslims secretly stay true to Islam in their hearts. Regardless of when Raza first heard the word *taqqiya*, 3:28 and 16:106 have been in the Koran since the 7th Century.

<u>Conclusion</u>

In her book *Their Jihad – Not My Jihad* (pp. 69-70), Raza wrote:

> *Since Islam is a way of life, everything we do is ruled by*
> *parameters laid down for us in the Qur'an and the*
> *traditions of the Prophet.*

However, we have seen a number of examples where Raza has simply picked and chosen among those parameters, and provided her own interpretation of Koran verses for the sake of creating her personal version of Islam. But aren't the jihadists and other "radical" Muslims regularly accused of doing this very same thing in order to create what is called a "radical" version of Islam? In reality, the jihadists generally seem to accurately understand, follow and quote from the "parameters" established in the Koran and the *Sunnah*. On the other hand, Raza does not.

Welcome to Raheel Raza, a "radical" Muslim playing an excellent game of Fantasy Islam.

---

[99]   Raheel Raza, "Who is a 'Moderate Muslim'?" *Clarion Project*, August 15, 2016; accessed at: https://clarionproject.org/who-moderate-muslim/.

In Part 3 we will look at the third Muslim on the Clarion Project's Advisory Board: Dr. Elham Manea.

The Clarion Project's Advisory Board: Elham Manea[100]

Dr. Elham Manea is the third Muslim on the Clarion Project's Advisory Board. According to the Clarion Project:

> Dr. Elham Manea is an associate professor specialized on the Middle East [sic], a writer, and a human rights activist. She is a Fulbright scholar who holds a PhD degree in political science from the University of Zurich, a Masters degree in comparative politics from the American University in Washington D.C, and a Bachelor degree in political science from Kuwait University.

Manea also plays Fantasy Islam with her advocacy of *Humanistic Islam.*

In her paper titled *For a Humanistic Islam* Manea noted that the base of her argument for a *Humanistic Islam* was the assumption that all religions have been touched and transformed by human beings, all are subject to change, and all are or had been in need of reform.[101]

---

[100]   This appeared in *Militant Islam Monitor* on February 7, 2017, with the title "The Clarion Project's Advisory Board Plays Fantasy Islam – Part 3: Elham Manea Rejects the Koran": http://www.militantislammonitor.org/article/id/7486.

[101]   Manea's paper *For a Humanistic Islam* is accessible at: http://inclusivemosqueinitiative.org/wp-content/uploads/2013/08/2013-London-IMI-For-a-Humanistic-Islam.pdf.

Turning the focus to *Humanistic Islam*, Manea explained on p. 2:

> *A humanistic Islam argues that any religion is shaped and molded by the humans who propagated and embraced its teachings, and as such, it reflects these humans' beliefs, traditions, Weltbild, and most importantly, it reflects the historical and social settings of the societies it sprang from.*

She wrote that "much of what we consider integral to the teaching of Islam are historically shaped." Her first example of this was the punishment of cutting off the hand of a thief. She said punishments like this were "neither holy nor divine, but tools of punishment used 14 centuries ago"; consequently she believed they could be declared "cruel" and replaced with modern approaches to punishment, such as prison and rehabilitation.

For Manea to claim that the amputation of a hand for theft is "neither holy nor divine" means that she ignores 5:38 of the Koran, which is a command from Allah for just such a punishment. It also requires her to ignore the teachings and example of Muhammad, who ordered the amputation of the hands of many thieves and said it was "one of the legal punishments prescribed by Allah":

> *A lady committed theft during the lifetime of Allah's Messenger...Her folk went to Usama bin Zaid to intercede for her (with the Prophet). When Usama interceded for her with Allah's Messenger, the colour of the face of Allah's Messenger changed and he said, "Do you intercede with me in a matter involving one of the legal punishments prescribed by Allah?* "[102]

Manea also mentioned stoning as a punishment "that reflects the historical moment where society stands." She pointed out that although this was

---

[102] *Sahih Al-Bukhari*, Vol. 5, Book 64, No. 4304, p. 361.

another outdated form of punishment, Saudi Arabia and Iran had adopted it despite the fact that stoning "was never mentioned in the Quran" (pp. 2-3). The statement that stoning was not mentioned in the Koran, and therefore implying that it is not a part of Islamic Doctrine, is a "red herring." Muhammad ordered the stoning to death of many adulterers, and he even said he was "the first to revive the order of God and His book and to practice it [stoning]."[103]

Manea wrote on p. 4:

> *The fact of the matter is there are core issues in the Islamic religion that should be reviewed and reformed.*

This review and reformation was to be done using *Humanistic Islam*. Manea explained:

> *A humanistic Islam is an approach - an approach to religion and life. It does not claim to be the true manifestation of anything [!]. It is just a framework. Its aim is to provide an alternative to the Islamists' argument that their "Islam" is the only "Islam". Its message is composed of four components. Identity, freedom of choice and rationality, crossing the Forbidden Areas of Thinking' (the nature of the Quran), and the gender issue* [sic].

On p. 8 Manea wrote that:

> *A serious reformation of Islam should start with this principle – Freedom of choice – and set it as its ideological core.*

Unfortunately, Manea's belief about freedom of choice goes against Islamic Doctrine established during the time of Muhammad. As I pointed

---

[103]   *The Life of Muhammad (Sirat Rasul Allah)*, p. 267.

out in my latest book, *Islam's Militant Prophet, Muhammad and Forced Conversions to Islam,* the idea of forcing non-Muslims to convert to Islam was a doctrine that started developing during the early years of Islam. The "no compulsion" verse (2:256) was "revealed" in August 625. Its doctrinal validity lasted only until it was abrogated by the actions of Muhammad in December 627. From December 627 until Muhammad's death in 632, forced conversions to Islam were commanded by Muhammad and by later verses of the Koran, and became the doctrinal norm for subsequent Muslim rulers. Advocating freedom of choice in religion would require Muslims to ignore the commands of Allah and the teachings and example of Muhammad.

On p. 8 Manea wrote that the most important component of *Humanistic Islam* for the reformation of Islam was the necessity of disregarding the Koran if it

> *stood against universal Human Rights as we understand them today, citizenship rights, or gender equality.*

How can one so blithely dismiss the commands of Allah in the Koran simply because they conflict with modern, man-made concepts of human rights and gender equality? Manea does so by claiming that the Koran was also man-made and a product of, and applicable mainly to an earlier time. Manea explained on p. 10:

> *I think that the nature of Quran is a human one. I think that the Prophet Mohammad is the one who composed much of the verses of the Quran, and that these verses were gathered afterwards by humans and it was these humans who wrote down these verses. As a result the social and historical context of the seventh century, when Mohammad the prophet lived, has been accurately mirrored in many Quranic versus [sic]. The Quran as such cannot be separated from its historical context.*
>
> *By saying that, I am challenging the orthodox assumption reiterated repeatedly in Islamic and Arabic school and*

university curriculums, in the media, and in any public
discourse, that the verses of Quran were said by God,
literally.

Manea referred to this God as "he/she" and said that *Humanistic Islam*
"does not ignore the human nature of Quran [sic]" (pp. 11 and12).

Manea even wrote on p. 13 about the irrelevance of this man-made Koran
for Muslims:

> *...it is possible to remain a Muslim while treating Quran*
> *as a text, written and gathered by different people. The*
> *text I respect, and treat with reverence. It is my tradition.*
> *But I see its human nature, and I see therefore its limits. I*
> *see its limits when it comes to regulating society in the*
> *twenty first century. But my faith, my faith, is not revolved*
> *around Quran* [sic]*, and therefore is not shaken by my*
> *conclusion regarding its nature. My faith is based on my*
> *belief in God himself/herself.*

According to Manea, the Koran "should therefore cease to be relevant
when regulating the social reality of family and state in the 21st century"
(p. 14). She wrote on p. 15 that one should

> *stop using Quran* [sic] *as a reference in regulating family*
> *relations and replace it with the stipulations of the* [United
> Nations] *Convention on the Elimination of All Forms of*
> *Discrimination against Women (CEDAW), which truly*
> *provide just parameters that ensure equality between*
> *sexes in family and society.*

So according to Manea, the Koran is largely man-made, with Muhammad
having "composed much of the verses"; it is a work reflecting mainly 7th
Century values and should be replaced in many respects by modern man-
made laws. Consequently, she feels free to challenge "the orthodox
assumption" of most Muslims, dismiss Koran verses and teachings of
Muhammad, and to create her own version of Fantasy Islam.

Conclusion

According to the Clarion Project's website, its Muslim Advisory Board has two purposes:

1. Advise management how to best achieve the organization's goals of educating the public about Islamic extremism; and

2. Provide a platform for Muslim human rights activists.

In terms of the first purpose, the "education" about "Islamic extremism" will come from three Muslims who acknowledge that they disagree with, and even challenge mainstream religious teachings in the Muslim world. All three believe that individual Muslims can reject canonical texts and interpret their faith however they want. Both Jasser and Raza recognize that other Muslims could consider them heretics, and Manea boldly implies the same.

If one understands the phrase "Islamic extremism" as an interpretation of Islam that selectively ignores some teachings while distorting the understanding of others to support a particular approach, then we have seen that in reality Jasser, Raza and Manea are Islamic "extremists." So in terms of the first purpose, the Advisory Board will be successful. Unfortunately, this Board will not be educating the public about the Islam that was commanded by Allah, taught by Muhammad, and acknowledged as mainstream for most of the 1,400 years of Islamic history. Instead, each will be propagating their own Fantasy Islam.

For the second purpose there will also be success for the Advisory Board. All three acknowledge that they deviate from mainstream teachings about Islamic Doctrine and that their approach to Islam is rejected by many, if not most, Muslims. A good indication of this is that these three do not talk about the number of mosques or the wide variety of Muslim organizations in which they have been allowed to speak about their own versions of Islam. So instead of being members of mosque advisory boards or large Muslim organizations, Jasser, Raza and Manea have found their "platform" on the board of a non-Muslim organization.

What are their prospects for changing Islam? As I have written before about "Americanized Muslim Reformers,"[104] and as Jasser, Raza, and Manea realize, their beliefs are heretical. Because they are heretics, they have little, if any support for their reforms from the greater Muslim community in the United States. Consequently, the reformers have to appeal to non-Muslims to help them reform Islam. This would be as if Martin Luther had relied on Muslims for his main support during the Reformation.

So what are the chances of success for Americanized Muslim heretics and their non-Muslim followers to change Islam from that which was taught by Muhammad to versions advocated by the heretics? Zero. And what are the chances for an Americanized Muslim heretic to convince non-Muslims that Islam can be modernized and "reformed"? Great. Because many non-Muslims know little about Islamic Doctrine and prefer to play Fantasy Islam.

Thus, these aspiring Muslim "reformers" will retain their non-Muslim platform as a beacon of false hope and encouragement for those wishing that Islam truly was a "Religion of Peace."

---

[104]   Stephen M. Kirby, "Why Americanized Muslim Reformers are Failing," *FrontPage Mag*, November 12, 2015; accessible at: http://www.frontpagemag.com/fpm/260743/why-americanized-muslim-reformers-are-failing-dr-stephen-m-kirby.

8

The Muslim Reform Movement
Plays Fantasy Islam[105]

In December 2015, a small group of "Muslim reformers" met in Washington DC to discuss the reform of Islam. They stated they were "Muslims who live in the 21st century" who were "in a battle for the soul of Islam." They proclaimed that they stood for "a respectful, merciful and inclusive interpretation of Islam." They called their meeting the Summit of Western Muslim Voices of Reform and named themselves the Muslim Reform Movement. On December 4, 2015, fourteen "founding authors" from this movement signed the *Declaration for Muslim Reform*,[106] laying out their beliefs.

At the conclusion of the event, two participants posted a signed copy of this *Declaration* on the door of the Islamic Center of Washington DC (a la Martin Luther nailing his *95 Theses* on the door of the Wittenberg Castle church in 1517). The document was quickly removed, and so far there has been little, if any, support for this reform movement from the greater Muslim-American community.

Here is the reason for that lack of support: the *Preamble* and *Declaration* are only two pages in length. But in those two pages these "founding

---

[105]   This appeared in *FrontPage Mag* on December 10, 2015: http://www.frontpagemag.com/fpm/261067/muslim-reform-movement-plays-fantasy-islam-dr-stephen-m-kirby.

[106]   This declaration is available at: http://aifdemocracy.org/declaration-of-the-muslim-reform-movement-signed-by-aifd-december-4-2015/.

authors" fundamentally rejected the commands of Allah in the Koran and the teachings of Muhammad in an effort to create their own *Fantasy Islam* that is more compatible with Western, Judeo-Christian values. Let's examine some parts of that *Declaration for Muslim Reform*.

We reject interpretations of Islam that call for any violence...

So starts out the second paragraph of the *Preamble*. But the commands of Allah in the Koran and the teachings of Muhammad are rife with violence.

The Koran commands Muslims specifically to kill non-Muslims (9:5), specifically to fight against Jews and Christians (9:29), and generally to fight against and be violent toward non-Muslims (e.g., 2:216, 4:74, 5:33, 8:12, 8:39, 8:57, 9:14, 9:73, 9:111, 9:123, 48:29, and 66:9).

Muhammad was proud that he had been made victorious through terror and fear.[107] He even said, "My livelihood is under the shade of my spear".[108] "Under the shade of my spear" means war plunder.

Muhammad is the standard of conduct for Muslims. Muhammad supervised the beheading of 600-900 captured Jewish males, including non-combatants, and over the years ordered individuals killed for criticizing Islam. Muhammad even ordered poets to be killed. The following is a portion of a letter written shortly after the Muslim conquest of Mecca in 630 AD. It was sent to a non-Muslim poet who used to satirize Muhammad, from the poet's brother:

> *Allah's Messenger killed some men in Makkah who used to satirize and harm him, and the poets who survived fled in all directions for their lives. So, if you want to save*

---

[107]   E.g. *Sahih Al-Bukhari*, Vol. 4, Book 56, No. 2977, p. 140; and Abu 'Abdur-Rahman Ahmad bin Shu'aib bin 'Ali bin Sinan bin Bahr An-Nasa'i, *Sunan An-Nasa'i*, trans. Nasiruddin al-Khattab (Riyadh, Kingdom of Saudi Arabia: Darussalam, 2007), Vol. 1, No. 432, p. 254.

[108]   *Sahih Al-Bukhari*, Vol. 4, Book 56, Chapter 88, p. 108.

*your skin, hasten to Allah's Messenger. He never kills
those who come to him repenting. If you refuse to do as I
say, it is up to you to try to save your skin by any means.*[109]

Violence and Islam go hand-in-hand.

We reject bigotry, oppression and violence against all people based on any prejudice, including... sexual orientation...

We find this in A3 of the *Declaration*. But Muhammad cursed lesbians and gays[110] and said that whoever is caught in a homosexual act should be killed.[111]

We...consider all people equal...

This is found in B2 of the *Declaration*. Muhammad felt differently. He said that Jews and Christians were worth only half of a Muslim.[112] He said that women were deficient in intelligence and religion,[113] and that it took the freeing of two female slaves to equal the virtue of freeing one male slave.[114] The Koran forbids Muslim women from marrying a non-Muslim (2:221), but a Muslim man can marry Jewish and Christian women (5:5).

---

[109]   Safiur-Rahman al-Mubarakpuri, *The Sealed Nectar* (Riyadh, Kingdom of Saudi Arabia: Darussalam, 2008), p. 521.

[110]   *Sahih Al-Bukhari*, Vol. 7, Book 77, No. 5886, p. 418.

[111]   *Tafsir Ibn Kathir*, Vol. 2, p. 402.

[112]   *Sunan Ibn Majah*, Vol. 3, No. 2644, p. 521.

[113]   *Sahih Al-Bukhari*, Vol. 1, Book 6, No. 304, p. 210.

[114]   Abu 'Eisa Mohammad ibn 'Eisa at-Tirmidhi, *Jami' At-Tirmidhi*, trans. Abu Khaliyl (Riyadh, Kingdom of Saudi Arabia: Darussalam, 2007), Vol. 3, No. 1547, pp. 318-319.

67

And the Koran states that Jews and Christians are among the worst of people (98:6), while Muslims are the best of people (98:7).

We support equal rights for women, including equal rights to inheritance, witness...

This is found in B3 of the *Declaration*. But this statement is a specific rejection of two verses in the Koran. 4:12 states that a woman only inherits one half of what a man would get, and this means that if there is more than one wife, all the wives will have to share that one-half portion. 2:282 states that in property matters it takes the testimony of two women to equal that of one man. Are these verses not the words of Allah?

Sharia is manmade.

This is an amazing claim made in C1 of the *Declaration*. In reality, Sharia Law is Islamic Sacred Law based on the commands of Allah found in the Koran and on the teachings and example of Muhammad, who spoke for Allah. Does the word *blasphemy* come to mind?

Every individual has the right to publicly express criticism of Islam.

This is another amazing claim, found in C2 of the *Declaration*. After all, in the Koran Allah states that Islam was perfected during the time of Muhammad (5:3). How then can something that is perfect be criticized? And there are many verses that specifically prohibit criticism of Islam, Allah, or Muhammad (e.g. 4:59, 4:115, 9:63, 33:36, 33:57, and 59:7).

Muhammad did not like criticism. For example, he personally ordered the killing of certain individuals who had criticized him or Islam ('Amsa' Bint Marwan, Abu 'Afak, Ka'b bin al-Ashraf, and Abu Rafi'). And he gave retroactive approval to the separate killings by Muslims of three individuals who had earlier criticized him or Islam.

Apostasy is not a crime.

This statement is in C3 of the *Declaration*. These reformers are rejecting 4:89 of the Koran which commands the killing of those who leave Islam. They are also rejecting specific statements from their prophet Muhammad, who stated that death was the penalty for those who left Islam;[115] and *Al-Muwatta of Imam Malik ibn Anas*, 36.18.15, in which Muhammad specified death by beheading for apostasy).

Conclusion

In an effort to "reform" Islam, a small band of aspiring Muslim reformers met in the capital of a non-Muslim country, proclaimed themselves to be "founding authors" (why not go all the way and say Founding Fathers?), created a document that rejected Muhammad's Islam in favor of Western, Judeo-Christian values, and then followed the example of an earlier non-Muslim who wanted to "reform" his own non-Muslim religion.

If folks are serious about religious reform, one thinks they would like to maintain some connection to their own religious traditions as a basis for that reform. But the Muslim Reform Movement has apparently decided otherwise and seems more interested in establishing a connection with the non-Muslim Western world as the basis for their reform. Such is the luxury of playing *Fantasy Islam*. And this is the reason why there seems to be little, if any, support coming from the greater Muslim-American community for this small group of aspiring reformers. It is only attention from the non-Muslim world that will sustain the Muslim Reform Movement.

---

[115]   E.g. *Sahih Al-Bukhari*, Vol. 4, Book 56, No. 3017, p. 159; and Vol. 9, Book 87, No. 6878, p. 20.

The Muslim Reform Movement is Irrelevant[116]

In December 2015, a small group of Muslims met in Washington DC to discuss the reform of Islam. With media fanfare, they named themselves the Muslim Reform Movement (MRM), issued a *Declaration for Muslim Reform*,[117] and became the new face of "Muslim reformers."

There was just one fundamental problem: the MRM never had support from the larger Muslim community.

Dr. Zuhdi Jasser, one of the MRM founders, admitted this on January 30, 2017, when he was interviewed in an article in *The Federalist* about the MRM's recent one year anniversary: *A Muslim Reformer Speaks Out About His Battle Against Islamism And PC*.[118] Jasser was asked about how many mosques the MRM had initially approached for support in 2015 and the nature of the responses from those mosques. Jasser's answer was eye-opening:

---

[116]   This appeared in *Jihad Watch* on February 24, 2017, with the title "Muslim Reform Group Reached Out to 3,000 US Mosques, Got Only 40 Responses": https://www.jihadwatch.org/2017/02/muslim-reform-group-reached-out-to-3000-us-mosques-got-only-40-responses.

[117]   This declaration is available at: http://aifdemocracy.org/declaration-of-the-muslim-reform-movement-signed-by-aifd-december-4-2015/.

[118]   Steve Postal, "A Muslim Reformer Speaks Out About His Battle Against Islamism And PC," *The Federalist*, January 30, 2017; accessed at: http://thefederalist.com/2017/01/30/muslim-reformer-speaks-battle-islamism-pc/.

We spent significant resources on this outreach over a period of ten months. We reached out through snail mail, e-mail, and telephone to over 3,000 mosques and over 500 known public American Muslims. We received only 40-plus rather dismissive responses from our outreach, and sadly less than ten of them were positive. In fact, one mosque in South Carolina left us a vicious voice mail threatening our staff if we contacted them again.

So the MRM made over 3,500 contacts within the Muslim community, but received only a little over 40 responses, of which *less than ten* were positive. So to work with these numbers, let's say the MRM made 3,500 contacts and received nine positive responses. That means that only .0026 (a touch over one-quarter of one percent) of the Muslim organizations and Muslim individuals the MRM contacted responded in a positive manner. And the MRM had even received a "vicious voicemail" from a mosque as a result of these initial contacts.

The irrelevance of the MRM was further revealed when Jasser was asked about the MRM's accomplishments during the first year of its existence. Jasser stated:

Our greatest accomplishment to date is our declaration.

The MRM's declaration is a two page document created at their first meeting, posted on the door of a nearby mosque (and quickly removed), and available on the websites of various Muslim "reform" organizations. As I noted in my first article about the MRM,[119] this declaration is "a document that rejected Muhammad's Islam in favor of Western, Judeo-Christian values," and in terms of Islamic Doctrine, it is rife with blasphemy.

Jasser also admitted that after a year of the MRM's existence,

---

[119]   Kirby, "The Muslim Reform Movement Plays Fantasy Islam."

we are disappointed in the relative silence from most
Muslim leaders...

Jasser blamed a lack of money for the poor support from the Muslim community:

> *I can guess why we had shortcomings in outreach. If we*
> *had more funding, we could study this more*
> *scientifically...No one knows truly how that majority of*
> *Muslims feels about Islamist ideologies. National security*
> *is in desperate need of helping us study that. ...We have*
> *not been able to effectively reach out to the majority of*
> *Muslims because of resources and the absence of effective*
> *platforms.*

So for the sake of "national security" the MRM needs to study the attitudes of Muslims in order to find out why the MRM has been generally rejected by those Muslims. And in order for the MRM to complete this study, they need money. The money has to, by default, come from non-Muslims.

But I would like to save the MRM time and non-Muslims money. Instead of a new study on why the MRM has virtually no Muslim support, I will provide the answer: in terms of Islamic Doctrine, the MRM declaration is blasphemous, and the MRM should not be surprised that over 99% of the larger Muslim community does not want to join in with that blasphemy.

It is only attention from the non-Muslim world that will enable the Muslim Reform Movement to remain on life-support, visible but irrelevant.

10

Why Americanized Muslim Reformers are Failing[120]

For many years we in the United States have regularly heard from a small number of Muslim American "reformers" who aspire to change Islam in ways that will make it more "modern" and compatible with American values such as freedom of speech and religion, and the equality of all people. According to these reformers, such change would rescue Islam from the "perverted" and "radical" interpretations of the *jihadists*, and return it to the way the reformers claim Muhammad originally taught it: as a religion that commanded peace and tolerance toward all, and promoted the rights of women.

These aspiring reformers seem to be generally Muslim males who were either born in the United States, or have spent a significant portion of their life in the United States. They have used the freedoms in the United States to explore Islam and to strike out on their own in providing an interpretation of that religion that conforms largely to American values. These personal interpretations commonly focus on Islam as a religion of peace that has been perverted by a few radical *jihadists*, and the aspiring reformers present Islam as such to non-Muslim audiences. I use the term "Americanized Muslim reformer" as a general reference to these aspiring Muslim reformers.

But what most non-Muslims don't realize is that Islam prohibits exactly what these Americanized Muslim reformers are trying to do. Let's look in

---

[120]   This appeared in *FrontPage Mag* on November 12, 2015: http://www.frontpagemag.com/fpm/260743/why-americanized-muslim-reformers-are-failing-dr-stephen-m-kirby.

the Koran, the holy book of Islam considered by Muslims to consist of the timeless, perfect, unchangeable words of their god Allah.

Islam was Perfected during the Time of Muhammad

Allah states in 5:3 of the Koran that the religion of Islam was perfected and finalized during the time of Muhammad:

>...*This day, I have perfected your religion for you, completed My Favour upon you, and have chosen for you Islam as your religion...*

In 15:9 Allah states that the Koran cannot be changed. According to Muslim scholars, 2:85 of the Koran prohibits picking and choosing among its verses.[121]

And to reiterate this, the prophet Muhammad said the penalty for denying a verse of the Koran was death:

>*It was narrated from Ibn 'Abbas that the Messenger of Allah said: "Whoever denies a Verse of the Qur'an, it is permissible to strike his neck (i.e. execute him)..."*[122]

And Muhammad talked about being in Paradise to greet the Muslims who died after him, and seeing some of those Muslims taken away because of changes they had made to Islam after he died:

>...*There will come to me some people whom I know and they know me, and then a barrier will be set up between me and them."* Abu Sa'id Al-Khudri added that the Prophet further said, "I will say those people are from me

---

[121]   E.g., *Tafsir Ahsanul-Bayan*, Vol. 1, p. 88.

[122]   *Sunan Ibn Majah*, Vol. 3, No. 2539, p. 455.

*(i.e. they are my followers). It will be said, 'You do not
know what new changes and new things (heresies) they
did after you.' Then I will say, 'Far removed (from
mercy), far removed (from mercy), those who changed,
did new things in (the religion) after me!'".*[123]

And once an issue has been decided in the Koran and/or in the teachings of
Muhammad, it is blasphemy for a Muslim to disagree with that decision.
This is plainly stated in the Koran, e.g:

> *It is not for a believer, man or woman, when Allah and
> His Messenger, have decreed a matter that they should
> have any option in their decision. And whoever disobeys
> Allah and His Messenger, he has indeed strayed into a
> plain error.* (33:36)

Their god and their prophet say that Islam cannot be changed after the time
of Muhammad, so what are the Americanized Muslim reformers to do?
Below are some of the major approaches I have found taken among these
reformers. These approaches are not necessarily mutually exclusive, and
the use of more than one of these approaches, or variations thereof, is not
uncommon.

The Koran Only

There are Muslims known as "Koranists." They believe that the only
source of Islamic Doctrine is what is found in the Koran. The Koranists
reject the *Sunnah* (the teachings and example of Muhammad).

But the Koran itself specifically rejects the premise of the Koranists.
These are some of the Koran verses that stress the importance of the
Sunnah of Muhammad:

---

[123]   *Sahih Al-Bukhari*, Vol. 9, Book 92, Nos. 7050-7051, pp. 123-124.

*He who obeys the Messenger (Muhammad), has indeed
obeyed Allah...* (4:80)

*And whoever contradicts and opposes the Messenger
(Muhammad) after the right path has been shown clearly
to him, and follows other than the believers' way, We shall
keep him in the path he has chosen, and burn him in Hell -
what an evil destination!* (4:115)

*Indeed in the Messenger of Allah (Muhammad) you have a
good example to follow for him who hopes for (the
Meeting with) Allah and the Last Day, and remembers
Allah much.* (33:21)

*...And whatsoever the Messenger (Muhammad) gives you,
take it; and whatsoever he forbids you, abstain (from it).
And fear Allah; verily, Allah is Severe in punishment.*
(59:7)

In the Koran Allah specifically commands Muslims to obey and follow the
teachings and example of Muhammad. So where does a Muslim find such
teachings and example, including in matters such as how to pray, actions
to be taken during the Hajj, or ablution? They are not in the Koran, they
are in the *Sunnah.*

The Koranists not only ignore the words of Allah, but they ignore the
words of their prophet Muhammad:

*Yahya related to me from Malik that he heard that the
Messenger of Allah, may Allah bless him and grant him
peace, said, "I have left two things with you. As long as
you hold fast to them, you will not go astray. They are the
Book of Allah and the sunna* [sic] *of His Prophet.*[124]

Al-Muwatta of Imam Malik ibn Anas, 46.3.

So in defiance of the commands and teachings of their god and prophet, the Koranist Muslims ignore the *Sunnah*.

Personal Interpretations of Salad Bar Islam

This approach is probably the one most used among the aspiring Americanized Muslim reformers and was the genesis for my first article about Fantasy Islam.[125] With this approach, changing Islamic Doctrine runs the gamut from a few tweaks here and there, to Islam being simply whatever the individual Muslim wants it to be. The common denominator is that the changes are based on the personal opinion of the aspiring reformer.

With this approach, *hadith* collections that have been considered authoritative since the 9th Century are questioned, with certain *hadiths* among them actually being deemed false, solely on the basis of the individual Muslim's opinion.

Verses of the Koran that are specific can be deemed allegorical, the eternal words of Allah can be judged applicable only to a specific time period, and verses of the Koran can be completely dismissed, solely on the basis of the individual Muslim's opinion.

With this approach, the Doctrine of Abrogation, based on 2:106 of the Koran, is frequently dismissed. This Doctrine is fundamental to understanding Islam, and it states that if there is a conflict between the messages of two "revelations" in the Koran, then the most recent "revelation" is the one to be followed. Consequently, a "revelation" made in Medina would supersede a similar, earlier "revelation" made in Mecca if there was a conflict between the messages of the two. The significance is that the "revelations" in Mecca tended to be more peaceful and accommodating toward non-Muslims than the verses later "revealed" in

---

[125]   Kirby, "The Lure of Fantasy Islam."

Medina. The verses from Medina are generally more belligerent and intolerant, and more inclined to make sharp differentiations between Muslims and non-Muslims. By ignoring the Doctrine of Abrogation, the aspiring Muslim reformer can concentrate on the Meccan verses, which, however, while more appealing to non-Muslim ears, simply don't carry the weight of Islamic Doctrine anymore.

This approach also dismisses centuries of accepted Muslim scholarship in the form of authoritative Koran commentaries (*tafsirs*), such as the *Tafsir Al-Qurturbi*, *Tafsir Ibn Kathir*, and *Tafsir Al-Jalalayn*. This approach also dismisses such 20th Century *tafsirs* as *Tafsir Ahsanul-Bayan* and *Tafsir As-Sa'di*. Dismissing authoritative *tafsirs* allows the aspiring reformer to then rely on new, personal interpretations of the meaning of verses in the Koran, even though such interpretations might directly conflict with the writings in authoritative *tafsirs* over the centuries. These new interpretations are based solely on the individual Muslim's opinion.

These aspiring reformers apparently ignore the fact that Muhammad had his own opinions about Muslims following this approach:

> *Muhammad bin Jarir reported that Ibn 'Abbas said that the Prophet said, 'Whoever explains the Qur'an with his opinion or with what he has no knowledge of, then let him assume his seat in the Fire.'*[126]

> Muhammad said: *The most truthful speech is Allah's Speech, and the best guidance is the guidance of Muhammad. The worst matters are the newly invented (in religion), every newly invented matter is an innovation, and every innovation is a heresy, and every heresy is in the Fire.*[127]

---

[126]   *Tafsir Ibn Kathir*, Vol. 1, pp. 32-33.

[127]   *Tafsir Ibn Kathir*, Vol. 2, p. 588.

Inaccurate Historical Information

It is not unusual to find Americanized Muslim reformers presenting historical information that is simply inaccurate. Here are three common examples:

<u>The peaceful conquest of Mecca</u>: You will hear that when Muhammad led an army of 10,000 Muslim warriors against Mecca in 630 AD, the Meccans surrendered peacefully and there was no bloodshed. You might even hear that Muhammad specifically prohibited the killing of any individuals. In reality, there was some resistance by the Meccans that resulted in the battle deaths of 2-3 Muslims and 12-13 Meccans. And before entering Mecca, Muhammad had ordered the killing of nine specific individuals, including four women. Some of these individuals were subsequently captured and killed, while others saved themselves by converting to Islam before they could be killed. As Muhammad explained it:

> *If anyone should say, The apostle killed men in Mecca, say God permitted His apostle to do so but He does not permit you.*[128]

<u>The Verse of the Sword is a pejorative term created by non-Muslims</u>: You might hear Muslims claim that non-Muslims created the term "Verse of the Sword" to disparage 9:5 of the Koran. Here is the first part of that verse:

> *Then when the Sacred Months have passed, then kill the Mushrikun* [non-Muslims] *wherever you find them, and capture them and besiege them, and lie in wait for them in every ambush...*

In reality, Muslim scholars have referred to this verse as the "Verse of the Sword" for centuries.[129]

---

[128]   *The Life of Muhammad (Sirat Rasul Allah)*, p. 555.

The Verse of the Sword was revealed before it was revealed: You might hear Muslims claim that 9:5 was among the verses "revealed" during the early period of Islam, when aggressive threats by militarily strong non-Muslims were being made against the young, weak Muslim community. You might also hear the claim that this verse was applicable only to a particular time period and/or circumstance in the past (e.g., Zuhdi Jasser claimed it was "revealed" in and applicable only to 623 AD).[130]

In reality, 9:5 was among the verses "revealed" in late 630 AD and early 631 AD. By this time Muhammad had already conquered Mecca, and the remaining non-Muslim tribes on the Arabian Peninsula, confronted by the burgeoning Muslim armies, were flocking to Medina to convert to Islam. And these verses were not related to a specific battle or to a specific tribe, but rather were directed toward all non-Muslims.[131]

And there is no basis in Islamic Doctrine for the claim that 9:5 has no relevance today. Such a claim ignores the facts that Muslims believe the Koran consists of the eternal words of Allah, and Chapter 9 of the Koran was the last chapter to be "revealed" to Muhammad. Consequently, the commands found in Chapter 9 were Allah's final, timeless instructions to the Muslims on how to deal with non-Muslims.

Their Audience Appears to be Mainly Non-Muslims

Americanized Muslim reformers appear on non-Muslim media and in front of non-Muslim organizations on a frequent basis, and almost always after a major *jihadist* attack.

---

[129]   E.g. *Tafsir Ibn Kathir*, Vol. 4, pp. 375 and 377.

[130]   Kirby, "The Lure of Fantasy Islam."

[131]   *Life of Muhammad (Sirat Rasul Allah)*, pp. 617-619; *The History of al-Tabari: The Last Years of the Prophet*, pp. 77-79; and *Tafsir Ibn Kathir*, Vol. 4, pp. 370-376.

But what I have yet to hear about is the number of mosques and Muslim organizations that allow these aspiring reformers to come in and advocate for their personal version of Islam. The Muslim reformers are vocal about their appearances on non-Muslim media and in front of non-Muslim organizations, but when it comes to any occurrence of similar appearances in mosques and in front of Muslim organizations, there seems to be silence.

Based on my research into the Tri-Faith Initiative in Omaha, Nebraska, I think these Americanized Muslim reformers are silent because they seldom, if ever, are allowed to present their personal version of Islam in a mosque or in front of a Muslim organization. The Tri-Faith Initiative is an experiment in interfaith dialogue and coexistence between Muslims, Jews, and Christians. However, in a series of articles I have shown that Islamic Doctrine prohibits such a venture and actually maligns, and preaches violence against, Jews and Christians.[132] And I have also shown that most of the money for this initiative comes from non-Muslim organizations and

---

[132]   Stephen M. Kirby, "Islam and the Omaha Tri-Faith Initiative," *FrontPage Mag*, April 30, 2015; accessible at: http://www.frontpagemag.com/2015/dr-stephen-m-kirby/islam-and-the-omaha-tri-faith-initiative/.

Stephen M. Kirby, "Don't Take Jews and Christians as Friends?" *FrontPage Mag*, May 11, 2015; accessible at: http://www.frontpagemag.com/2015/dr-stephen-m-kirby/dont-take-jews-and-christians-as-friends/.

Stephen M. Kirby, "The Fraud of Omaha's Tri-Faith Initiative," *FrontPage Mag*, May 19, 2015; accessible at: http://www.frontpagemag.com/2015/dr-stephen-kirby/the-fraud-of-omahas-tri-faith-initiative/.

Stephen M. Kirby, "The Omaha Tri-Faith Initiative: Nebraska's Potemkin Village?" *FrontPage Mag*, June 4, 2015; accessible at: http://www.frontpagemag.com/2015/dr-stephen-m-kirby/the-omaha-tri-faith-initiative-nebraskas-potemkin-village/.

a few aspiring Muslim reformers, with apparently no support for the initiative from mosques and Muslim organizations in Nebraska.[133]

When I have corresponded with Tri-Faith partners and proponents, and Nebraska mosques and Muslim organizations, about what Islamic Doctrine teaches and the lack of support for the Tri-Faith from the greater Muslim community in Nebraska, there has been only silence from the Muslims and character attacks on me from the non-Muslims.

<u>Conclusion</u>

Here are reasons why Americanized Muslim reformers are failing:

1. They create their own versions of Islam, relying on their own personal opinions and interpretations, and arbitrarily dismissing parts of Islamic history and centuries of established Muslim scholarship.

2. They claim to follow the Koran, but actually go against verses of the Koran by arbitrarily dismissing one of the two columns upon which Islam rests: the *Sunnah* of Muhammad.

3. They go against the commands of Allah in the Koran and the teachings of Muhammad by picking and choosing, and actually dismissing verses in the Koran.

4. They personally decide which *hadiths* are authentic, again arbitrarily dismissing centuries of established Muslim scholarship.

---

[133]   Kirby, "The Omaha Tri-Faith Initiative: Nebraska's Potemkin Village?"; and Stephen M. Kirby, "Nebraska Muslims and Omaha's Tri-Faith Initiative," *FrontPage Mag*, June 23, 2015; accessible at: http://www.frontpagemag.com/2015/dr-stephen-kirby/nebraska-muslims-and-omahas-tri-faith-initiative/.

5. As a result, their beliefs are heretical. And as Muhammad said above, every heresy sends one to the Fires of Hell.

6. Because these reformers are heretics, they have little, if any support for their reforms from the greater Muslim community in the United States.

7. Consequently, the reformers have to appeal to non-Muslims to help them reform Islam. This would be as if Martin Luther had relied on Muslims for his main support during the Reformation.

8. So what are the chances of success for an Americanized Muslim heretic and his non-Muslim followers to change Islam from that which was taught by Muhammad to that which is advocated by the heretic? Zero.

Does it really matter that Americanized Muslim reformers are going around trying to create personalized, "modern" versions of Islam? Yes, because they are relying on non-Muslims for support. And to get that support, the reformers are presenting "the true" Islam as a religion of peace, similar to Christianity and Judaism, and able to be modified and modernized. And the reformers are presenting the *jihadists* as outliers who have perverted and hijacked that religion. But the reality is that the Muslim reformers are perverting and hijacking the religion, and it is the jihadists who are following the Islam taught by Muhammad.

How one understands a religion, whether correctly or incorrectly, is a major factor in how one welcomes it adherents. In terms of the mass migration of Muslim "refugees" into Europe, the European leadership and many Europeans in general appear to think that Islam is as the aspiring reformers have presented it. So the Muslim "refugees" have been generally welcomed with open arms. But would there have been such a welcome if the realization had been more wide spread that the reformers are heretics with little support in the greater Muslim community?

There is support in the United States for the Obama administration's call to bring in tens of thousands of these Muslim "refugees." But before allowing this to happen, we must ask the question that the Europeans should have asked, but for whom now it is too late to ask: Will these Muslim "refugees" follow the Islam of our Americanized Muslim heretics, or will these "refugees" follow the centuries-old intolerant, supremacist, violent teachings of their god Allah and their prophet Muhammad? The fate of Western culture lies in the answer.

> *Just as it is obligatory to accept the commandments proven by the textual evidence from the Qur'an, and that it is utter disbelief to reject them, so are the commandments proven by the hadeeths of the Messenger of Allah. It is obligatory to act by them, and it is sheer disbelief to deny them.*[134]

---

[134]   *Tafsir Ahsanul-Bayan*, Vol. 1, pp. 622-623.

11

"ISNA Condemns Terrorism," & other Acts of Legerdemain[135]

The Islamic Society of North America (ISNA) presents itself as "an association of Muslim organizations and individuals that provides a common platform for presenting Islam…" Leaders of ISNA are accorded access to all levels of government in the United States, and are looked to as authorities on Islam and representatives of the Muslim-American community.

But there are two things in particular that need to be remembered about ISNA:

1. ISNA was, and still is, considered an unindicted co-conspirator in the federal terrorism case against the Holy Land Foundation for Relief and Development. On November 24, 2008, the Holy Land Foundation and five of its leaders were convicted on charges of providing material support to Hamas, a federally designated foreign terrorist organization. The five leaders subsequently received sentences ranging from 15 to 65 years in federal prison.

2. ISNA is connected to the Muslim Brotherhood. Among the evidence submitted by the federal prosecutors in the Holy Land Foundation case was a document titled *An Explanatory Memorandum on the General Strategic Goal for the Group in North America, May 22, 1991*. This document stated

---

[135]   This appeared in *FrontPage Mag* on September 4, 2015: http://www.frontpagemag.com/fpm/259993/isna-condemns-terrorism-and-other-acts-legerdemain-dr-stephen-m-kirby.

The Ikhwan [Muslim Brotherhood] *must understand that their work in America is a kind of grand Jihad in eliminating and destroying the Western civilization from within and "sabotaging" its miserable house by their hands and the hands of the believers* [Muslims] *so that it is eliminated and God's religion* [Islam] *is made victorious over all other religions.*

This document listed "our organizations and the organizations of our friends." Number 1 on this list was ISNA.

In spite of ISNA's links to the Holy Land Foundation case and its relationship with the Muslim Brotherhood, ISNA makes much of its condemnation of terrorism and refers to ISNA's 2005 brochure titled "Against Terrorism and Religious Extremism: Muslim Position and Responsibilities."[136] The brochure appears to condemn terrorism and refute claims that Islam has anything to do with such violence. But, as with acts of legerdemain, things in this brochure are not what they seem.

ISNA Condemns Terrorism

In this brochure ISNA states that in the absence of "a universally agreed upon definition of terrorism," it has chosen to define terrorism as "any act of indiscriminate violence that targets innocent people." The idea of "indiscriminate violence" means random violence that fails to make a distinction among its recipients. It can even mean killing someone by accident.

But there are problems with this definition and the rationale for it. In the first place, due to the different cultures, religions and values in the world, there can never be "a universally agreed upon definition of terrorism." But

---

[136]   https://makkah.files.wordpress.com/2007/01/isna-anti-terrorism-and-anti-extremism-brochure.pdf

that is irrelevant because our focus should be on how the concept of terrorism is understood in the United States. In the United States "terrorism" is commonly understood to be an act of violence used to create fear among people in order to further particular goals of the perpetrator. With this understanding of the word, there is no such thing as "indiscriminate violence" because there is a reason, and usually advanced planning, for the use of that violence.

We can probably all agree that innocent people should not be targeted for violence. But the crux of the matter is defining who is "innocent." ISNA is an Islamic organization that wants to, among other things, foster a better understanding of Islam. So who are innocent people according to Islamic Doctrine? Let's consider what Muhammad and the Koran have to say:

> *Abu Huraira reported that Allah's Messenger (may peace be upon him) had said...A Muslim is the brother of a Muslim. He neither oppresses him nor humiliates him nor looks down upon him...All things of a Muslim are inviolable for his brother in faith; his blood, his wealth and his honour.*[137]

So Muhammad said that Muslims are not to harm each other. This was expanded on in Chapter 4, Verses 92-93 of the Koran:

> *It is not for a believer [Muslim] to kill a believer except (that it be) by mistake...And whoever kills a believer intentionally, his recompense is Hell to abide therein; and the Wrath and the Curse of Allah are upon him, and a great punishment is prepared for him.*

In general, then, a Muslim is prohibited from intentionally killing another Muslim. But there are three exceptions to that:

---

[137]   *Sahih Muslim*, Vol. 7, No. 2564, p. 173.

It was narrated from 'Aishah that the Messenger of Allah said: "It is not permissible to shed the blood of a Muslim except in three cases: A [sic] *adulterer who had been married, who should be stoned to death; a man who killed another man intentionally* [and without legal authority], *who should be killed; and a man who left Islam and waged war against Allah, the Mighty and Sublime, and His Messenger, who should be killed, or crucified, or banished from the land."[138]*

So there are three circumstances that allow a Muslim to kill another Muslim.

On the other hand,

It was narrated from 'Amr bin Shu'aib, from his father, from his grandfather that the Messenger of Allah said: "A Muslim should not be killed in retaliation for the murder of a disbeliever."[139]

Muhammad tells Muslims that they can kill non-Muslims without a penalty. In contrast, Islam forbids Muslims from intentionally killing other Muslims who are staying true to their faith, and Allah will punish them with Hell if they do such a thing. So according to Islamic doctrine, the only innocent people are devout Muslims.

It appears then, that ISNA's definition of terrorism only applies to the random and/or accidental killing of devout Muslims.

---

[138]   *Sunan An-Nasa'i*, Vol. 5, No. 4053, pp. 56-57.

[139]   *Sunan Ibn Majah*, Vol. 3, No. 2659, p. 528.

The Word *Jihad* does not mean "Holy War"

The brochure states, "Contrary to common misperceptions and mistranslations, the word *jihad* does not mean "Holy War"…" If this is true, then such "misperceptions and mistranslations" of the word *jihad* are rampant in the Muslim community, e.g.:

1. *Jihad: Striving, holy war.*[140]

2. *…the earliest (and therefore fundamental) Qur'anic reference to the question of jihad, or holy war…*[141]

3. *…he was taken prisoner in a jihad - that is, a holy war…*[142]

4. *…a woman taken captive in a "holy war" (jihad)…*[143]

5. *And He (Allah) said: Jihad (Islamic holy war) is ordained for you (Muslims)…*[144]

6. *…the Prophet nevertheless said to his companions that they had returned from the lesser holy war to the greater holy war, the*

---

[140]   Mahmoud Ismail Saleh, *Dictionary of Islamic Words & Expressions*, 3rd ed. (Riyadh, Kingdom of Saudi Arabia: Darussalam, 2011), p. 116.

[141]   *The Message of the Qur'an*, trans. Muhammad Asad, (Bristol, England: The Book Foundation, 2003), n. 167, p. 51. This is the translation of the Koran endorsed and distributed by the Council on American-Islamic Relations (CAIR).

[142]   Ibid., n. 72, p. 284.

[143]   Ibid., n. 58, p. 727.

[144]   Sheikh 'Abdullah bin Muhammad bin Humaid, "The Call to Jihad (Fighting For Allah's Cause) in the Qur'an," *Interpretation of the Meanings of The Noble Qur'an*, trans. Muhammad Muhsin Khan and Muhammad Taqi-ud-Din Al-Hilali (Riyadh, Kingdom of Saudi Arabia: Maktaba Dar-us-Salam, 1994), p. 1046.

greater jihad being the inner battle… - Seyyed Hossein Nasr, *The Spiritual Significance of Jihad.* This article is found at a website titled *MyJihad*;[145] a major focus of this website is the attempt to redefine the word *jihad* away from any connection to war. (It should be noted that the distinction between a lesser and a greater *jihad* is a fabrication).[146]

7. *The holy war (jihad) is a collective duty…*[147]

Perhaps ISNA will contact CAIR, and the authors and publishers of these works, and let them know they are perpetuating "misperceptions and mistranslations."

Cutting and Pasting from the Koran

The ISNA brochure is quite critical of "detractors of Islam" who take a "cut-and-paste" approach to verses of the Koran by ignoring their historical context and "textual analysis." ISNA states that contrary to what

---

[145]   This website, http://myjihad.org, appears to have closed down in early 2017. Here is a link to this website on December 3, 2016: http://web.archive.org/web/20161203232440/http://myjihad.org/.

Clicking on the *Resources* tab shows Nasr's article listed as of November 3, 2016: http://web.archive.org/web/20161103144013/http://myjihad.org/resources/.

Nasr's article can be found at: https://www.al-islam.org/al-serat/vol-9-no-1/spiritual-significance-jihad-seyyed-hossein-nasr.

[146]   Stephen M. Kirby, *Islam According to Muhammad, Not Your Neighbor* (CreateSPace: Charleston, South Carolina, 2014), pp. 115-123.

[147]   Imam Muwaffaq ad-Din Abdu'llah ibn Ahmad ibn Qudama al-Maqdisi, *The Mainstay Concerning Jurisprudence (Al-Umda fi 'l-Fiqh)*, trans. Muhtar Holland (Ft. Lauderdale, FL: Al-Baz Publishing, Inc., 2009), "The Book of the Holy War (*Kitab al-Jihad*), p. 313.

these "detractors" say, "...nowhere does the Qur'an call for violence against anyone merely on the grounds that he/she rejected Islam." This is followed by the mentioning of a number of verses apparently in support of that claim, and the dismissal of verses 9:5, 9:29, and 9:123, that are used by the "detractors" against that claim. ISNA states that these last three verses were relevant only to a particular historical period.

So what is the historical context of these three verses, according to ISNA? ISNA claims that these three verses from Chapter 9 were "revealed" during a period of threatening "aggression and gross oppression" against the "nascent Muslim community." ISNA is wrong. In reality, the verses in Chapter 9 were "revealed" in late 630 AD and early 631 AD. By this time Muhammad had already conquered Mecca and the remaining non-Muslim tribes on the Arabian Peninsula, confronted by the burgeoning Muslim armies, were flocking to Medina to convert to Islam.

And ISNA has a problem in that these three verses from Chapter 9 were among the last verses to be "revealed" to Muhammad. According to the Islamic Doctrine of Abrogation, if there is a conflict between the message of a verse in Chapter 9 and that of a verse in another chapter, the verse in Chapter 9 abrogates (supersedes) the other verse; that other verse is still a valid part of the Koran, but the verse in Chapter 9 is the one now carrying the doctrinal weight. In reality, the verses in Chapter 9 were Allah's final instructions to the Muslims on how to deal with non-Muslims.

ISNA has an additional problem in that Islam teaches that the Koran consists of the perfect and eternal commands of Allah. So there is nothing in the Koran or Islamic doctrine that limits the messages of verses 9:5, 9:29, and 9:123 to the time period in which they were "revealed." The messages of these verses are as valid today as they were in the 7th Century.

Let's do a textual analysis. 9:5 is referred to by Muslim scholars as the "Verse of the Sword"; it commands Muslims to kill non-Muslims wherever they can be found, and to besiege and ambush them. The non-Muslims have only two choices: either fight to the death or convert to Islam. Here is that verse:

91

*Then when the Sacred Months have passed, then kill the
Mushrikun wherever you find them, and capture them and
besiege them, and lie in wait for them in every ambush.
But if they repent [by rejecting Shirk (polytheism) and
accept Islamic Monotheism] and perform As-Salat (the
prayers), and give Zakat (obligatory charity), then leave
their way free. Verily, Allah is Oft-Forgiving, Most
Merciful.*

9:29 commands Muslims to fight Jews and Christians, but it gives Jews
and Christians an additional option along with the options of fighting to
the death or converting to Islam. Jews and Christians can instead pay the
jizyah (protection money) and live as second-class citizens under Muslim
rule, feeling themselves subdued. Here is that verse:

*Fight against those who believe not in Allah, nor in the
Last Day, nor forbid that which has been forbidden by
Allah and His Messenger (Muhammad), and those who
acknowledge not the religion of truth (i.e. Islam) among
the people of the Scripture (Jews and Christians), until
they pay the Jizyah with willing submission, and feel
themselves subdued.*

9:123 commands Muslims (believers) to fight non-Muslims (disbelievers)
who are nearby and let those non-Muslims feel the harshness of the
Muslims:

*O you who believe! Fight those of the disbelievers who
are close to you, and let them find harshness in you; and
know that Allah is with those who are Al-Muttaqun (the
pious).*

There is no ambiguity in these three verses. And the attempt by ISNA to
suggest that these three verses only applied to a time period when the
"nascent Muslim community" was under attack is disproved by the facts
that they were "revealed" during a time when the Muslims were the most

powerful of the people on the Arabian Peninsula, and that the commands of Allah in the Koran are timeless.

And to further undermine ISNA's claim that the Koran does not call for violence against anyone for rejecting Islam, in 4:89 Allah commands death for any Muslim leaving Islam:

> ...But if they turn back (from Islam), take (hold of) them and kill them wherever you find them...

Taking Verses of the Koran out of Context

A regular response from ISNA is that critics of Islam have taken Koran verses out of context. But is interesting to see that ISNA is quite willing to do that very thing. Here are two examples.

In the brochure, ISNA makes a blanket statement that war is described in the Koran "as a hated act," and refers to 2:216. Here is that verse:

> Jihad (holy fighting in Allah's Cause) is ordained for you (Muslims) though you dislike it, and it may be that you dislike a thing which is good for you and that you like a thing which is bad for you. Allah knows but you do not know.

Authoritative Koran commentaries (tafsirs) explain that this verse does not say that war is "a hated act." On the contrary, this verse says that war (jihad) is obligatory and "good" for Muslims, even though some Muslims might not like it. The "bad" thing that some Muslims might like is to not participate in war; and this is bad because it means the enemy can win.[148]

---

[148] *Tafsir Ibn Kathir*, Vol. 1, pp. 596-597; *Tafsir Al-Qurtubi*, pp. 544-546; *Tafsir Al-Jalalayn*, p. 79; *Tafsir As-Sa'di*, Vol. 1, pp. 152-153; and *Tafsir Ahsanul-Bayan*, Vol. 1, pp. 190-191.

ISNA's statement that 2:216 proclaims that war is "a hated act" completely distorts the meaning of this verse and has no doctrinal basis.

The ISNA brochure mentions 60:8-9 to support the statement that

> *a basic rule governing the relationship between Muslims and people of other faiths is that of peaceful coexistence, justice and compassion.*

Here are those two verses:

> [8] *Allah does not forbid you to deal justly and kindly with those who fought not against you on account of religion nor drove you out of your homes. Verily, Allah loves those who deal with equity.* [9] *It is only as regards those who fought against you on account of religion, and have driven you out of your homes, and helped to drive you out, that Allah forbids you to befriend them. And whosoever will befriend them, then such are the Zalimun (wrongdoers – those who disobey Allah).*

Authoritative Koran commentaries explain that in 60:8 Allah allows Muslims to be kind to non-Muslims who don't want to fight the Muslims (e.g. women and weak non-Muslims) or help other non-Muslims against the Muslims.[149] Although one commentary stated that this was allowed only up until the time that Muslims had been commanded to fight the non-Muslims in "*jihad*".[150]

---

[149]   E.g., *Tafsir Ibn Kathir*, Vol. 9, pp. 595-597; and *Tafsir Ahsanul-Bayan*, Vol. 5, pp. 421-422.

[150]   *Tafsir Al-Jalalayn*, p. 1194.

Our authoritative Koran commentaries explain that in 60:9 Allah forbids Muslims from being kind toward, and/or having friendship with non-Muslims who are openly hostile and/or fought against Muslims.[151]

So we can see that ISNA's blanket statement about 60:8-9 supporting "peaceful coexistence, justice and compassion" is not an accurate explanation of the meaning of these two verses.

Conclusion

ISNA proclaims that it condemns "terrorism," but ISNA's unique definition of terrorism means that this condemnation apparently only applies to the random and/or accidental killing of devout Muslims.

ISNA is critical of those who take a "cut and paste" approach to verses of the Koran and take verses out of context. However, as was pointed out above, ISNA appears to be quite willing to present erroneous historical contexts and provide new, doctrinally unsupported interpretations of verses in the Koran.

Perhaps ISNA should heed the following advice from the section of their brochure talking about Muslims' responsibilities:

> *Educate Muslims, especially leaders and imams, about relevant Islamic teachings....Hold leaders responsible for un-Islamic teachings, and encourage them to seek training...*

Hopefully, such training will give the folks at ISNA a better understanding of Islam and minimize ISNA's un-Islamic teachings.

---

[151]   *Tafsir Ibn Kathir*, Vol. 9, pp. 597-598; *Tafsir Al-Jalalayn*, pp. 1194-1196; and *Tafsir Ahsanul-Bayan*, Vol. 5, pp. 422-423.

Fantasy Islam (Kafir Edition)

Fantasy Islam (Kafir Edition): A game in which an audience of non-Muslims wish with all their hearts that Islam was a "Religion of Peace," and a Kafir (non-Muslim) strives to fulfill that wish by presenting a version of Islam that has little foundation in Islamic Doctrine.

Stephen M. Kirby

12

John Esposito's Fairy Tale Version of Islam[152]

John Esposito is Professor of Religion and International Affairs and Professor of Islamic Studies at Georgetown University. He is also the Founding Director of the Alwaleed Center for Muslim-Christian Understanding. He is the author of *What Everyone Needs to Know about Islam*, a book in its second edition and presented as "the best single source…for answers to basic questions about Islam…"

The reality is that with his well-known book, Esposito played the Kafir Edition of Fantasy Islam. Here are some examples:

70 Virgins waiting in Paradise? – On pp. 143-144 Esposito wrote that there was nothing in the Koran that supported the idea of martyrs being rewarded with 70 virgins in Paradise. He noted that:

> *The reward of seventy virgins to martyrs is based on a "weak" Prophetic tradition used in medieval times to encourage Muslims to military activities…*

Esposito is half right. There is no mention in the Koran of 70 virgins as a reward. However, he is wrong with his numbers and when he ascribes it

---

[152]   This appeared in *FrontPage Mag* on December 22, 2016, with the title "Fantasy Islam (Kafir Edition) – John Esposito's fairy tale version of Islam": http://www.frontpagemag.com/fpm/265178/fantasy-islam-kafir-edition-dr-stephen-m-kirby.

simply to a "weak" tradition. In reality, Muhammad himself promised martyrs the reward of 72 virgins in paradise, and the following is from one of the six authoritative collections of Muhammad's teachings (*hadiths*) compiled in the ninth century:

> *Al-Miqdam bin Ma'diykarib narrated that the Messenger of Allah said: "There are six things with Allah for the martyr...he is married to seventy-two wives among Al-Huril-'Ayn* [virgins] *of Paradise...* "[153]

At-Tirmidhi himself stated this *hadith* was *"Hasan Sahih"* (lit. Good Sound/Authoritative). Was a "Professor of Islamic Studies" not aware of *Jami' At-Tirmidhi*?

Greater Jihad* vs. *Lesser Jihad – On pp. 133-134, and again in the Glossary, Esposito made a distinction between the *Greater Jihad*, supposedly the struggle with oneself, and the *Lesser Jihad*, supposedly fighting in defense of Islam. He claimed this distinction was based on a "well-known Prophetic tradition."

The reality is the opposite. Such a distinction between *Jihads* is based largely on two things: 1) Weak or fabricated *hadiths*; and 2) The 19th Century commentary inserted into *Reliance of the Traveller*, a 14th Century Shafi'i manual of Sharia Law; this commentary has been erroneously considered to be part of the original manual. I covered this fabricated distinction in more detail on pp. 115-123 of my book *Islam According to Muhammad, Not Your Neighbor*.

***Jihad* and Holy War** – On p. 134 Esposito wrote that *Jihad* "is not associated with the words *holy war* anywhere in the Quran." This is mildly interesting, but, on the other hand, Esposito did not mention

---

[153]   *Jami' At-Tirmidhi*, Vol. 3, No. 1663, p. 410.

98

numerous examples of other works where such an association is made, e.g.:

1. *Jihad: Striving, holy war.*[154]

2. *...the earliest (and therefore fundamental) Qur'anic reference to the question of jihad, or holy war...*[155]

3. *...he was taken prisoner in a jihad - that is, a holy war...*[156]

4. *...a woman taken captive in a "holy war" (jihad)...*[157]

5. *And He (Allah) said: Jihad (Islamic holy war) is ordained for you (Muslims)...*[158]

6. *The holy war (jihad) is a collective duty...*[159]

<u>Birth Control in Islam</u> – On p. 174 Esposito wrote:

> *The Quran does not address family planning measures, but a few hadith (traditions) mention coitus interruptus.*

---

[154]   *Dictionary of Islamic Words & Expressions*, p. 116.

[155]   *The Message of the Qur'an*, n. 167, p. 51.

[156]   Ibid., n. 72, p. 284.

[157]   Ibid., n. 58, p. 727.

[158]   Sheikh 'Abdullah bin Muhammad bin Humaid, *The Call to Jihad (Fighting For Allah's Cause) in the Qur'an*, p. 1046.

[159]   "The Book of the Holy War (*Kitab al-Jihad*)," *The Mainstay Concerning Jurisprudence (Al-'Umda fi 'l-Fiqh)*, p. 313.

Here is a well-known *hadith* about *coitus interruptus* that includes, to a certain degree, family planning. It addressed the problem of whether or not the ransom the Muslims were expecting for particular female captives would be affected if the captives were returned pregnant. In response to the question about whether the Muslim warriors should therefore engage in *coitus interruptus* with their rape victims, Muhammad, instead of prohibiting the rapes, merely said that *coitus interruptus* would not matter because every soul that was destined to be born would be born:

> *O Abu Sa'id, did you hear Allah's Messenger (SAW) mentioning al-'azl* [coitus interruptus]? *He said: Yes, and added: We went out with Allah's Messenger (SAW) on the expedition to the Bi'l-Mustaliq. We took captive some excellent Arab women. We desired them, for we were suffering from the absence of our wives, (but at the same time) we also desired ransom for them. So we decided to have sexual intercourse with them but by observing 'azl...But we said: We are doing an act whereas Allah's Messenger is amongst us; why not ask him? So we asked Allah's Messenger (SAW), and he said: It does not matter if you do not do it, for every soul that is to be born up to the Day of Resurrection will be born.*[160]

Jesus returns to Earth – In the spirit of ecumenical harmony, Esposito wrote that Islam teaches that Jesus would return to earth to "establish justice, and reign over the world for forty years as an upright and just ruler" (p. 29). But that is not how Muhammad had described Jesus' return. Here is what Muhammad said:

> *He* [Jesus] *will descend...He will break the cross, kill the pig, and banish the Jizyah and will call the people to Islam. During his time, Allah will destroy all religions*

---

[160]   *Sahih Muslim*, Vol. 4, No. 1438, p. 373.

except Islam...'Isa [Jesus] *will remain for forty years and then will die...*[161]

So during those forty years after he returned, Jesus would be destroying Christianity and calling the people to Islam.

And, according to Muhammad, Jesus would also be judging mankind by the laws of the Koran:

> *Narrated Abu Hurairah: Allah's Messenger said, "How will you be when the son of Maryam (Mary) ['Isa (Jesus)] descends amongst you, and he will judge people by the law of the Qur'an and not by the law of the Gospel."*[162]

Islam teaches that Jesus will return to earth to destroy Christianity, call the people to Islam, and judge by the Koran; according to Esposito this is an example of Jesus establishing "justice" and ruling as an "upright and just ruler."

The Apostasy Law was Man-Made – On p. 74 Esposito wrote that

> *Prominent Muslim scholars maintain that the Islamic law on apostasy, which prescribes the death penalty, was not based on the Quran but was a man-made effort in early Islam to prevent and punish the equivalent of desertion or treason...*

On the contrary, in 4:89 of the Koran Allah commands Muslims to take hold of those apostates who have left Islam and "kill them wherever you find them." So the death penalty for apostasy from Islam is in the Koran.

---

[161]   *Tafsir Ibn Kathir*, Vol. 3, p. 32.

[162]   *Sahih Al-Bukhari*, Vol. 4, Book 60, No. 3449, p. 412.

In addition, Muhammad said that death was the penalty for a Muslim who left Islam.[163] And Muhammad even specified the nature of that death:

> *If someone changes his religion - then strike off his head![164]*

Are these "prominent Muslim scholars" really saying that the Koran and the words of Muhammad were "man-made"?

Muslim Women in the Afterlife – On p. 31 Esposito wrote about the rewards the Koran says are waiting for women in paradise, pointing out that the Koran "makes no gender distinction as to the reward or punishment of the afterlife." But Esposito left out the fact that Muhammad made such a gender distinction:

> *Imran b. Husain reported that Allah's Messenger (may peace be upon him) said: Amongst the inmates of Paradise the women would form a minority.[165]*

And where was the final destination for most women?

> *Narrated 'Imran bin Husain: The Prophet said, "I looked at Paradise and found poor people forming the majority of its inhabitants; and I looked at Hell and saw that the majority of its inhabitants were women."[166]*

---

[163]   E.g., *Sahih Al-Bukhari*, Vol. 9, No. 6878, p. 20

[164]   *Al-Muwatta of Imam Malik ibn Anas*, 36.18.15, in a section titled "Judgement on Abandonment of Islam."

[165]   *Sahih Muslim*, Vol. 8, No. 2738, p. 253.

[166]   *Sahih Al-Bukhari*, Vol. 4, No. 3241, p. 290.

It is interesting to note that on p. 13 Esposito had pointed out that *Sahih Muslim* and *Sahih Al-Bukhari* were two collections of Muhammad's teachings that "enjoy special authoritative status" in most of the Muslim world. These two collections did not enjoy that same status in this section of Esposito's book.

Homosexuality – On p. 173 Esposito wrote that while homosexuality is forbidden in Islam, "Muslims are divided over how to respond to gay Muslims." This is strange because Esposito wrote in a number of places about Muhammad embodying the Koran and providing the example for Muslims to follow (pp. 11-12, 128, and 159), and Muhammad was explicit about what to do with homosexuals:

> *Ibn 'Abbas said that the Messenger of Allah said,*
> *"Whoever you catch committing the act of the people of Lut (homosexuality), then kill both parties to the act."*[167]
>
> *It was narrated from Abu Hurairah that the Prophet said concerning those who do the action of the people of Lut: "Stone the upper and the lower, stone them both."*[168]

Conclusion

Esposito wrote about the "common future" of the West and the Muslim world, and he stressed the importance of the "knowledge of what Islam teaches" (xv-xvi). Unfortunately, Esposito chose instead to play Fantasy Islam.

But there is more to Esposito's game playing. Part 2 will look at Esposito's version of the Koran.

---

[167] *Tafsir Ibn Kathir*, Vol. 2, p. 402.

[168] *Sunan Ibn Majah*, Vol. 3, No. 2562, p. 469.

John Esposito Channels the Koran[169]

In Part 1, I showed how John Esposito, a Professor of Islamic Studies at Georgetown University, played the Kafir Edition of Fantasy Islam with his book, *What Everyone Needs to Know about Islam.* In this article we look specifically at how Esposito also provided his own interpretation of the Koran.

Are Koran Verses General and Timeless? - When a Koran verse was "revealed," was its message specific only to a particular occurrence and/or time period? Or is the message of a Koran verse generally applicable without time restrictions?

There are a few Koran verses that were specific to a particular occurrence and cannot be applied generally (e.g., 24:11-20, 33:50, and 66:1-5). But with the exception of a few verses such as these, Muslim scholars have for centuries believed that most Koran verses are general in meaning with no time restrictions. As Yasir Qadhi pointed out:

> ...*it is not possible to restrict the ruling to the circumstances of its revelation, for the Qur'aan was*

---

169   This appeared in *FrontPage Mag* on December 26, 2016, with the title "Fantasy Islam (Kafir Edition) – John Esposito Channels the Koran": http://www.frontpagemag.com/fpm/265248/fantasy-islam-kafir-edition-part-ii-dr-stephen-m-kirby.

revealed as a guidance for all the nations until the Day of Judgement...[170]

As we shall see below, there is significance in whether a verse's message is general and timeless, or specific and restricted.

9:5 (The Verse of the Sword) – Esposito wrote on p. 138 that 9:5 started out with this command from Allah:

> *When the sacred months have passed, slay the idolaters wherever you find them...*

Esposito claimed that 9:5 applied to only a certain group of people during a certain time period:

> *Critics use the verse to demonstrate that Islam is inherently violent...it is a distortion to apply this passage to all non-Muslims or unbelievers; the verse is specifically referring to Meccan "idolaters" who are accused of breaking a treaty and continuously warring against the Muslims.*

Esposito then claimed that 9:5 was "immediately qualified" by the last portion of that verse:

> *But if they repent and fulfill their devotional obligations and pay the zakat [the charitable tax on non-Muslims], then let them go their way, for God is forgiving and kind.*

There are numerous problems with Esposito's examination of 9:5, starting with the claim that 9:5 was referring only to specific Meccan idolaters, for which he provided no supporting evidence.

---

[170]   *An Introduction to the Sciences of the Qur'aan*, p. 118.

Chapter 9 of the Koran was the last chapter to be "revealed" to Muhammad, so Allah's statements in that chapter are the final, timeless words on the topics addressed. And with regard to 9:5, the Muslim scholar Yasir Qadhi made this sobering comment about its timeless message:

> *This was one of the last verses to be revealed, and perhaps the last verse that dealt with the treatment of the disbelievers.*[171]

So this verse dealt with how the Muslims were to treat all non-Muslims, not just the Meccan idolaters.

According to the authoritative 14th Century Muslim scholar Ibn Kathir, 9:5 was reported to have abrogated every peace treaty between Muhammad and all non-Muslims and prevented any new treaties of that kind:

> *This honorable Ayah (9:5) was called the Ayah of the Sword, about which Ad-Dahhak bin Muzahim said, "It abrogated every agreement of peace between the Prophet and any idolator, every treaty, and every term." Al-'Awfi said that Ibn 'Abbas commented: "No idolator had any more treaty or promise of safety ever since Surah Bara'ah [Chapter 9] was revealed.*[172]

Ibn Kathir noted that the command to *slay the idolaters wherever you find them* was a "general statement" and meant Muslims could slay them "anywhere on earth you meet them."[173]

---

171   Ibid., p. 252.

172   *Tafsir Ibn Kathir*, Vol. 4, p. 377.

173   Abu al-Fida' 'Imad Ad-Din Isma'il bin 'Umar bin Kathir al-Qurashi Al-Busrawi, *Tafsir Ibn Kathir* (Abridged), abr. Sheikh Muhammad Nasib Ar-Rafa'i, trans. Chafik Abdelghani ibn Rahal (London: Al-Firdous Ltd., 1998), Part 10, p. 90.

Despite Esposito's claim to the contrary, the message of 9:5 is general and timeless.

Esposito then claimed that the last part of 9:5 restricted the command to slay non-Muslims found in the first part of that verse. To support this claim, he stated that the last part of 9:5 allowed non-Muslims to save themselves by paying the *zakat*, which he then erroneously defined as a *charitable tax on non-Muslims*. This was a strange definition, because Esposito had correctly noted on pp. 20-21 and in his Glossary that *zakat* was charitable giving by Muslims and one of the Five Pillars of Islam.

In spite of Esposito's claim, the real meaning of the last part of 9:5 is that the only way non-Muslims can save themselves is by converting to Islam.[174] But by erroneously defining *zakat*, Esposito enabled the reader to believe that 9:5 provided non-Muslims the option of paying the *charitable tax* on themselves to save themselves from the Muslims, instead of understanding the true command of 9:5, which is *convert to Islam or be killed*.

9:60 and *Zakat* – Esposito wrote about *zakat* on pp. 20-21. There he referred to 9:60, which states that *zakat* is allowed to be given for only certain purposes. One of those purposes was the "cause of God," and Esposito provided some examples of that "cause":

> *...to support those working in the "cause of God" (e.g., construction of mosques, religious schools, and hospitals, etc.).*

His were rather curious examples of the "cause of God," especially when considering how the "cause of God" mentioned in 9:60 was explained in other sources, e.g.:

---

174   E.g. *Tafsir Ibn Kathir*, Vol. 4, p. 376; and *Tafsir Al-Jalalayn*, p. 398.

1. *...(i.e. for Mujahidun – those fighting in a holy battle)...*[175]

2. *And for (fighters in) the cause of Allah...*[176]

3. *...is exclusive for the benefit of the fighters in Jihad...*[177]

4. *...to enable those who do not have booty to undertake jihad...*[178]

5. *For the cause of Allah means jihad. Zakah may be spent to buy weapons and help a fighter...*[179]

6. *...for the fighters for the cause of Allah...*[180]

No talk of construction projects here.

47:4 (How to Treat Prisoners) – Esposito pointed out on p. 140 that Islam "places limits on the use of violence," and the Koran provided guidelines regarding war. One of his examples was Koran verse 47:4, which he said explained "how to treat prisoners" in war. Esposito did not elaborate on what 47:4 actually stated, so here is the beginning of that verse:

---

[175]   *Interpretation of the Meanings of The Noble Qur'an*, trans. Muhammad Muhsin Khan and Muhammad Taqi-ud-Din Al-Hilali (Riyadh, Kingdom of Saudi Arabia: Darussalam, 2007), p. 266.

[176]   *English Translation of the Message of the Quran*, trans. Dr. Syed Vickar Ahamed (Lombard, IL: Book of Signs Foundation, 2007), p. 101.

[177]   *Tafsir Ibn Kathir*, Vol. 4, p. 458.

[178]   *Tafsir Al-Jalalayn*, p. 415.

[179]   *Tafsir Ahsanul-Bayan*, Vol. 2, p. 371.

[180]   *Tafsir Ibn 'Abbas*, p. 238.

So, when you meet (in fight – Jihad in Allah's Cause)
those who disbelieve, smite (their) necks till when you
have killed and wounded many of them, then bind a bond
firmly (on them, i.e. take them as captives)...

So according to Esposito, Islam "limits" violence by commanding that
Muslims can start taking captives only after they have killed and wounded
many of the enemy. An interesting definition of "limits."

2:256 (No Compulsion in Islam) – Esposito wrote on p. 91 that 2:256

is often used by scholars to illustrate Islam's acceptance
of freedom of religion, that other believers should not be
forced to convert to Islam.

In my latest book, *Islam's Militant Prophet: Muhammad and Forced*
Conversions to Islam, I show that the doctrinal authority of 2:256 lasted
only from the time of its "revelation" in August 625 until it was abrogated
by the actions of Muhammad in December 627. Prior to August 625 there
were a few examples of forced or attempted forced conversions to Islam.
From December 627 until Muhammad's death in 632, Islam was spread
across the Arabian Peninsula by Muhammad and the Muslims offering
most of the non-Muslim tribes the choice of Islam or the sword.
Muhammad believed that non-Muslims could, and should be forced to
convert to Islam, and he acted accordingly.

27:23-44 (The Queen of Sheba) – In a section titled "What kinds of roles
did women play in early Islam?" Esposito wrote on p. 105 about how in
27:23-44 the Koran portrayed the Queen of Sheba as a positive role model
and an "effective political leader." However, a look at those verses tells us
the opposite.

In 27:23-27 a "hoopoe" bird reported to King Solomon about the
Queen of Sheba, telling him that the Queen had many

possessions and a great throne. However, the Queen and her people worshipped the sun instead of Allah.

In 27:28-34 Solomon sent a letter to the Queen calling on her to become a Muslim. The Queen told her chiefs that she was afraid of what Solomon would do to them if he marched into Sheba.

In 27:35-41 the Queen sent Solomon a gift hoping he would not attack them, but Solomon told her messengers that he would come to them with a force they could not resist and drive them out in disgrace. Solomon then asked for someone from among his own people and *Jinn* to bring him her throne, and it was done by one of the *Jinn*.

In 27:42-44 the Queen went to Solomon, admitted that she had wronged herself by not believing in Allah, and then became a Muslim.

The theme of these verses is not on the Queen as a positive role model and effective leader, but rather as a Queen facing an overwhelming, hostile Muslim force and consequently deciding to convert to Islam.

Conclusion

In Part 1, we saw how adept Esposito was in playing the Kafir Edition of Fantasy Islam with the religion of Islam in general. Now we see that Esposito took a similar approach in presenting selected verses of the Koran. Perhaps his book would have been better titled *What Everyone Needs to Know about John Esposito's Version of Islam*.

14

Lutheran Social Service of MN: Play or Being Played?[181]

In 2015 the Lutheran Social Service of Minnesota produced a 61 page booklet titled *My Neighbor is Muslim, Exploring the Muslim Faith.*[182] The purpose of the booklet was to enable Lutherans to learn about Islam in order to better understand their "new neighbors" who were arriving as refugees.

On p. 3 of the booklet we find an endorsement by, and a picture of, Imam Hassan Ali Mohamud, the founder, Imam, and Director of the Minnesota Da'wah Institute. A brief biography of Mohamud can be found at the Institute's site. But there are a few additional items in Mohamud's background that are of particular interest and make him a curious choice as the endorser of a book welcoming Muslims into non-Muslim communities.

Hassan Ali Mohamud praised Hamas

The United States government declared Hamas a Foreign Terrorist Organization in 1997. On March 22, 2004, Sheikh Ahmed Yassin (Yaasin), the founder of Hamas, was killed in an Israeli airstrike. On

---

[181]   This appeared in *FrontPage Mag* on March 4, 2016, with the title "Fantasy Islam (Kafir Edition) – Lutheran Social Service of Minnesota: Play or Being Played?": http://www.frontpagemag.com/fpm/262027/fantasy-islam-kafir-edition-lutheran-social-dr-stephen-m-kirby.

[182]   http://lirs.org/myneighborismuslim/

March 26, 2004, Mohamud wrote an article in *Somalitalk – Minneapolis* expressing his condolences for Yassin's death.[183] The article was titled *Hambalyo Shahiid Sh. Ahmed Yaasin*, (Congratulations to Sheikh Ahmed Yaasin, the *Shahiid*). *Shahiid* is the term used for those who achieve martyrdom by being killed in the cause of Allah.

Mohamud noted that Yassin had founded Hamas and referred to the Hamas mujahidin (*mujaahidiinta*), who were fighting for the liberation of the Al-Aqsa Mosque and of Palestine (mujahidin are those fighting in the Cause of Allah). Mohamud hoped that Allah would consider Yassin a martyr, and he referred to Yassin as the Sheikh of the Mujahidin (*Sheikhul Mujaahidiin*). Mohamud referred to the Israelis as terrorists.

This article had the following byline: "Sh. Xasan Jaamici, xasanjaamici@yahoo.com, Minneapolis, MN, USA." How do we know this is our Hassan Ali Mohamud? An internet search of this name and e-mail address will show the connection to Mohamud (…which also include a telephone number).[184] The aforementioned telephone number is also connected to Mohamud.[185]

---

183   http://www.somaliatalk.com/2004/march/26mar404.html

184   Here are the sites:
1. http://nwaneri.com/
2. http://www.somaliatalk.com/2003/aug/jaamici2.html
3. http://somalitalk.com/kiish/shir.html (includes a telephone number)
4. http://www.somalitalk.com/hajj/hajj.html (includes a telephone number)
5. http://web.archive.org/web/20160422134539/http://www.somalicurrent.com/author/imam/
6. http://www.somaliatalk.com/2003/aug/2aug3003.html

185   Here are the sites:
1. http://www.naseeb.com/villages/journals/roseville-librarian-47627
2. http://somalitalk.com/kiish/civil.html
3. http://web.archive.org/web/20070109055820/http:/www.masmn.org/documents/pressreleases/MASMN_Media_Kit.pdf (on the page titled *Expert Resources Available To Media*)
4. http://documents.mx/documents/history-of-somalia.html (on p. 15 of the slide presentation)

Muslim cab drivers at the Minneapolis-St. Paul International Airport

For a number of years some Muslim cab drivers had refused to pick up passengers at the airport if those passengers were carrying sealed bottles of wine and/or liquor, even if those bottles were in the passenger's luggage. Controversy grew, and on June 6, 2006 the Muslim American Society of Minnesota (MAS) stepped in and issued a religious ruling (*fatwa*) stating that it violated Islamic law for the cab drivers to be involved in the transportation of alcohol. Hassan Ali Mohamud was one of the four members of the committee that issued this *fatwa*.

A few weeks later, when interviewed by NPR,[186] Mohamud stated:

> *Islamic identity is important because it is like keeping the faith. For that reason, Muslims here believe - Somalis are the majority of the Muslims in Minnesota- they believe it's important to have, like, our own village, what you can call like Muslim village.*

And what would this Muslim-majority "village" in the United States be like? Here is an excerpt from an article published later that year; this excerpt starts off with comments from Omar Jamal, a Muslim cab driver, and ends with comments from Mohamud:[187]

> *Jamal...says MAS is an organization of Middle Eastern Muslims attempting to fold Minnesota's large population of Somali Muslims into its divisive political campaign... "They've been driving the taxis for the last 20*

---

[186]   Sea Stachura, "More Somalis in Minnesota Turn to Islam," *NPR*, July 9, 2006; accessible at: http://www.npr.org/templates/story/story.php?storyId=5544610.

[187]   Mark Bergin, "Get out of the Cab," *Student News Daily*, November 7, 2006; accessible at: https://www.studentnewsdaily.com/world-current-events/get_out_of_the_cab/.

years. How come it became an issue now all of a sudden?
Were all the Muslims born again?"

MAS leader Mohamud, who is Somali, contends that just
such a revival occurred, that nominal Muslims began
practicing their faith. He says that as more Muslims do
the same, similar issues will continue to spring up
throughout the country. Asked if he believes local
governments should enforce Shariah law in communities
dominated by Muslim immigrants, Mohamud replied, "I
believe in American democracy, which is majority rules."

So according to Mohamud, as more Muslims return to their faith there will
be more conflicts springing up between Shariah Law and American law.
And if localities have a Muslim majority, then he believes that Shariah
Law should be enforced, even in the United States.

This approach by Mohamud should not be surprising, because of what he
wrote for his law school student newspaper in 2000; the article was titled
Law in the Islamic Perspective:[188]

Law, both as jurisprudence and as a normative system is
an articulation and an expression of God's will. As a
consequence, within the Islamic outlook, it is difficult to
conceive of a secular state or a secular legal system.

If one cannot conceive of a "secular legal system" then it is only natural to
come to the defense of Muslim cab drivers who are trying to impose
Allah's law on non-Muslims.

Omar Jamal would later state:[189]

---

[188]   Hassan Mohamud, "Law in the Islamic Perspective," *The Opinion*,
Winter 2000, p. 19; accessible at: http://mitchellhamline.edu/students/wp-
content/uploads/sites/9/2011/08/winter2000.pdf.

[189]   Mark Bergin, "Get out of the Cab."

"They have a political agenda, and they want to hijack the faith of Islam," he said of MAS leaders. "They're looking for an issue to get Muslims to rally behind to drive a wedge in the community between Muslims and non-Muslims."

Somali youth leaving Minneapolis to fight with al-Shabab

For many years there has been concern within the Somali community in Minneapolis, and among federal government officials, about Somali youth going overseas to fight for the *jihadist* terror group al-Shabab. In late 2008 and early 2009 there were two articles that mentioned Mohamud and his mosque.

On December 19, 2008 *USA Today* had an article that included an interview with a former *jihadist* living in Minneapolis.[190] Below he describes how *jihadists* recruit new members at one particular mosque, and he stated that similar activities were occurring at Mohamud's mosque, the Minnesota Da'wah Institute:

> *Yusuf Shaba...says he decided to speak out about what he considers Islamic indoctrination at Minneapolis mosques because he doesn't want his sons to follow the same path he did.*
>
> *Shaba, 34, joined Al Ittihad Al-Islami (Islamic Union) at age 16 and was wounded at age 19 in Somalia. Al Ittihad was Somalia's largest Islamic terrorist group in the 1990s...*

---

[190]   Oren Dorrell, "Somalis may be leaving Minn. for jihad," *USA Today*, December 19, 2008; accessible at:
http://usatoday30.usatoday.com/news/nation/2008-12-18-somalis_N.htm.

*Shaba says he and his three teenage sons attended a
program two months ago at Abubaker As-Saddique
Islamic Center, where a former Somali warrior sat in a
circle with other young people and delivered a passionate
recitation of his experiences during the Somali civil war.*

*Some mosques also screen videos about the war in
Afghanistan and about Muslim victims of perceived
injustices... "They give them all the grievances that
Osama Bin Laden has," Shaba says. "They talk about
nothing but jihad and it's the best thing that can happen to
a Muslim."...*

*Shaba says similar activities occur at Minnesota Da'wah
Institute in St. Paul, another mosque. Sheik Mahamud
Hassan [sic], the institute's imam, says nothing like that is
happening as his mosque. "It's liars," he says. "I'm not
missing any members."*

In February 2009 *NPR* did a similar report.[191] The report noted this about
the missing youth:

*All of them were reared by single mothers, and all of them
were particularly devout Muslims. They all prayed and
signed up for youth programs at two local mosques...*

Mohamud was the imam of one of those two mosques. And it was in
Mohamud's mosque where the parents said their missing boys spent a lot
of time, and even spent the night. In reply to the NPR interviewer,
Mohamud stated, "We are not missing any single student who is connected
to the mosque and the Dawah Islamic center." The interviewer pointed out
that when Mohamud and his mosque's youth director were being
interviewed, they were both "defensive."

---

[191]   Dina Temple-Raston, "Missing Somali Teens May Be Terrorist
Recruits," *NPR*, February 5, 2009; accessible at:
http://www.npr.org/templates/story/story.php?storyId=100287439.

Mohamud was refused clearance for an airport tour

In January 2016 Mohamud and other community leaders were invited to tour the Minneapolis - St. Paul International Airport and review its operations and screening procedures.[192] Each had to be cleared in advance to access the secure areas of the airport. But a few hours before the tour started on February 18th, Mohamud was notified that he had not been cleared to access the secure areas. Government officials would not discuss the matter.

Conclusion

Lutheran Social Service of Minnesota created a booklet seeking to educate non-Muslims about Islam and encouraging them to have a welcoming attitude toward Muslim refugees coming into their neighborhoods. Ironically, the Muslim imam selected to endorse this booklet appears to be a Hamas supporter, believes that Shariah Law should be enforced in American communities where Muslims are the majority, heads one of two mosques that have been the focus of articles about Somali youth leaving Minneapolis to fight for a terrorist organization, and was recently refused a government security clearance. Welcome to the neighborhood!

Part 2 will look at how Islam is presented in this booklet.

---

[192]   Mukhtar Ibrahim, "St. Paul imam barred from Twin Cities airport tour blames feds," *MPR News*, February 24, 2016; accessible at: http://www.mprnews.org/story/2016/02/24/st-paul-imam-barred-from-twin-cities-airport-tour.

15

Lutheran Social Service of MN: Who is "reforming" who?[193]

In 2015 the Lutheran Social Service of Minnesota produced a 61 page booklet titled *My Neighbor is Muslim, Exploring the Muslim Faith.*[194] The purpose of the booklet was to enable Lutherans to learn about Islam in order to better understand their "new neighbors" who were arriving as refugees. The booklet includes discussion questions after each chapter.

In my first article about this booklet, I looked at the interesting background of the imam who endorsed the booklet.[195] The focus of this article is on how the booklet presents Islam.

Statements Supported by Vague Terms

There was only one footnote in this booklet; it was on p. 48 and simply pointed out other names for the *jihadist* group ISIS. Throughout the booklet assertions about Islam and Islamic Doctrine were made, with only the occasional use of vague terms such as "mainstream Islamic tradition," "most Muslims," or "many scholars" to support these assertions. The

---

[193]   This appeared in *FrontPage Mag* on March 10, 2016, with the title "Fantasy Islam (Kafir Edition) – Lutheran Social Service of Minnesota: Who is "reforming" who?": http://www.frontpagemag.com/fpm/262094/fantasy-islam-kafir-edition-lutheran-social-dr-stephen-m-kirby.

[194]   http://lirs.org/myneighborismuslim/

[195]   Kirby, "Fantasy Islam (Kafir Edition) – Lutheran Social Service of Minnesota: Play or Being Played?"

booklet does have a suggested reading list of ten books by modern authors, but there is no indication where among those ten books one could go for further reading about any particular statement made about Islam.

Islam's Jesus – the Rest of the Story

The booklet has a chapter titled "What Does the Qur'an Say about Jesus?" This chapter pointed out similarities and differences "between the Qur'an's presentation of Jesus and traditional Christian understandings of Jesus." There were three differences the booklet found worth of considering: 1) Jesus Is Not the Son of God; 2) Jesus Is Not a Savior; and 3) Jesus Was Not Crucified. On p. 17 we find that these differences are not "insurmountable":

> *While the differences between the Muslim and Christian Jesus are significant, they are not insurmountable hurdles for interfaith dialogue. The reverence and respect Muslims have for Jesus is considerable. If Christians can develop an appreciation for the prominent role that Jesus has in Islam, they may discover Jesus is more of an opportunity than an obstacle for developing interfaith relationships with their Muslim sisters and brothers.*

But to really understand "the prominent role that Jesus has in Islam," we must turn to the teachings of Muhammad (the *hadiths*). Here is what Muhammad said would happen when Jesus returned to earth:

> *He [Jesus] will descend…He will break the cross, kill the pig, and banish the Jizyah and will call the people to Islam. During his time, Allah will destroy all religions except Islam…*[196]

---

[196]   *Tafsir Ibn Kathir*, Vol. 3, p. 32.

And, according to Muhammad, Jesus would also be judging mankind by the laws of the Koran:

> *Narrated Abu Hurairah: Allah's Messenger said, "How will you be when the son of Maryam (Mary) ['Isa (Jesus)] descends amongst you, and he will judge people by the law of the Qur'an and not by the law of the Gospel."*[197]

So Islam teaches that Jesus will return to earth to destroy Christianity, call the people to Islam, and judge mankind by the Koran. In terms of "interfaith dialogue," these three issues should be priorities for discussion. But the Islamic message of these three issues raises interesting questions about the "opportunity" they create for "interfaith relationships" between Muslims and those who are to be destroyed by Islam's Jesus.

No Compulsion Under Islam

On p. 24 we find:

> *The first point to note is that the general policy in Islamic empires in premodern history was not to force Jews and Christians to convert. The source of this policy is the Qur'an.*

> *Let there be no compulsion in religion. Surely, Truth stands out clearly from error. Whoever rejects evil and believes in God has held the most trustworthy handhold that never breaks. And God is All-Hearing, All-Knowing (Q. 2:256).*

> *...Islam's primary emphasis when it comes to conversion is that one must accept Islam through free will.*

---

[197]   *Sahih Al-Bukhari*, Vol. 4, Book 60, No. 3449, p. 412.

2:256 of the Koran is used as the basis for claiming that there is no compulsion under Islam for the conversion of non-Muslims. However, this claim ignores the Doctrine of Abrogation, which is fundamental to understanding Islam. Here is a summary of that Doctrine:

The verses of the Koran are "revelations" Muhammad received from 610 AD until his death in 632 AD. While in Mecca, the religion of Islam was just starting and it was generally not well received. Perhaps as a result of this, the verses of the Koran "revealed" in Mecca were generally more peaceful and accommodating toward non-Muslims than the verses later "revealed" in Medina. The verses from Medina had a general tendency to be more belligerent and intolerant, and more inclined to make sharp differentiations between Muslims (believers) and non-Muslims (disbelievers).

This can lead to a conflict between the message of a Meccan verse and that of a Medinan verse addressing the same general topic. But how can there be such a conflict if the Koran is the infallible, eternal, "revealed" word of Allah? This was covered in a Medinan verse in the Koran that introduced the concept of "abrogation":

Chapter 2, Verse 106

> *Whatever a Verse (revelation) do We abrogate or cause to be forgotten, We bring a better one or similar to it. Know you not that Allah is Able to do all things?*

Abrogation means that if there is a conflict between the messages of two "revelations" in the Koran, then the most recent "revelation" is the one to be followed. Both verses remain in the Koran because they are considered the words of Allah; but it is the most recent "revelation" that now carries the doctrinal weight. So let's take a brief chronological look at this claim of "no compulsion under Islam."

121

2:106 was "revealed" around February 624.[198] 2:256 was "revealed" around August 625.[199] So as of August 625 Allah had "revealed" that verses of the Koran could be abrogated and no one was to be forced to become a Muslim.

Around March 629, 2:193 was "revealed"[200]:

> *And fight them until there is no more Fitnah (disbelief and worshipping of others along with Allah) and (all and every kind of) worship is for Allah (Alone). But if they cease, let there be no transgression except against Az-Zalimun (the polytheists and wrongdoers).*

The authoritative Muslim scholar al-Qurtubi explained the meaning of this verse:

> *It is an unqualified command to fight without any precondition of hostilities being initiated by the unbelievers [non-Muslims]...The Prophet said, "I was commanded to fight people until they say, 'There is no god but Allah.'...If they cease, there should be no enmity towards any but wrongdoers. If they stop and become Muslim or submit by paying jizya...Otherwise they should be fought....The wrongdoers are either those who initiate fighting or those who remain entrenched in disbelief and fitna.[201]*

---

[198]   *Tafsir Al-Qurtubi*, p. 321.

[199]   Abu'l-Hasan 'Ali ibn Ahmad ibn Muhammad ibn 'Ali al-Wahidi, *Al-Wahidi's Asbab al-Nuzul*, trans. Mokrane Guezzou (Louisville, KY: Fons Vitae, 2008), pp. 36-37.

[200]   *Al-Wahidi's Asbab al-Nuzul*, p. 23; and *Tafsir Ahsanul-Bayan*, Vol. 1, pp. 171-172.

[201]   *Tafsir Al-Qurtubi*, p. 496.

Chapter 9 of the Koran was "revealed" in 630-631. In that chapter is Verse 5:

> *Then when the Sacred Months have passed, then kill the Mushrikun [non-Muslims] wherever you find them, and capture them and besiege them, and lie in wait for them in every ambush. But if they repent [by rejecting Shirk (polytheism) and accept Islamic Monotheism] and perform As-Salat (the prayers), and give Zakat (obligatory charity), then leave their way free. Verily, Allah is Oft-Forgiving, Most Merciful.*

So 9:5 commands Muslims to aggressively seek-out and attack non-Muslims, and to kill some, and to capture some. And the only way non-Muslims could save themselves would be to convert to Islam.

Just with these few Koran verses the Doctrine of Abrogation shows us that the idea there is "no compulsion in Islam" has been abrogated by at least two subsequent verses of the Koran. Unfortunately, the booklet *My Neighbor is Muslim* does not address the Doctrine of Abrogation. And by ignoring this doctrine, the booklet was then able to present any Koran verse as still carrying doctrinal weight.

Conclusion

The purported purpose of this booklet is to provide introductory information about Islam that can be used in group discussions. Space limits for this article enabled us to examine just a few of the issues I found with this booklet. Nevertheless, it is hard to see how a version of Islam that includes significant omissions and broad assertions can possible contribute to a better understanding of the Islam of Muhammad. However, it will certainly help one better understand the Lutheran Social Service Reformed Islam.

Christian and Political Leaders

Quo vadis?

16

Do We All Believe in the Same God?[202]

A commonly heard claim is that Jews, Christians and Muslims all believe in "the same God." These are comforting words and of great assistance to those wishing to engage in interfaith dialogues and tri-faith ventures. But is this true? To answer that question, let's look at what is said and taught about Jews and Christians by Allah, the god of Islam, and Muhammad, Allah's prophet. We'll start with the Koran.

The Koran

Muslims believe the Koran is the infallible, timeless and perfect word of Allah. So what does Allah say in the Koran about Jews and Christians?

To set the stage, Allah states that the only religion acceptable to him is Islam (e.g., 3:19 and 3:85). And Allah states that Islam is to be made superior over all other religions, even if the non-Muslims don't like it (e.g., 9:33, 48:28, and 61:9).

Allah states that he is angry with the Jews, and the Christians are misguided in their beliefs (1:7). In fact, Allah curses the Jews and Christians (9:30). He states that the Jews and Christians are among the worst of creatures who "will abide in the fire of Hell" (98:6), while Muslims are the best of creatures (3:110 and 98:7). He forbids Muslims

---

[202]   This appeared in *FrontPage Mag* on December 22, 2014: http://www.frontpagemag.com/2014/dr-stephen-m-kirby/do-we-all-believe-in-the-same-god.

from being friends with Jews and Christians (5:51). Instead, Allah commands Muslims to fight the Jews and Christians until those Jews and Christians pay the *jizyah* (protection tax), with willing submission and feeling themselves subdued (9:29).

Allah specifically states that the Jews are among the worst enemies of Islam (5:82).

Allah states that Christianity is a false religion. Allah says that Jesus was not crucified, but it only appeared so (4:157-158). Allah states that he took Jesus bodily into paradise and made one of Jesus' disciples look like Jesus; it was that disciple who was crucified. So Muslims who know their religion look at a crucifix or a painting of the Crucifixion and see an imposter hanging on the cross. And of course, if there was no Crucifixion, there was no Resurrection. So Islam teaches that Christianity is based on a fraud.

Allah also states that those who believe that Jesus is the Son of God commit the one unforgiveable sin in Islam, *Shirk* (e.g., 4:48 and 4:116). In fact, Allah curses Christians specifically for this belief (9:30) and says that those who so believe will go to Hell (e.g., 3:151 and 5:72-73).

Muhammad

Islam teaches that Muhammad spoke for Allah (4:80), and Allah commands Muslims to obey Muhammad (59:7). And Muhammad is considered the timeless standard by which Muslims should conduct themselves (33:21). So what did Muhammad have to say?

He said Jews and Christians are worth only half as much as a Muslim,[203] and he gave the following advice about what to do when meeting Jews and Christians:

---

[203]   *Sunan Ibn Majah*, Vol. 3, No. 2644, p. 521.

*Do not greet the Jews and the Christians before they greet
you and when you meet any one of them on the roads force
him to go to the narrowest part of it.*[204]

Muhammad said that the Jews were grave robbers,[205] and he said,

*The Hour will not be established until you fight against
the Jews, and the stone behind which a Jew will be hiding
will say, 'O Muslim! There is a Jew hiding behind me, so
kill him.*[206]

Muhammad said that on the Day of Resurrection, mountains of sins would
be removed from the backs of Muslims and put onto the Jews and
Christians.[207] Muhammad even said that Jews and Christians would take
the place of Muslims in Hell.[208]

And on his death bed Muhammad said:

*I will expel the Jews and Christians from the Arabian
Peninsula and will not leave any but Muslims.*[209]

These are timeless commands and statements from Allah and Muhammad,
and Muslims are not allowed to disagree with them (33:36).

---

[204]   *Sahih Muslim*, Vol. 6, No. 2167, p. 439.

[205]   *Sahih Al-Bukhari*, Vol. 4, Book 60, No. 3452, p. 413.

[206]   *Sahih Al-Bukhari*, Vol. 4, Book 56, No. 2926, p. 113.

[207]   *110 Ahadith Qudsi: Sayings of the Prophet Having Allahs Statements*, 3rd
ed., trans. Syed Masood-ul-Hasan (Riyadh, Kingdom of Saudi Arabia:
Darussalam, 2006), No. 8, titled *Superiority of the believers in the Oneness of
Allah and the punishment of Jews and Christians*, pp. 19-20.

[208]   *Sahih Muslim*, Vol. 8, No. 2767R1, p. 269.

[209]   *Sahih Muslim*, Vol. 5, No. 1767, p. 189.

So if Allah is God and the Koran consists of statements and commands from Allah, if Muhammad spoke for Allah, and if Jews, Christians and Muslims all believe in that same God, then Jews and Christians believe in and worship a God who hates and curses them, orders Muslims to fight them, and condemns them to Hell simply because they are not Muslims.

Either we are talking about a pagan god of multiple, compartmentalized personalities, or the claim that Jews, Christians and Muslims all believe in the same God is theological nonsense.

17

Islam and the Role of the Shepherd[210]

A good shepherd protects the flock and defends it from anything harmful or dangerous. The priest, as the shepherd making present Jesus the Good Shepherd, does this through the function of teaching as well as by preaching and catechizing.[211]

I was recently advised of an article titled "Extremists don't accurately represent the faith of Muslims" that appeared in the *Catholic Voice* on December 4, 2015. Looking online, I found that this article has appeared in a number of publications since the latter part of November under titles such as "Our Muslim Brothers and Sisters" and "Muslims, our brothers and sisters."[212]

---

[210] This was written on December 19, 2015, for the Global Faith Institute, Omaha, NE (http://globalfaithinstitute.org/). The article is accessible at: https://islamseries.files.wordpress.com/2016/01/gfi-islam-and-the-role-of-the-shepherd.pdf.

[211] Bishop Paul S. Loverde, "The Priest: A Shepherd After the Heart of Christ," *The Arlington Catholic Herald*, August 5, 2009; accessible at: http://catholicherald.com/Faith/Bishop_Loverde/Homilies/The_Priest__A_Shepherd_After_the_Heart_of_Christ/.

[212] For example:
1. http://catholicvoiceomaha.com/spiritual-life/extremists-don%E2%80%99t-accurately-represent-faith-muslims.
2. http://ronrolheiser.com/our-muslim-brothers-and-sisters/#.WO6XoWnyuM9.
3. http://www.pilotcatholicnews.com/Opinion/article.asp?ID=175305.
4. http://www.catholic-sf.org/news_select.php&newsid=27&id=58007/https:/ns.php?newsid=7&id=63998

The article was written by Oblate Father Ron Rolheiser, a theologian, teacher, and president of the Oblate School of Theology in San Antonio, Texas. The focus of the article was on getting Christians to understand that Islam was being misrepresented *by jihadist* groups like ISIS, and that "moderate Muslims" were not only being physically victimized by these *jihadist* groups, but these "moderate Muslims" were also being psychologically victimized by non-Muslims who were becoming hostile to Islam as a result of the *jihadists'* activities.

Let's consider some of the statements that Father Rolheiser made about Islam in his article.

Violence is not Inherent to Islam

Father Rolheiser mentioned that violence being done by "radical Islamic groups" was becoming more prevalent. He noted:

> *Popular opinion more and more blames the Muslim religion for that violence, suggesting there is something inherent in Islam that's responsible for this kind of violence. That equation needs to be challenged, both in the name of truth and in the name of what's best in us as Christians. First of all, it's untrue.*

So let's examine his claim.

Islamic Doctrine is based on the commands of Allah in the Koran and the teachings and example of Allah's Messenger Muhammad (the *Sunnah*). Here is some of what the verses in the Koran and the *Sunnah* have to say about violence:

1. *Jihad* (holy fighting) is "ordained" for Muslims, whether they like it or not (2:216).

2. Muslims are commanded to kill non-Muslims in general, and are allowed to kill non-Muslim women, children, and other non-combatants (9:5 and *Sunnah*).

3. Muslims are commanded to fight against Jews and Christians (9:29).

4. Muslims are commanded to be harsh toward non-Muslims (e.g. 9:14, 9:73, 9:123, 48:29, and 66:9), and can even severely punish and torture non-Muslim captives (8:57 and *Sunnah*).

5. Amputation is a punishment for theft (5:38 and *Sunnah*).

6. Adulterers should be stoned to death (*Sunnah*).

7. Apostates from Islam should be killed (4:89 and *Sunnah*).

8. Crucifixion is allowed (5:33).

9. Flogging is a legitimate punishment (24:2 and *Sunnah*).

10. A Muslim man can beat his wives (4:34 and *Sunnah*).

11. Muslims can take non-Muslim female captives as sex slaves (4:24 and *Sunnah*).

12. Non-Muslims can be beheaded (8:12, 47:4, and *Sunnah*).

13. Mutilation of non-Muslims is allowed (5:33, 8:12, and *Sunnah*).

14. Non-Muslims can be burned alive (*Sunnah*).

15. Non-Muslims who criticize Islam, Allah, and/or Muhammad can be killed (e.g. 5:33, 33:57, and *Sunnah*).

The only way to maintain that there is nothing inherently violent about Islam is to deny Islamic Doctrine. Nevertheless, Father Rolheiser wrote:

Any interpretation of Islam by a radicalized group that gives divine sanction to terrorist violence is false and belies Islam.

Untrue - *jihadist* groups who commit any of the above acts of violence have already been given divine sanction.

We Have the Same God

Father Rolheiser repeats the mantra that, "We have the same God." If this is so, what does Allah, the god of Islam, have to say about Jews and Christians? Consider the following:

1. Allah states that the only religion acceptable to him is Islam (e.g., 3:19 and 3:85). And Allah states that Islam is to be made superior over all other religions, even if the non-Muslims don't like it (e.g., 9:33, 48:28, and 61:9).

2. Allah states that he is angry with the Jews, and the Christians are misguided in their beliefs (1:7). In fact, Allah curses the Jews and Christians (9:30). He states that the Jews and Christians are among the worst of creatures who "will abide in the fire of Hell" (98:6), while Muslims are the best of creatures (3:110 and 98:7). He forbids Muslims from being friends with Jews and Christians (5:51). Instead, Allah commands Muslims to fight the Jews and Christians until those Jews and Christians pay the *jizyah* (protection tax), with willing submission and feeling themselves subdued (9:29).

3. Allah specifically states that the Jews are among the worst enemies of Islam (5:82).

4. Allah states that Christianity is a false religion. Allah says that Jesus was not crucified, but it only appeared so (4:157-158). Allah states that he took Jesus bodily into paradise and made one of Jesus' disciples look like Jesus; it was that disciple who was

crucified. So Muslims who know their religion look at a crucifix or a painting of the Crucifixion and see an imposter hanging on the cross. And of course, if there was no Crucifixion, there was no Resurrection. So Islam teaches that Christianity is based on a fraud.

5. Allah also states that those who believe that Jesus is the Son of God commit the one unforgiveable sin in Islam, *Shirk* (e.g., 4:48 and 4:116). In fact, Allah curses Christians specifically for this belief (9:30) and says that those who so believe will go to Hell (e.g., 3:151 and 5:72-73).

And speaking of Hell, Father Rolheiser wrote about a Trappist monk who was killed by Islamic terrorists in Algeria in 1996. The monk had earlier written to his family that if he was to be killed by the terrorists, he had already forgiven them and he foresaw himself and his killers "in the same heaven, playing together under God's gaze." The reality is that Islamic doctrine says otherwise; Muhammad said that the sins of Muslims would be removed and placed on the backs of the Jews and Christians,[213] Jews and Christians would actually take the place of Muslims in Hell,[214] and Jews and Christians who died without converting to Islam would go to Hell.[215]

So if Jews, Christians and Muslims all have the same God, then Jews and Christians believe in and worship a God who hates and curses them, orders Muslims to fight them, and condemns them to Hell. And only Muslims will be playing together in Heaven.

---

[213]   *110 Ahadith Qudsi: Sayings of the Prophet Having Allahs Statements*, No. 8, titled *Superiority of the believers in the Oneness of Allah and the punishment of Jews and Christians*, pp. 19-20.

[214]   *Sahih Muslim*, Vol. 8, No. 2767R1, p. 269.

[215]   *Sahih Muslim*, Vol. 1, No. 153, p. 103.

Authentic, God-fearing Muslims are the First Victims of Jihadists

Father Rolheiser states that *jihadists* "have killed thousands more Muslims than they have killed Christians or persons of any other religion." This is a common statement made by those who are trying to claim that the violence done by *jihadists* is not supported by Islamic Doctrine.

This claim is best addressed in a recent article by Raymond Ibrahim titled *But ISIS Kills More Muslims than Non-Muslims!*[216] Ibrahim makes the following observations:

1. ISIS does not consider its victims to be Muslim. ISIS is a Sunni Muslim organization and views all non-Sunnis as false Muslims (and, on the other hand, Shia Muslims view all non-Shias as false Muslims).

2. If fellow Sunnis are accidently killed by ISIS, those Sunni victims are considered martyrs, destined to enter Islam's paradise.

3. Sunnis who are intentionally killed by ISIS are considered to be infidels and, therefore, to be non-Muslims.

Ibrahim aptly summed it up:

> *In short, to Sunni jihadis – not just ISIS, but al-Qaeda, Boko Haram, Hamas, et al – all non-Sunni peoples are infidels and thus free game. As for fellow Sunnis, if they die accidentally, they are martyrs...and if fellow Sunnis intentionally get in the way, they are denounced as infidels and killed accordingly.*

---

[216]   Raymond Ibrahim, "But ISIS Kills More Muslims than Non-Muslims!" *FrontPage Mag*, December 18, 2015; accessible at: http://www.frontpagemag.com/fpm/261156/isis-kills-more-muslims-non-muslims-raymond-ibrahim.

Hitler was a Christian?

Father Rolheiser paraphrases a scholar who wrote that

> *we should always judge a religion by its best expressions,*
> *by its saints and graced history, rather than by its*
> *psychopaths and aberrations.*

Father Rolheiser then proceeds to state, "Hitler was somehow a product of the Christian West, as was Mother Teresa."

It is unfortunately common to hear attempts to excuse the violence done in the name of Islam by equating the actions and beliefs of Hitler with Christianity. But what is unanswered, even by Father Rolheiser, is where in the teachings of Jesus is there Christian doctrinal support for the Nazi concentration camps and the slaughter of millions of civilians? This question is not pursued by such folks because the answer undermines any attempt to link Hitler's beliefs and actions with Christianity. The answer is simple: there is nothing in the teachings of Jesus to support such beliefs and actions.

Conclusion

In his role as a priest, Father Rolheiser is called upon to protect his flock from danger and harm. One of the ways of doing so is by teaching his flock about the sources of that danger and harm. To varying degrees Islam has been at war with non-Muslims since the 7th Century. This war is based on the commands of Allah and the teachings and example of Muhammad. The shepherd does his flock a great disservice by denying this, for the flock will perceive a sheep dog where they should recognize a wolf.

18

The True Meaning of ISNA's Christmas Greeting[217]

On December 29, 2015, the Islamic Society of North America (ISNA) extended a Christmas greeting to "Our Christian Brothers and Sisters." ISNA, it must be remembered, was, and still is considered an unindicted co-conspirator in the successfully prosecuted federal terrorism case against the Holy Land Foundation for Relief and Development. ISNA is also Number One on the list of the Muslim Brotherhood's "organizations and the organizations of our friends."

The tone of the greeting was how much in common Muslims have with their Christian brothers and sisters. This should not be surprising because at the bottom of the greeting was: Dr. Sayyid M. Sayeed, ISNA Office of Interfaith and Community Alliances Director.

So let's examine some of the claims of commonality in this greeting.

---

[217] This appeared in *FrontPage Mag* on January 5, 2016: http://www.frontpagemag.com/fpm/261331/true-meaning-isnas-christmas-greeting-dr-stephen-m-kirby.

136

Mary, the Mother of Jesus

The Christmas greeting makes much of the fact that Mary appears to be equally revered by both Muslims and Christians. To show that Muslim reverence, ISNA points out there is an entire chapter of the Koran named after Mary (Chapter 19). But the greeting fails to mention that of the 98 verses in that chapter, only fourteen are actually devoted to Mary (Verses 16-29).

And Islam has an interesting, but different, approach to the virgin birth of Jesus. 21:91 and 66:12 of the Koran state that Mary became pregnant by the Angle Gabriel blowing into an opening of the garment she was wearing. Ibn Kathir explained:

> *Then the breath descended until it entered into her vagina and she conceived the child by the leave of Allah.*[218]

The nature of Gabriel's involvement in this would be an interesting topic for interfaith dialogue.

ISNA rejects certain interpretations and understandings of the Koran?

ISNA's greeting included this eye-opening statement:

> *We reject those interpretations and that understanding of our scriptures that set us up against each other...*

In the Koran Allah states that Islam is the only acceptable religion and is to be supreme over all other religions (e.g., 3:85, 9:33, 48:28, and 61:9). Allah commands Muslims to kill non-Muslims (9:5) and to specifically

---

[218]   *Tafsir Ibn Kathir*, Vol. 6, p. 244; also see *Tafsir Al-Jalalayn*, pp. 704 and 1223.

fight the Christians (9:29). Allah prohibits Muslims from being friends with Christians (5:51), he curses Christians (9:30), and states that Christians are among the worst of creatures and will go to Hell (98:6).

The Koran specifically states the Jesus was not the son of Allah (e.g., 4:171, 5:72, 9:30, and 19:35). The Koran also states that Jesus was not crucified, but it only appeared so (4:157-158). The authoritative Muslim scholar Ibn Kathir explained how this worked: One of Jesus' followers volunteered to take Jesus' place; so Allah made that follower look like Jesus, Allah took Jesus bodily to paradise, and that follower was crucified.[219]

According to Islamic Doctrine then, Jesus was not crucified, which means there was no Resurrection. Consequently, the Christian brothers and sisters receiving ISNA's greeting believe in a religion that is based on a fraud. And Muslims who know their religion look at a crucifix or a painting of the Crucifixion and see an imposter hanging on the cross. No commonality between Muslims and Christians here.

Muslims believe that the Koran consists of the timeless, perfect, and unchangeable commands of Allah. Is ISNA now saying that, for the sake of getting along with Christians, they have decided to pick and choose which commands of Allah they will follow, and which ones they will ignore?

The Divine Command that "binds" Muslims and Christians

ISNA's greeting stated:

> We stand committed to the divine command that binds us
> to cooperate in promoting good and forbidding what is
> evil and harmful for God's creation (Quran 5:2).

---

[219]   *Tafsir Ibn Kathir*, Vol. 3, p. 28.

So ISNA states there are "divine commands" that bind Muslims and Christians together in promoting good and forbidding evil, and this is based on 5:2 of the Koran. Here is how 5:2 starts off:

> *O you who believe! Violate not the sanctity of the*
> *Symbols of Allah...*

What are these *Symbols of Allah*? They are what Allah has made permissible and what Allah has made impermissible; they are the hallmarks of Islam.[220] The rest of 5:2 focuses on other aspects of Islamic Doctrine: the Sacred Month, animal sacrifices, and the pilgrimage to Mecca.

So according to ISNA, Christians and Muslims are bound together by the "divine command" to promote good and to forbid evil. Except, the basis for this claim is a Koran verse that states this "divine command" comes from the god of Islam and pertains to only what is good and evil in Islamic terms.

The Teachings and Example of Jesus Christ

ISNA's Christmas greeting ended with these words:

> *Let the teachings and example of Jesus Christ continue to*
> *energize us all with love, tolerance, religious freedom and*
> *mutual respect.*

So let's consider some of what Islam tells us about the teachings and example of Jesus.

The Koran states that Jesus was one of the Messengers of Allah (e.g. 3:49, 3:53, 4:171, 5:75, and 61:6), and a "slave" of Allah (e.g. 4:172, 21:26, and

---

[220]   *Tafsir Ibn Kathir*, Vol. 3, p. 76; *Tafsir Al-Jalalayn*, p. 235; and *Tafsir As-Sa'di*, Vol. 1, p. 471.

43:59). As a baby in his cradle, Jesus himself proclaimed that he was "a slave of Allah" (19:30).

Here is what Muhammad said would happen when Jesus first returned to earth:

> He [Jesus] *will descend while wearing two long, light yellow garments. His head appears to be dripping water, even though no moisture touched it. He will break the cross, kill the pig, and banish the Jizyah and will call the people to Islam. During his time, Allah will destroy all religions except Islam... 'Isa [Jesus] will remain for forty years and then will die, and Muslims will offer the funeral prayer for him.*[221]

So during those forty years after Jesus returned, Allah would destroy all religions except Islam, and Jesus would be breaking the cross of Christianity and calling the people to Islam. The *Jizyah* is the protection money demanded of Jews and Christians in 9:29 of the Koran in lieu of fighting to the death or converting to Islam. So when Islam's Jesus returns to earth, the *Jizyah* will be banished simply because the only religion allowed will be Islam.

And, according to Muhammad, Jesus would also be judging mankind by the laws of the Koran:

> *Narrated Abu Hurairah: Allah's Messenger said, "How will you be when the son of Maryam (Mary) ['Isa (Jesus)] descends amongst you, and he will judge people by the law of the Qur'an and not by the law of the Gospel."*[222]

Here is what 4:159 of the Koran has to say about Jesus and religious freedom:

---

[221]   *Tafsir Ibn Kathir*, Vol. 3, p. 32.

[222]   *Sahih Al-Bukhari*, Vol. 4, Book 60, No. 3449, p. 412.

And there is none of the people of the Scripture (Jews and Christians) but must believe in him ['Isa (Jesus), son of Maryam (Mary), as only a Messenger of Allah and a human being] before his ['Isa (Jesus) or a Jew's or a Christian's] death (at the time of the appearance of the angel of death). And on the Day of Resurrection, he ['Isa (Jesus)] will be a witness against them.

This verse means that Jews and Christians only have up until *the point of death* to believe that Jesus was just a Messenger of Allah and a human being. Some Islamic scholars believed that *the point of death* pertained to the death of the individual Christian or Jew; other scholars believed that the Jews and Christians only have up until the point of Jesus' actual death, after he returns and fights the final battle, to so believe.[223] So regardless of whose death, if Jews and Christians want to be saved, they have to believe that Jesus was just a Messenger of Allah and a human being.

And it is interesting to note that most of the authoritative Islamic commentators stated that 4:159 also meant that Jesus would kill all of the Jews and Christians, and leave only Muslims on the earth.[224]

Conclusion

ISNA's Christmas greeting to Christians is filled with the ideas of interfaith tolerance, respect, and love, and the many commonalities between Muslims and Christians. Unfortunately, the message of this greeting flies in the face of Islamic Doctrine. The fact that ISNA is able to put out such a greeting shows the extent to which willful ignorance of Islamic Doctrine for the sake of "interfaith dialogue" has become the norm among most of the leaders of Western Christendom. ISNA is aware of this, and that is the true meaning of ISNA's Christmas greeting.

---

[223]   *Tafsir Ibn Kathir*, Vol. 3, p. 29; *Tafsir Ahsanul-Bayan*, Vol. 1, p. 549; *Tafsir As-Sa'di*, Vol. 1, p. 457; and *Tafsir Ibn 'Abbas*, p. 128.

[224]   *Tafsir Ahsanul-Bayan*, Vol. 1, p. 549.

141

19

Congressman Ellison and Jefferson's Koran[225]

On January 4, 2007, newly elected Congressman Keith Ellison made history. He became not only the first Muslim to be elected to the United States Congress, but he also took the ceremonial oath of office holding his hand on the Koran that had been owned by Thomas Jefferson. Dozens of television cameras, including one from the Arab network Al-Arabiya, were on hand to record this historical event.

Ellison had explained the importance of this ceremony in an interview the day before, "...in a private ceremony...I'll put my hand on a book that is the basis of my faith, which is Islam..."[226]

A few weeks after the swearing-in, Ellison said that the Koran "is the scripture that I read every day and it's the book that I draw inspiration from."[227]

---

[225]   This appeared in *FrontPage Mag* on April 19, 2015: http://www.frontpagemag.com/2015/dr-stephen-m-kirby/congressman-ellison-and-jeffersons-koran/.

[226]   John Nichols, "Keith Ellison and the Jefferson Koran," *The Nation - The Beat Blog*, January 3, 2007; accessible at: https://www.thenation.com/article/keith-ellison-and-jefferson-koran/.

[227]   Askia Muhammad, "Rep. Keith Ellison: First Muslim in Congress," *FinalCall.com News*, January 20, 2007; accessible at: http://www.finalcall.com/artman/publish/National_News_2/Rep_Keith_Ellison_First_Muslim_in_Congress_3200.shtml.

The significance of this event was even recognized two years later, on June 4th, 2009, as President Obama was giving a speech in Cairo, Egypt. In the portion of the speech when Obama was talking about how Muslim-Americans had "enriched" the United States, he pointed out that Congressman Ellison had taken his oath on Jefferson's "Holy Koran."

So President Obama and Congressman Ellison proclaimed that Ellison had placed his hand on an actual Koran for this ceremony.

Jefferson's Koran

The Koran Ellison used was a two volume translation of the Koran done by George Sale, a non-Muslim. It was titled *The Koran, Commonly Called the Alcoran of Mohammed*. It was first printed in 1734, but the two volume translation used by Ellison was from a second printing done in 1764. Digital copies of both volumes of this second printing can be located online. So let's examine this particular Koran.

In the first volume Sale had three sections before his actual translation of the Koran began: *Dedication, Introduction*, and *Preliminary Discourse*. In the *Dedication*, Sale lamented the "detestation" with which the name Muhammad was laden. But then Sale contrasted the religion and laws of Muhammad to the laws of Jesus and Moses, "whose laws came really from heaven." So according to Sale, Muhammad's religion and laws had not come from heaven. Sale then went on to note that Muhammad used "an imposture [fraud] to set up a new religion."

In the *Introduction*, Sale wrote that the Koran was a "forgery" (p. vii) and it "pretends to be the Word of God" (p. xiii). Sale criticized Muhammad for "imposing a false religion on mankind" (p. x). And Sale explained that he was providing "an impartial version of the Koran" because

> it is absolutely necessary to undeceive those who, from the
> ignorant or unfair translations which have appeared, have
> entertained too favourable an opinion of the original, and

143

also to enable us effectually to expose the imposture
[fraud]... (pp. vii-viii)

In the *Preliminary Discourse*, Sale repeatedly pointed out that Muhammad had "pretended" to be a messenger from God (pp. 52-53, 93, and 96). Sale stated that Muhammad had "pretended" to receive the "revelations...which compose his Koran" (p. 55). And on numerous pages Sale repeated his assertion that Muhammad had "pretended" to receive those revelations (pp. 56, 64, 66, 82, 84, 100, 143, 190, and 192).

Sale addresses Muhammad's "Night Journey" on pp. 61-62 of the *Preliminary Discourse*. In this journey Muhammad claimed to have traveled from Mecca to the seven levels of Heaven. He claimed he was accompanied by the angel *Jibril* (Gabriel) and rode on *Al-Buraq*, a white, horse-like animal, smaller than a mule and bigger than a donkey. Muhammad claimed that he had visited the first six levels of Heaven, meeting one or more of the earlier prophets on each level. On the seventh level he had met Abraham and Allah, and received certain instructions from Allah. Sale wrote that Muhammad "feigns to have made a journey to heaven," and only pretended that he had spoken with Allah. Sale summed up his feelings about Muhammad's "Night Journey":

> *And I am apt to think this fiction, notwithstanding its extravagance, was one of the most artful contrivances Mohammed ever put in practice...*

And Sale believed that Islam was simply a "human invention" based on violence:

> *It is certainly one of the most convincing proofs that Mohammedism was no other than a human invention, that it owed its progress and establishment almost entirely to the sword...*

> (*Preliminary Discourse*, p. 65)

144

Questions Sent to Congressman Ellison

There had been much excitement over Congressman Ellison using Jefferson's Koran for his ceremonial swearing-in. Jefferson's Koran had been declared an official Koran by Ellison and President Obama. Yet this translation of the Koran had been done by a non-Muslim who not only considered Islam to be a manmade religion "that it owed its progress and establishment almost entirely to the sword," but who also considered Muhammad to be a charlatan, and the Koran itself to be false and a forgery.

With this in mind, on March 13, 2015, I sent an e-mail to Congressman Ellison in Washington DC, in care of his Communications Director, Mike Casca. The e-mail summarized the information above with regard to Sale's beliefs about Islam, Muhammad, and the Koran, and I presented the following two questions for the Congressman's consideration:

1. Do you think Sale's negative beliefs about Islam affected the accuracy of his translation of the meaning of each of the verses in the Koran? If they did, how might they have affected that translation, and can his translated work then be accurately referred to as a Koran?

2. If you consider his work to be an accurate translation of the meaning of the verses in the Koran, how would you explain to your Christian and Jewish constituents verses such as these found in this work:

   They are infidels, who say, Verily God is Christ, the son of Mary.
   >> Vol. 1, p. 133   (Koran 5:17)
   >> (So Christians are infidels.)

   War is injoined [sic] *you against the Infidels...*
   >> Vol. 1, p. 38   (Koran 2: 216)

145

...for the infidels are your open enemies.
            Vol. 1, p. 114   (Koran 4:101)

Take not the Jews, or Christians for your friends; they are friends one to the other...
            Vol.1, p. 141   (Koran 5:51)

Thou shalt surely find the most violent of all men in enmity against the true believers [Muslims], *to be the Jews, and the idolators...*
            Vol. 1, p. 147   (Koran 5:82)

My first e-mail to the Congressman went unanswered. After I had sent a second e-mail on March 19th, Casca responded that same day asking when I needed the answers. I replied that with the Congressman's busy schedule, one or two weeks would be fine.

Now, four weeks, and two unanswered e-mails to Casca later, it appears that the Congressman has decided not to respond.

Based on the available evidence, Congressman Ellison apparently considers Sale's work to be an accurate translation of the meaning of the verses in the Koran, and to also be a legitimate Koran. Consequently, it might be worthwhile for the congressman's Jewish and Christian constituents to ask him why he has such high esteem for a book that speaks ill of Jews and Christians, and specifically calls Christians the "open enemies" of Muslims.

So let's close with some verses from the book upon which Congressman Ellison placed his hand, and from which he said he draws inspiration:

As for the infidels...they shall be the fewel [fuel] *of hell fire.*
            Vol. 1, p. 55   (Koran 3:10)

O true believers [Muslims]*! wage war against such of the infidels as are near you; and let them find severity in you...*

　　　　Vol. 1, p. 265　(Koran 9:123)

When ye encounter the unbelievers [non-Muslims], *strike off their heads, until ye have made a great slaughter among them...*

　　　　Vol. 2, p. 376　(Koran 47:4)

Mohammed is the apostle of God: and those who are with him are fierce against the unbelievers, but compassionate towards one another.

　　　　Vol. 2, p. 387　(Koran 48:29)

Interfaith "Dialogue"

The opening prayer of the Koran being seen as really the Lord's Prayer of Islam is something that if you shared that with a group of Christians in Middle America they would probably fall over and need resuscitation. You know, I marvel when, when people ask me the question about or they say did you know that the opening prayer in the Koran is, is, is sometimes referred to as the Lord's Prayer of Islam? And my response is, so what? It is true. How did it get there? Common, common heritage, common linkages. Common pieces of respectful dialogue and information sharing. Recognizing that we are connected. We do have a common source. There is one God.

The Rt. Rev. John B. Chane, Episcopal Bishop of Washington, DC, *Three Faiths, One God: Judaism, Christianity, Islam* (Documentary Preview, 2011)

148

20

Twisting Islam to Enable an Interfaith Dialogue?[228]

A popular book for "interfaith dialogue" among Christians, Jews and Muslims is *Islam's Jesus* by Professor Zeki Saritoprak.[229] Most of the book focused on the Islamic theological beliefs about Jesus's return to earth, with an extensive look at different approaches to, and theories about, understanding what the Koran and the teachings of Muhammad say about this event.

But throughout the book Saritoprak also stressed the idea of interfaith cooperation and dialogue, especially between Christians and Muslims. He hoped to use this book to further that idea by showing how much Christians and Muslims had in common in terms of Jesus. Saritoprak relied on what he called the "interpretive" approach to find this commonality. He stated that this approach is a "middle way to understanding" the texts of Islam that avoids the "extremism" of literalism and the "extremism" of "esoteric understandings" that can border on, or even become heretical (p. 122).

The reliance on the "interpretive" approach created significant problems for the book.

---

[228]   This appeared in *FrontPage Mag* on April 2, 2015: http://www.frontpagemag.com/2015/dr-stephen-m-kirby/twisting-islam-to-enable-an-interfaith-dialogue.

[229]   Zeki Saritoprak, *Islam's Jesus* (Gainesville, FL: University Press of Florida, 2014).

Jesus Returns

Saritoprak wrote that "Jesus's descent is one of the most significant events in Islamic eschatological literature" (p. 72). Saritoprak refers to the following *hadith* from Muhammad to explain this descent:

> *Imam Ahmad recorded that Abu Hurayrah said that the Prophet said...He* [Jesus] *will descend while wearing two long, light yellow garments. His head appears to be dripping water, even though no moisture touched it. He will break the cross, kill the pig, and banish the Jizyah and will call the people to Islam. During his time, Allah will destroy all religions except Islam...*[230]

This *hadith* seems to be easily understood: Jesus will return to earth, destroy Christianity (break the cross), call non-Muslims to Islam (thus having no more need for the *Jizyah*), and Allah will destroy all religions except for Islam. But I am taking what Saritoprak calls the "literalist" approach to understanding this *hadith*.

Saritoprak uses the "interpretive" approach. With this approach, he is able to suggest that this *hadith* could mean, *inter alia*, that Jesus will return to "restore the messages of the Gospel and the Qur'an"; or there will be "a renewal of Christianity, allowing it to be freed of elements that have been added over the centuries and are not necessary or compatible with the core teachings of Jesus" (p. 124). Although the "interpretive" approach may seem somewhat vague and open-ended, in this instance it is certainly more conducive to promoting dialogue between Christians and Muslims than is the "literalist" approach.

Saritoprak relies extensively on verses of the Koran. However, it is curious that he sometimes uses verses that have been abrogated, selectively quotes portions of verses, and even takes verses out of context:

---

[230] *Tafsir Ibn Kathir*, Vol. 3, pp. 31-32.

150

Abrogation and Partial Quotes of Koran Verses

On pp. 52 and 140, Saritoprak writes about how the Koran ensures salvation not only to Muslims, but also to Christians and Jews. He refers especially to verses 2:62 and 5:69. Unfortunately for his premise, I have previously shown that both of these verses were abrogated by 3:85;[231] 3:85 states that the only religion acceptable to Allah is Islam and those who follow another religion will go to Hell.

On p. 144 he writes that the Koran "praises Christians who are humble," and then he quotes the last portion of 5:82 which states that Christians are "closest in affection" to Muslims. It is interesting that he left out the beginning of 5:82:

> *Verily, you will find the strongest among men in enmity to the believers (Muslims) the Jews...*

And in Endnote No. 44 on p. 200, he quotes only this portion of 9:30:

> *"The Jews say, 'Ezra is the son of God'; the Christians say, 'The Messiah is the son of God.' That is what they say with their mouths. They imitate the sayings of the disbelievers of old...*

Here is what he left out: *Allah's Curse be on them, how they are deluded away from the truth.* So Allah curses Christians for saying Jesus is the Son of God.

Does the "interpretive" approach really allow the use of abrogated Koran verses and selective, partial quotes of other verses?

---

[231]   Stephen M. Kirby, *Letting Islam Be Islam: Separating Truth From Myth* (Charleston, SC: CreateSpace, 2012), pp. 159-162.

151

Koran Verses Taken Out of Context

On p. 48, Saritoprak wrote, "A general theological principle of the Islamic tradition is that Muslims are to make peace instead of war...The Qur'an says, 'Peace is Better' (4:128)."

In reality, this verse has nothing to do with peace between peoples or nations. 4:128 specifically addresses the relations between a man and wife:

> *And if a woman fears cruelty or desertion on her husband's part, there is no sin on them both if they make terms of peace between themselves; and making peace is better.*

On p. 135, while discussing the theme of Muslim-Christian Cooperation, Saritoprak wrote,

> *The Holy Book of Islam instructs its audience to initiate dialogue with others by showing a way of greeting, the same way Jesus used to greet his disciples: "When you are greeted, respond with an equal or better greeting" (4:86).*

Is this a proper understanding of Verse 4:86? We will turn to two sources to understand the meaning of this verse. The first source consists of authoritative Koran commentaries (*tafsirs*). Here we find that 4:86 pertains only to Muslims greeting each other, and non-Muslims are excluded.[232]

Our second source is the *hadith* collection in *Sahih Muslim*, which Saritoprak said was one of the two most reliable collections of the sayings of Muhammad (p. 66). Here is what Muhammad said about the idea of a Muslim greeting Jews and Christians:

---

[232]   *Tafsir Ibn Kathir*, Vol. 2, pp. 534-535; *Tafsir Al-Jalalayn*, p. 205; and *Tafsir Ahsanul-Bayan*, Vol. 1, p. 492.

Abu Huraira reported that Allah's Messenger (may peace be upon him) had said: Do not greet the Jews and the Christians before they greet you and when you meet any one of them on the roads force him to go to the narrowest part of it.[233]

So we can see that Christians are excluded from the message of 4:86; and Muhammad not only prohibits Muslims from being the first to greet Christians, he commands Muslims to force Christians to go to the narrowest part of the road. Yet Saritoprak uses 4:86 while discussing Muslim-Christian cooperation.

He continued this theme of cooperation on p. 139:

Likewise, the Qur'an praises the People of the Book [Jews and Christians] *for their good deeds and faith in God: "As for those who believe in God and remain steadfast in their faith, God will enter them in His mercy and grace. He will lead them to the path of righteousness, the straight path" (4:175).*

Again, authoritative Koran commentaries are important here. They explain to us that Verse 4:175 has nothing to do with Jews and Christians. The "straight path" is Islam,[234] and this verse admonishes Muslims to believe in Allah, and to hold fast to the Koran and Islam.[235]

Does the "interpretive" approach really allow Koran verses to be taken out of context?

---

[233]   *Sahih Muslim*, Vol. 6, No. 2167, p. 439.

[234]   *Tafsir Ibn Kathir*, Vol. 1, p. 84; *Tafsir Ahsanul-Bayan*, Vol. 1, pp. 23-24, and *Tafsir As-Sa'di*, Vol. 1, p. 3.

[235]   *Tafsir Ibn Kathir*, Vol. 3, p. 63, *Tafsir Al-Jalalayn*, p. 233, and *Tafsir As-Sa'di*, Vol. 1, p. 466.

Saritoprak also makes some curious claims in his effort to promote Christian-Muslim dialogue:

A "Landmark" Event

While Muhammad was still in Mecca getting Islam started, the Meccan polytheists sent a request to the Negus, the Christian king of Abyssinia, to return a small group of Muslims who had sought refuge in his country. While the king was considering this request, one of those Muslims recited verses from the Koran, which brought tears to the eyes of the Negus and his court, and the Muslims were allowed to stay. After the Negus died, Muhammad performed a funeral prayer in Medina for him, setting "the precedent in Islamic law" for what would be called the "funeral prayer in absentia"; Saritoprak lauded this as a "land-mark in the history of Muslim-Christian cooperation" (p. 145).

But what Saritoprak left out was that the Negus had secretly converted to Islam shortly after the verses were recited to him, and when later questioned about this by his subjects, he had actually lied to them about his conversion. Muhammad was advised of this and later performed the funeral prayer simply because the Negus was a Muslim (Muhammad had referred to the Negus as a "brother" [in Islam]).[236] So this "land-mark" event of Muslim-Christian cooperation was actually an early incident of Muslim deception toward Christians!

Muhammad the Multiculturalist

Saritoprak wrote that Muhammad's family life and later marriages were "a good example of the multicultural environment in which the Qur'an was revealed" (p. 135). He mentioned Safiyya, a Jew, and Maria, a Coptic Christian.

---

[236]   *Sahih Al-Bukhari*, Vol. 5, Book 63, Nos. 3877 and 3880, pp. 128-129.

Safiyyah was among the captives taken when the Muslims conquered Khaybar in May 628; her father was killed during the battle. Muhammad bought her from another Muslim warrior for the price of seven slaves. Muhammad married her after ordering the torture and beheading of her husband, Kinanah b. al-Rabi'.

Maria was not even a wife of Muhammad. She was a Coptic Christian given as a slave to Muhammad. She bore Muhammad a son named Ibrahim, who died as a young child.

If Safiyyah and Maria are to be examples of the "multicultural environment in which the Qur'an was revealed," then this environment consisted of slave trading, torture, beheading, and the violent conquest of non-Muslims.

The "Tender Tone" in the Koran

Saritoprak wrote that the Koran encourages "dialogue" and cooperation with non-Muslims, especially Jews and Christians (e.g. pp. 136, 137, 139, and 140). He pointed out that, "In the Qur'anic passages regarding the People of the Book in general and the Christians in particular, one often finds a tender tone" (p. 140).

Here are some examples of the dialogue and "tender tone" in the Koran: Allah states that he is angry with the Jews, and the Christians are misguided in their beliefs (1:7). Allah curses the Jews and Christians (9:30). He states that the Jews and Christians are among the worst of creatures who "will abide in the fire of Hell" (98:6). Allah commands Muslims to fight the Jews and Christians until those Jews and Christians pay the *jizyah* (protection tax), with willing submission and feeling themselves subdued (9:29). And Allah specifically states that the Jews are among the worst enemies of Islam (5:82).

Saritoprak wrote that, "Intentionally denying anything in the Qur'an drives an individual outside the pale of Islam" (p. 32). He is apparently not using the Koran I rely on, so what Koran is he using to find that "tender tone" toward Jews and Christians?

Muslims, Jews and Christians Believe in the "Same God"

Saritoprak stated that Muslims, Jews and Christians all believe in the "same God" (p. 153). If this is the case, that means that Jews and Christians believe in and worship a God who hates and curses them, orders Muslims to fight them, and condemns them to Hell simply because they are not Muslims.

I have addressed this topic in more detail in a previous article.[237]

Conclusion

Saritoprak wanted his book to be used to enhance interfaith dialogue, especially between Christians and Muslims. But his "interpretive" approach appears to be based largely on personal opinion, great freedom in the selective use and personal interpretation of Koran verses, the making of some curious claims, and it tends toward the esoteric. Saritoprak said that Muhammad never spoke in vain, and whatever Muhammad spoke was a direct revelation from Allah or divinely inspired (p. 34). So when considering the use of the "interpretive" approach, one should probably heed these cautionary words of Muhammad:

> *Muhammad bin Jarir reported that Ibn 'Abbas said that the Prophet said, 'Whoever explains the Qur'an with his opinion or with what he has no knowledge of, then let him assume his seat in the Fire.'*[238]

---

[237] Kirby, "Do We All Believe in the Same God?"

[238] *Tafsir Ibn Kathir*, Vol. 1, pp. 32-33.

21

Don't Take Jews and Christians as Friends?[239]

Some claim that Chapter 5, Verse 51 of the Koran prohibits Muslims from being friends with Jews and Christians. Others claim that there are various ways of interpreting this verse, and that this verse is only advising Muslims not to take Jews and Christians as, for example, legal or spiritual advisers. Because the Koran is considered the timeless Word of Allah to be followed by Muslims, let's see which claim is supported by Islamic doctrine.

The Koran

Since most Muslims do not speak Arabic, the Koran has been translated into numerous languages to help Muslims learn about their faith. Since it is blasphemy to provide an incorrect translation of the meaning of a Koran verse, there is a tremendous burden on the shoulders of the translator to make sure the translation accurately reflects the Arabic verse. With this in mind, let's look at how 5:51 has been translated into English by Muslim scholars in five different modern translations of the Koran:

> *O you who believe! Take not the Jews and the Christians as Auliya' (friends, protectors, helpers), they are but Auliya' of each other. And if any amongst you takes them as Auliya', then surely, he is one of them. Verily, Allah*

---

239   This appeared in *FrontPage Mag* on May 10, 2015: http://www.frontpagemag.com/2015/dr-stephen-m-kirby/dont-take-jews-and-christians-as-friends/.

guides not those people who are the Zalimun (polytheists and wrongdoers and unjust).

> *Interpretation of the Meanings of The Noble Qur'an*, trans. Khan and Al-Hilali (2007)

O ye who believe! Take not the Jews and the Christians for friends. They are friends one to another. He among you who taketh them for friends is (one) of them. Lo! Allah guideth not wrongdoing folk.

> *The Meaning of the Glorious Koran*, trans. Marmaduke Pickthall (1930; rpt. 1992)

You who believe! do [sic] *not take the Jews and Christians as your friends; they are the friends of one another. Any of you who takes* [sic] *them as friends is one of them. Allah does not guide wrongdoing people.*

> *The Noble Qur'an: A New Rendering of its Meaning in English*, trans. Abdalhaqq and Aisha Bewley (2011)

O ye who believe! take [sic] *not the Jews and the Christians for your friends and protectors: They are but friends and protectors to each other. And he amongst you that turns to them (for friendship) is of them. Verily Allah guideth not a people unjust.*

> *The Meaning of the Holy Qur'an*, trans. Abdullah Yusuf Ali (2010)

For some years the Council on American-Islamic Relations (CAIR) has been distributing a particular translation of the Koran at no charge. This

158

translation was done by Muhammad Asad, and here is how he translated 5:51:

> *O YOU who have attained to faith! Do not take the Jews and the Christians for your allies: they are but allies of one another – and whoever of you allies himself with them becomes, verily, one of them; behold, God does not guide such evildoers.*

> *The Message of the Qur'an*, trans. Muhammad Asad (2003)

In Footnote 72 for this verse, Asad explained that "allies" meant "friendship":

> *According to most of the commentators (e.g. Tabari), this means that each of these two communities extends genuine friendship only to its own adherents – i.e., the Jews to the Jews, and the Christians to the Christians – and cannot, therefore, be expected to be really friendly towards the followers of the Qur'an.*

The Koran Commentaries (*Tafsirs*)

Asad referred to *commentators* who have provided an explanation for this verse. Asad is referring to authoritative Islamic scholars who have written commentaries (*tafsirs*) on the Koran that Muslims have used for centuries to understand the meaning of each verse. So let's see how some of those authoritative scholars have explained 5:51.

In a section titled *The Prohibition of Taking the Jews, Christians and Enemies of Islam as Friends*, Ibn Kathir explained this verse by pointing out that,

> *Allah forbids His believing servants from having Jews and Christians as friends, because they are the enemies of Islam and its people, may Allah curse them. Allah then*

159

states that they are friends of each other and He gives a
warning threat to those who do this, And if any among you
befriends them, then surely he is one of them.[240]

The *Tafsir Al-Jalalayn* (p. 256) explained that this verse meant Muslims were not to join Jews and Christians "in mutual friendship and love," or "in their unbelief."

The *Tafsir Ibn 'Abbas* (p. 143) stated that Muslims who take Jews and Christians as friends are "not included in Allah's protection and safety."

One might point out that these three *tafsirs* were written centuries ago, and then make the claim that the understanding of this verse has surely been "modernized." So let's look at two, more recent *tafsirs*.

The *Tafsir as-Sa'di* was written in the early 20th century. Here is how 5:51 is explained:

> *Allah, while describing to His believing servants the*
> *ignorant condition and unethical demeanor of the Jews*
> *and the Christians, orders them to not maintain alliance*
> *with them. This is because the Christians and the Jews*
> *aid one another and are united in their opposition of*
> *others. You should not make them your allies; rather, they*
> *are your enemies and they care not the least concerning*
> *your loss; they will leave no stone unturned to misguide*
> *you. Only a person who is like them will make alliance*
> *with them.*[241]

The *Tafsir Ahsanul-Bayan* was first published on 1995; here is how this *tafsir* explained 5:51:

---

[240]   *Tafsir Ibn Kathir*, Vol. 3, p. 204.

[241]   *Tafsir as-Sa'di*, Vol. 1, p. 512.

*The verse forbids Muslims to keep intimate relations with
them and take them as protectors and helpers, because
they are the enemies of Allah, the Muslims, and Islam. It
should be noted that those who take them as protectors
and helpers will be considered among them.*[242]

So here we have five authoritative *tafsirs* joining together in explaining
that 5:51 prohibits Muslims from being friends with Jews and Christians;
and in the context of this verse, three of these *tafsirs* (including the two
most modern) specifically refer to Jews and Christians as the *enemies* of
Islam.

Additional Evidence

The idea that Muslims should not take Jews and Christians as friends is
reinforced in the following verses of the Koran:

Chapter 5, Verse 82

*Verily, you will find the strongest among men in enmity to
the believers (Muslims) the Jews...*

Chapter 9, Verse 29

*Fight against those who believe not in Allah, nor in the
Last Day, nor forbid that which has been forbidden by
Allah and His Messenger (Muhammad), and those who
acknowledge not the religion of truth (i.e. Islam) among
the people of the Scripture (Jews and Christians), until
they pay the Jizyah with willing submission, and feel
themselves subdued.*

---

[242]   *Tafsir Ahsanul-Bayan*, Vol. 1, p. 616.

Chapter 98, Verse 6

> *Verily, those who disbelieve (in the religion of Islam, the Qu'ran and Prophet Muhammad) from among the people of the Scripture (Jews and Christians) and Al-Mushrikun, will abide in the fire of Hell. They are the worst of creatures.*

These ill-feelings towards Jews and Christians were repeated in teachings of Muhammad, e.g.:

> *Abu Huraira reported that Allah's Messenger (may peace be upon him) had said: Do not greet the Jews and the Christians before they greet you and when you meet any one of them on the roads force him to go to the narrowest part of it.*[243]

> *Narrated Abu Hurairah: Allah's Messenger said, "The Hour will not be established until you fight against the Jews, and the stone behind which a Jew will be hiding will say, 'O Muslim! There is a Jew hiding behind me, so kill him.'"*[244]

Muhammad even said that Jews and Christians would take the place of Muslims in Hell:

> *Abu Burda reported on the authority of his father that Allah's Apostle (may peace be upon him) said: No Muslim would die but Allah would admit instead of him a Jew or a Christian in Hell-Fire.*[245]

---

[243]   *Sahih Muslim*, Vol. 6, No. 2167, p. 439.

[244]   *Sahih Al-Bukhari*, Vol. 4, Book 56, No. 2926, p. 113.

[245]   *Sahih Muslim*, Vol. 8, No. 2767R1, p. 269.

And on his death bed Muhammad had this to say regarding Jews and Christians:

> It has been narrated by 'Umar b. Al-Khattab that he heard the Messenger of Allah (may peace be upon him) saying: I will expel the Jews and Christians from the Arabian Peninsula and will not leave any but Muslims.[246]

Conclusion

In 5:51 Allah commands Muslims not to be friends with Jews and Christians. This understanding is supported by five modern translations of the Koran; the message of additional verses of the Koran; five authoritative *tafsirs*, written at different times between circa 900-1995 AD; and the teachings of Muhammad.

But what about Muslims who appear to be friends with Jews and Christians in defiance of Allah's timeless command? There are a number of explanations:

1. In reality they might be following another command of Allah: Chapter 3, Verse 28 of the Koran allows Muslims to <u>pretend</u> to be friends with non-Muslims if those Muslims live in a non-Muslim society and fear for their safety.

2. They might just decide they can actively deny certain verses in the Koran. But Muhammad had a warning about this:

   > It was narrated from Ibn 'Abbas that the Messenger of Allah said: "Whoever denies a Verse of the Qur'an, it is permissible to strike his neck (i.e. execute him)..."[247]

---

[246] *Sahih Muslim*, Vol. 5, No. 1767, p. 189.

[247] *Sunan Ibn Majah*, Vol. 3, No. 2539, p. 455.

3. They might just use their own personal opinion in re-interpreting the commands of Allah. But Muhammad had a warning about this too:

> *Muhammad bin Jarir reported that Ibn 'Abbas said that the Prophet said, 'Whoever explains the Qur'an with his opinion or with what he has no knowledge of, then let him assume his seat in the Fire.'*[248]

4. Or they might just simply decide to passively ignore this timeless command from Allah.

Keep in mind that denying or ignoring a doctrine does not mean that doctrine is no longer valid. 5:51 is a valid part of Islamic doctrine and has been so since the 7th century. And anytime a wayward Muslim wants to, he can return to that doctrine.

---

[248] *Tafsir Ibn Kathir*, Vol. 1, pp. 32-33.

22

Islam and the Omaha Tri-Faith Initiative[249]

Currently underway in the Heartland of America is an experiment in interfaith dialogue and coexistence: the Tri-Faith Initiative in Omaha, Nebraska. The goal of the Tri-Faith Initiative is to have a synagogue, a mosque, and a church located on a common piece of land, each with its own separate building; the Tri-Faith hopes to later add a fourth building as a shared Tri-Faith Center. The location for this venture is 35 acres in the Sterling Ridge development in Omaha.

The original institutional members of the Tri-Faith Initiative were Temple Israel, the American Institute of Islamic Studies and Culture (AIISC), and the Episcopal Diocese of Nebraska. In 2014 the Episcopal Diocese asked Countryside Community Church to takes its place as the Christian partner in the Tri-Faith. On April 12, 2015, Countryside voted in favor of relocating its church to the Tri-Faith grounds and becoming the Christian partner.

The Tri-Faith's Memorandum of Understanding states, "In working together, our vision is to build bridges of respect, trust and acceptance..." Unfortunately, Islamic doctrine prohibits Muslims from respecting, trusting, or accepting Jews and Christians (unless of course the latter pay the *jizyah*).

So I decided to contact three non-Muslims who are heavily involved in the Tri-Faith Initiative: Rabbi Aryeh Azriel of Temple Israel; Reverend Eric

---

[249]   This appeared in *FrontPage Mag* on April 29, 2015: http://www.frontpagemag.com/2015/dr-stephen-m-kirby/islam-and-the-omaha-tri-faith-initiative/.

Elnes of Countryside Community Church; and Susie Buffett, daughter of multi-billionaire Warren Buffet, a member of Countryside Community Church, and Chairperson of the Sherwood Foundation.

I sent each of them the following e-mail:

> In light of your extensive involvement with the Tri-Faith Initiative, I am interested in your view on the following matter.
>
> The Vision Statement of the Tri-Faith Initiative talks about building "bridges of Respect, Trust and Acceptance" between Jews, Christians, and Muslims. This is a commendable idea, but how can such bridges be built when Islamic doctrine prohibits it? Please consider:
>
> The Koran says the following about Jews and Christians:
>
>> 1. Allah is angry with the Jews, and the Christians are misguided because they believe that Jesus is the son of God (1:7).
>>
>> 2. Muslims are commanded not to make friends with Jews and Christians (e.g. 5:51), although Muslims can pretend to be friends if the situation so dictates (3:28).
>>
>> 3. Jews are among the worst enemies of Islam (5:82).
>>
>> 4. Muslims are commanded to fight Jews and Christians until the Jews and Christians pay protection money with willing submission and feel themselves subdued (9:29).
>>
>> 5. Allah curses the Jews and the Christians (9:30).
>>
>> 6. Jews and Christians are among the worst of creatures and "will abide in the fire of Hell" (98:6).

Muhammad spoke for Allah (4:80), Muslims are commanded to obey Muhammad (59:7), and he is considered the timeless standard by which Muslims should conduct themselves (33:21).

Consider that Muhammad said:

1. Jews and Christians are each worth only half of a Muslim (*Sunan Ibn Majah*, No. 2644).

2. *Do not greet the Jews and the Christians before they greet you and when you meet any one of them on the roads force him to go to the narrowest part of it* (*Sahih Muslim*, No. 2167).

3. *The Hour will not be established until you fight against the Jews, and the stone behind which a Jew will be hiding will say, 'O Muslim! There is a Jew hiding behind me, so kill him* (*Sahih Al-Bukhari*, No. 2926).

4. The Jews were grave robbers (*Sahih Al-Bukhari*, No. 3452).

5. Jews and Christians will take the place of Muslims in Hell (*Sahih Muslim*, No. 2767R1).

6. *I will expel the Jews and Christians from the Arabian Peninsula and will not leave any but Muslims* (*Sahih Muslim*, No. 1767).

If the Koran truly consists of the commands of Allah, and if Muhammad truly spoke for Allah and is to be obeyed, how can Islam be a partner in building "bridges of Respect, Trust and Acceptance" with Jews and Christians?

Unfortunately, after sending the e-mail twice to each of the three, and after waiting a number of weeks, I have still not received replies from Azriel, Elnes, or Buffett.

Non-Muslims and Islamic Doctrine

Why would the non-Muslim portion of the Tri-Faith Initiative appear to deny or simply ignore the Islamic doctrine that undermines the idea of this venture? Due to the silence of Azriel, Elnes and Buffett, we do not know.

However, we do know that there are many millions of dollars involved in the Tri-Faith Initiative.

In December 2011, the Episcopal Diocese purchased 6.35 acres of land in the Sterling Ridge development for almost $1.3 million. At that same time the Tri-Faith Initiative organization itself purchased 3.6 acres in an adjoining lot for almost $800,000.00.

In December 2011, Rabbi Azriel and the congregation of Temple Israel purchased 13.54 acres of land in that development for almost $3 million; this was to be the site of their new synagogue. In August 2013, the congregation moved into their new synagogue. It is 58,500 square feet in size (a third larger than the previous synagogue), and features stone from a Jerusalem quarry and artwork done by an international group of artists.

With the successful vote on April 12, 2015, Countryside Community Church can now move forward. Countryside's new church will be an estimated 71,100 square feet in size; the existing church is only 58,000 square feet. The cost, including the land, is estimated to be about $25 million. Reverend Elnes stated that there was already $16.1 million in financial commitments, mostly from among the 1,500 congregation members.

Susie Buffett's Sherwood Foundation is extensively involved. She was quoted as saying that she would provide an unspecified amount of financial support for the new Countryside church. In fact, according to available IRS records (Form 990's), in 2011-2013 the Sherwood Foundation had contributed $191,000.00 to Countryside church. These records also showed that during that same time period the Sherwood Foundation had contributed $1,305,000.00 to the Muslim partner, the AIISC. This was almost 79% of the total amount of contributions received by AIISC during that time period. And during the years 2012-2013, the Sherwood Foundation contributed $270,000.00 to the Tri-Faith Initiative itself.

Millions of dollars have been spent, and many more millions will be spent, by non-Muslims to see the Tri-Faith Initiative a success. With so much money involved, non-Muslims could tend to view the Islamic doctrine that undermines the very goals of the Tri-Faith Initiative as a minor annoyance to be denied or ignored.

Muslims and Islamic Doctrine

We have commands of Allah in the Koran and teachings from Muhammad that prohibit the idea of the Tri-Faith Initiative. Non-Muslims can deny or ignore them. But what about the Muslims in AIISC (now known as the American Muslim Institute)? They are committed to the Tri-Faith Initiative. After all, in December 2011, AIISC spent a little over $800,000 to buy 3.85 acres in the Sterling Ridge development. So let's consider some additional, relevant Islamic doctrine.

Muhammad said that anyone denying a verse of the Koran could be killed:

> *It was narrated from Ibn 'Abbas that the Messenger of Allah said: "Whoever denies a Verse of the Qur'an, it is permissible to strike his neck (i.e. execute him)...* "[250]

In Chapter 59, Verse 7, the Koran specifically commands Muslims to obey Muhammad:

---

[250] *Sunan Ibn Majah*, Vol. 3, No. 2539, p. 455.

...And whatsoever the Messenger (Muhammad) gives you, take it; and whatsoever he forbids you, abstain (from it). And fear Allah; verily, Allah is Severe in punishment.

And Muslims are not only expected to know the Koran, but they are also expected to act on its commands. In the following authoritative *hadith*, Muhammad talks about the penalty for knowing the Koran, but not acting on it. He tells us what he saw when the angels Gabriel and Michael had taken him to visit the "Sacred Land":

> *...we went on till we came to a man lying in a prone position, and another man standing at his head carrying a stone or a piece of rock, and crushing the head of the lying man with that stone. Whenever he struck him, the stone rolled away. The man went to pick it up and by the time he returned to him, the crushed head returned to its normal state and the man came back and struck him again (and so on).*

When Muhammad asked about this man, the angels replied:

> *The one whose head you saw being crushed is the one whom Allah had given the knowledge of the Qur'an (i.e. knowing it by heart), but he used to sleep at night (i.e., he did not recite it then) and did not use to act upon it (i.e., upon its orders etc.) by day; and so this punishment will go on till the Day of Resurrection.* [251]

It is blasphemy for a Muslim to deny a verse of the Koran or a teaching of Muhammad. But it is also blasphemy, and potentially head-crushing, for a Muslim not to act on a command from Allah or a teaching of Muhammad. With this in mind, it will be interesting to see if the larger Muslim community in Nebraska decides to support the Tri-Faith Initiative, or follow the commands of Allah and the teachings of Muhammad.

---

[251]   *Sahih Al-Bukhari*, Vol. 2, Book 23, No. 1386, pp. 268-269.

23

The Fraud of Omaha's
Tri-Faith Initiative[252]

The Tri-Faith Initiative in Omaha has lofty goals for the Jewish, Christian, and Muslim partners involved. It is best summed up in the Tri-Faith's *Vision Statement*:

> *In working together, our vision is to build bridges of respect, trust and acceptance, to challenge stereotypes of each other, to learn from one another, and to counter the influence of extremists and agents of hate.*

Among the *Founding Principles* is this statement:

> *Each participant agrees to completely respect the beliefs and practices of the other participants. All beliefs shall be respected.*

These are noble ideals, but the reality is that the Muslim partners can never respect and accept the beliefs of their Christian partners. This is because Islam teaches that Christianity is a false religion, based on a fraud, and initially spread by those who knew it was a fraud. The crux of the issue revolves around Jesus.

---

[252]   This appeared in *FrontPage Mag* on May 18, 2015: http://www.frontpagemag.com/2015/dr-stephen-kirby/the-fraud-of-omahas-tri-faith-initiative/.

An Imposter on the Cross

Islam teaches that Jesus ('Isa) was not crucified; instead, someone took his place on the cross. This is explicitly stated in Chapter 4, Verses 157-158 of the Koran:

> *And because of their saying (in boast), "We killed Messiah 'Isa (Jesus), son of Maryam (Mary), the Messenger of Allah," - but they killed him not nor crucified him, but it appeared so to them [the resemblance of 'Isa (Jesus) was put over another man (and they killed that man)], and those who differ therein are full of doubts. They have no (certain) knowledge, they follow nothing but conjecture. For surely, they killed him not [i.e. 'Isa (Jesus), son of Maryam (Mary)]; But Allah raised him ['Isa (Jesus)] up (with his body and soul) to Himself (and he is in the heavens). And Allah is Ever All-Powerful, All-Wise.*

The authoritative Muslim scholar Ibn Kathir provided the explanation of these verses:

> *Ibn Abi Hatim recorded that Ibn 'Abbas said, "Just before Allah raised 'Isa to the heavens, 'Isa went to his companions, who were twelve inside the house. When he arrived, his hair was dripping water and he said, 'There are those among you who will disbelieve in me twelve times after he had believed in me.' He then asked, 'Who volunteers that his image appear as mine, and be killed in my place. He will be with me (in Paradise)?' One of the youngest ones among them volunteered and 'Isa asked him to sit down. 'Isa again asked for a volunteer, and the young man kept volunteering and 'Isa asking him to sit down. Then the young man volunteered again and 'Isa said, 'You will be that man,' and the resemblance of 'Isa was cast over that man while 'Isa ascended to heaven from*

a hole in the house. When the Jews came looking for 'Isa, they found that young man and crucified him..."[253]

So Islam teaches that instead of being crucified, Jesus first asked for a volunteer to take his place, and then was taken bodily to heaven while the volunteer, whom Allah had made to look like Jesus, was crucified in his place.

Ibn Kathir also made an interesting observation. He noted that those twelve companions in the house knew that Jesus ascended to heaven from the house and that it was the volunteer who was crucified.[254] And of course, if there was no Crucifixion, there was no Resurrection.

The implication is that it was the Twelve Apostles in the house, which would mean that those Apostles then went out and knowingly preached a lie, based on a fraud, which spread across the world as the Christian religion. The Muslim partners in the Tri-Faith Initiative are supposed to respect and accept this?

And to add another nail in the coffin of respect and acceptance, a Muslim who knows his religion will look at a crucifix or a painting of the Crucifixion and see an imposter hanging on the cross.

Commonality with Jesus?

But isn't there still a commonality in belief and acceptance among Christians and Muslims that Jesus will return to earth? Yes, both religions do believe that Jesus will return, but there is a vast difference in what is taught about the purpose of that return.

Here is what Muhammad said would happen when Jesus first returned:

---

[253]   *Tafsir Ibn Kathir*, Vol. 3, p. 28.

[254]   Ibid., p. 27.

173

He [Jesus] *will descend while wearing two long, light yellow garments. His head appears to be dripping water, even though no moisture touched it. He will break the cross, kill the pig, and banish the Jizyah and will call the people to Islam. During his time, Allah will destroy all religions except Islam...'Isa will remain for forty years and then will die, and Muslims will offer the funeral prayer for him.*[255]

So during those forty years after Jesus returned, Allah would destroy all religions except Islam, and Jesus would be breaking the cross of Christianity and calling the people to Islam. The *Jizyah* is the protection money demanded of Jews and Christians in 9:29 of the Koran in lieu of fighting to the death or converting to Islam. So when Islam's Jesus returns to earth, the *Jizyah* will be banished simply because the only religion allowed will be Islam.

And, according to Muhammad, Jesus would also be judging mankind by the laws of the Koran:

Narrated Abu Hurairah: Allah's Messenger said, "How will you be when the son of Maryam (Mary) ['Isa (Jesus)] descends amongst you, and he will judge people by the law of the Qur'an and not by the law of the Gospel."[256]

So when it comes to the meaning of Jesus' return to earth, there is no respect or acceptance extended to Christians by Islamic doctrine.

---

[255]   Ibid., p. 32.

[256]   *Sahih Al-Bukhari*, Vol. 4, Book 60, No. 3449, p. 412.

Shirk, the Unforgiveable Sin

Christians believe that Jesus is the Son of God. According to Islamic doctrine, this means that Christians are ascribing a "partner" to Allah; in Islam this is the sin of *Shirk*. And in 4:48 the Koran states that *Shirk* is the one sin that Allah will not forgive:

> *Verily, Allah forgives not that partners should be set up with Him (in worship), but He forgives except that (anything else) to whom He wills; and whoever sets up partners with Allah in worship, he has indeed invented a tremendous sin.*

And 3:151 of the Koran states what is to be done to those engaging in *Shirk*:

> *We shall cast terror into the hearts of those who disbelieve, because they joined others in worship with Allah, for which He had sent no authority; their abode will be the Fire and how evil is the abode of the Zalimun (polytheists and wrongdoers).*

So those engaging in *Shirk* will have terror cast into their hearts and they are destined for the Fires of Hell.

This was reiterated by Muhammad:

> *Narrated 'Abdullah: The Prophet said one statement and I said another. The Prophet said "Whoever dies while still invoking anything other than Allah as a rival to Allah, will enter Hell (Fire)." And I said, "Whoever dies without invoking anything as a rival to Allah, will enter Paradise."[257]*

---

[257]   *Sahih Al-Bukhari*, Vol. 6, Book 65, No. 4497, pp. 37-38.

So Christians, by definition, engage in *Shirk*, the unforgivable sin in Islam that condemns Christians to the Fires of Hell.

Conclusion

The Christian partners of Omaha's Tri-Faith Initiative are waiting in vain if they expect Islamic doctrine to respect Christianity. According to Islamic doctrine, Christianity is simply a false religion based on a fraud, and Christians are destined for Hell. How can a devout Muslim respect such a religion?

Although St. Paul wrote his letter to the Corinthians well before the birth of Muhammad, his letter aptly explains the significance of Islamic teachings about Jesus and Christianity:

> *...if Christ has not been raised, then our preaching is in vain and your faith is in vain. We are even found to be misrepresenting God, because we testified of God that he raised Christ, whom he did not raise if it is true that the dead are not raised. For if the dead are not raised, then Christ has not been raised. If Christ has not been raised, your faith is futile...*
>
> *1 Corinthians*, 15:14-17

24

The Omaha Tri-Faith Initiative-Nebraska's Potemkin Village?[258]

Potemkin village: An impressive façade or show designed to hide an undesirable fact or condition.

Merriam-Webster's Collegiate Dictionary, 11th Edition

The phrase "Potemkin village" is based on a supposed incident in which Russian Prince Grigory Potemkin erected fake settlements along the banks of the Dnieper River in order to fool and impress Russian Empress Catherine II and her entourage during a trip to "New Russia" (Crimea) in 1787. The supposed purpose of these fake settlements was to create an image of development and prosperity where there was none.

In the Heartland of the United States, along the banks of the Missouri River, lies the city of Omaha, Nebraska, where there is currently underway an experiment in interfaith dialogue and coexistence: the Tri-Faith Initiative. The goal of the Tri-Faith Initiative is to have a synagogue, a mosque, and a church located on a common piece of land, each with its own separate building; the Tri-Faith hopes to later add a fourth building as a shared Tri-Faith Center. The location for this venture is 35 acres in the Sterling Ridge development in Omaha. The religious partners are Temple Israel, the American Muslim Institute (formerly the American Institute of Islamic Studies and Culture), and Countryside Community Church, the new Christian partner.

---

[258]   This appeared in *FrontPage Mag* on June 3, 2015: http://www.frontpagemag.com/2015/dr-stephen-m-kirby/the-omaha-tri-faith-initiative-nebraskas-potemkin-village/.

The goal of the Tri-Faith "is to build bridges of respect, trust and acceptance" between Judaism, Christianity, and Islam. But Islamic doctrine prohibits Muslims from respecting, trusting, or accepting Jews and Christians, so how can Muslims support it? Does Nebraska have its own Potemkin village along the banks of the Missouri River? Let's first review Islamic doctrine.

Islamic Doctrine

We do not believe in the same God: A foundational belief of the Tri-Faith Initiative seems to be that Jews, Christians, and Muslims all believe in the same God, the God of Abraham. But the god of Islam hates and curses Jews and Christians, orders Muslims to fight them, and condemns Jews and Christians to Hell simply because they are not Muslims. I have addressed this topic in more detail in a previous article.[259]

Muslims cannot be friends with Jews and Christians: Building bridges of respect, trust and acceptance among these three religions requires a certain element of friendship between the adherents of these religions. But 5:51 of the Koran, and the teachings of Muhammad, specifically command Muslims not to be friends with Jews and Christians. There is only one exception found, and that is in 3:28 of the Koran, which allows Muslims to pretend to be friends with non-Muslims. I have provided more detail about this issue.[260]

Christianity is a false religion based on a fraud: Islam teaches that Jesus was not crucified; instead, Allah took Jesus bodily into Heaven and made one of Jesus' followers look like Jesus, and that follower was crucified. Islam also teaches that Jesus' apostles were aware of the substitution, but, nevertheless, they then proceeded to spread the new religion, knowing it was based on a fraud. So a Muslim who knows his religion will look at a crucifix or a painting of the Crucifixion and see an

---

[259] Kirby, "Do We All Believe in the Same God?"

[260] Kirby, "Don't Take Christians and Jews as Friends."

imposter hanging on the cross.   Given this, how can Muslims respect Christianity? For more details about this, see my previous article.[261]

There are three non-Muslims who are heavily involved in the Tri-Faith Initiative: Rabbi Aryeh Azriel of Temple Israel; Reverend Eric Elnes of Countryside Community Church; and Susie Buffett, daughter of multi-billionaire Warren Buffet, a member of Countryside Community Church, and Chairperson of the Sherwood Foundation. Many weeks ago I sent repeated e-mails to each of them asking how, considering what Islamic doctrine teaches, could Islam be a partner in building bridges of "respect, trust and acceptance" with Jews and Christians? I have yet to receive any reply.

So apparently non-Muslims have decided to ignore Islamic doctrine for the sake of the idea of the Tri-Faith Initiative.

Non-Muslim Money

A factor in this could be the millions of dollars of non-Muslim money that has been, and will be spent for this venture.

In December 2011, the Episcopal Diocese of Nebraska, the original Christian partner, purchased 6.35 acres of land in the Sterling Ridge development for almost $1.3 million. At that same time the Tri-Faith Initiative organization itself purchased 3.6 acres in an adjoining lot for almost $800,000.

Temple Israel: In December 2011, the congregation of Temple Israel purchased 13.54 acres of land in that development for almost $3 million; this was to be the site of their new synagogue. In August 2013, the congregation moved into that new synagogue, built at a cost of about $20 million.

---

[261]   Kirby, "The Fraud of Omaha's Tri-Faith initiative."

Countryside Community Church: The cost of Countryside's new church, including the land to be purchased from the Episcopal Diocese, is estimated to be about $25 million. Countryside's Reverend Elnes stated that there was already $16.1 million in financial commitments, mostly from among the 1,500 congregation members.

The Sherwood Foundation: The non-Muslim Sherwood Foundation is chaired by Susie Buffett. The Sherwood Foundation is extensively involved in the Tri-Faith Initiative. During the years 2009-2010 and 2012-2014, the Sherwood Foundation contributed $288,500 to the Tri-Faith Initiative organization; this was about 59% of the total contributions received by the Tri-Faith during those years. What is interesting to note is that in 2011, the year the Tri-Faith organization spent almost $800,000 to purchase its 3.6 acres in the Sterling Ridge development, the Sherwood Foundation made no contribution to the Tri-Faith organization. Nevertheless, the Tri-Faith organization received over $1 million dollars in contributions that year. There is more about this in the following section.

Ms. Buffet was quoted as saying that she would provide an unspecified amount of financial support for the new Countryside church. And according to available IRS records (Form 990's), during 2009-2014 the Sherwood Foundation contributed $504,000 to Countryside church. Of the money the Foundation contributed to the church in 2014, $30,000 was specifically designated for "Tri-Faith Expenses."

Form 990's also showed that during 2011-2013, the Sherwood Foundation had contributed about $1.3 million to the American Muslim Institute (AMI). This was almost 79% of the total amount of contributions received by AMI during that three year period; it was also almost 70% of the <u>total</u> contributions received by AMI during 2007-2014. It is interesting to note that of the $650,000 contributed by the Foundation to AMI in 2011, $600,000 was specifically designated for "Purchase of Land." 2011 was the year that AMI purchased its 3.85 acres in the Sterling Ridge development for $827,640.

Undisclosed Contributors

The Tri-Faith Initiative organization and the American Muslim Institute are not legally required to identify contributors. But there are some strategically timed contributions of interest:

Tri-Faith Initiative organization: 2011 was a significant year financially for the Tri-Faith organization, because it received $1,004,019 in contributions that year, and purchased land in the Sterling Ridge development. Had these contributions not been received, the Tri-Faith organization would not have been able to purchase that land. None of these contributions came from the Sherwood Foundation.

I contacted the Tri-Faith organization and asked for the names and contribution amounts of the contributors for 2011. I was advised that these contributors had requested anonymity, but that they were "all local Omaha donors."

American Muslim Institute (AMI): In a May 22, 2015, article in the *Omaha World-Herald*, Dr. Syed Mohiuddin, President of AMI, said that nearly all of the money had been raised for the construction of the mosque, estimated to cost around $5.5 million. But according to the Form 990 filed for 2014, excluding their land, AMI only had assets of a little over $400,000 at the end of 2014. If Dr. Mohiuddin's statement was accurate, this means that AMI had raised around $5 million in the first five months of 2015; in contrast, during the previous eight years AMI had raised a total of only about $1.8 million.

So I e-mailed Leigh Sittenauer, AMI Executive Director, asking for a list of the 2015 contributors and the amounts of their contributions. Ms. Sittenauer replied:

> *We are not obligated to share that information and have no plans to provide it to you or any other inquisitors.*

As pointed out above, during 2007-2014 almost 70% of the contributions to AMI came from a non-Muslim organization. If this pattern of

181

contributions holds for 2015, then the vast majority of the $5.5 million needed for mosque construction will have come from non-Muslims.

Conclusion

This leaves us with some fundamental questions:

1. If the major source of funding, even for mosque construction, comes from non-Muslims, is the venture really Tri-Faith?

2. Given that the Tri-Faith Initiative appears to be publically touted as a model for interfaith relations, why the opaqueness about the sources of millions of dollars necessary to support this venture?

3. Given that the Tri-Faith Initiative appears to be publically touted as a model for interfaith relations, why were contributions allowed to be made anonymously?

4. Given that the Tri-Faith Initiative appears to be publically touted as a model for interfaith relations, why don't contributors want to be publically recognized?

5. Are the new Christian partners at Countryside Community Church even aware of the sources for these millions of dollars given to the venture they have recently joined?

6. If all the partners, Muslims included, are required to ignore core doctrines of Islam to create the appearance of respect, trust and acceptance, can the venture really be Tri-Faith?

Instead of answers, at this point all we have is Tri-Faith Silence.

25

Nebraska Muslims and Omaha's Tri-Faith Initiative[262]

For those not familiar with it, there is currently underway an experiment in interfaith dialogue and coexistence: the Tri-Faith Initiative in Omaha, Nebraska. The Tri-Faith Initiative wants to have a synagogue, a mosque, and a church located on a common piece of land, each with its own separate building. The religious partners are Temple Israel, the American Muslim Institute, and Countryside Community Church.

The goal of the Tri-Faith "is to build bridges of respect, trust and acceptance" between Judaism, Christianity, and Islam. But Islamic doctrine prohibits Muslims from respecting, trusting, or accepting Jews and Christians, so how can Muslims support it?

With this question in mind, I tried to find out how much support there is for the Tri-Faith Initiative and its goal among the Muslims in Nebraska.

Nebraska Muslims

I located e-mail addresses for the following nine Muslim organizations/mosques in Nebraska:

---

[262]   This appeared in *FrontPage Mag* on June 22, 2015:
http://www.frontpagemag.com/2015/dr-stephen-kirby/nebraska-muslims-and-omahas-tri-faith-initiative/.

Al Hadi Islamic Center (Omaha)
Grand Island Masjid
Islamic Center of Omaha
Islamic Center of Siouxland
Islamic Foundation of Lincoln
Masjid Al-Huda (Omaha)
Masjid al-Wadood (Norfolk)
Millard Islamic Center (Omaha)
Nebraska Islamic Foundation (Lincoln)

I sent the following e-mail to each of them, twice:

The Omaha Tri-Faith Initiative is an experiment in interfaith dialogue and coexistence. The goal of the Tri-Faith Initiative is to have a synagogue, a mosque, and a church located on a common piece of land, each with its own separate building. The religious partners are Temple Israel, the American Muslim Institute, and Countryside Community Church.

The goal of the Tri-Faith "is to build bridges of respect, trust and acceptance" between Judaism, Islam, and Christianity. But Islamic doctrine prohibits Muslims from respecting, trusting, or accepting Jews and Christians; for example:

According to the Koran: Muslims are prohibited from being friends with Jews and Christians (5:51); Muslims are commanded to fight Jews and Christians until the Jews and Christians pay the jizyah with willing submission and feeling themselves subdued (9:29); Jews are among the worst enemies of Islam (5:82); Allah curses the Jews and the Christians (9:30); and Jews and Christians are among the worst of creatures and "will abide in the fire of Hell" (98:6).

Muhammad said such things as:

1. Jews and Christians are each worth only half of a Muslim (Sunan Ibn Majah, No. 2644);

184

2. Do not greet the Jews and the Christians before they greet you and when you meet any one of them on the roads force him to go to the narrowest part of it (Sahih Muslim, No. 2167);

3. The Hour will not be established until you fight against the Jews, and the stone behind which a Jew will be hiding will say, 'O Muslim! There is a Jew hiding behind me, so kill him' (Sahih Al-Bukhari, No. 2926);

4. Jews and Christians will take the place of Muslims in Hell (Sahih Muslim, No. 2767R1).

Consequently, I am interested in your response to the following questions:

1. Does your mosque/organization officially and publicly support the Tri-Faith Initiative and its goal? If so, what have you done to show that support, including any financial contributions and the amounts?

2. If your mosque/organization officially and publicly supports the Tri-Faith Initiative and its goal, how do you address the above verses of the Koran and teachings of Muhammad?

3. If your mosque/organization does not officially and publicly support the Tri-Faith Initiative and its goal, is it because Islamic doctrine prohibits such a venture on the part of Muslims?

4. Do you know of any Muslim organizations or individual Muslims who have provided financial support to the Tri-Faith Initiative, including for purchase of land, construction of the synagogue, or construction of the proposed mosque and/or church? If you know of any such organizations or individuals, what was the total amount of their respective contributions?

None of the nine have responded to my questions.

185

American Muslim Institute

Consequently, I decided to contact the Muslim partner in the Tri-Faith Initiative, the American Muslim Institute (AMI). I sent the following e-mail twice to Leigh Sittenauer, AMI Executive Director:

> *I am interested in finding out the extent of the support from Nebraska Muslims for 1) the Tri-Faith Initiative; 2) its goal of building "bridges of respect, trust and acceptance" between Judaism, Christianity, and Islam; and 3) the construction of the new mosque. Could you please advise me of the Muslim organizations and/or mosques that publicly support these items, and the number of members in each of the organizations and/or mosques that show that support? How are they showing their support?*
>
> *Also, since there are already mosques in the Omaha area, how specifically will your mosque differ, doctrinally or otherwise, from the existing mosques? If there is no difference, why should Muslims start attending your mosque after it is built? Do you already have members who are meeting for Friday prayer at some place other than the existing mosques? If so, how many current members do you have for your new mosque, who is the imam, and where are they meeting?*

Ms. Sittenauer has not responded.

I recently attended a presentation on Islam by Dr. Syed Mohiuddin, President of AMI. An attendee asked a multi-part question that included a request for the names of Muslim organizations that supported the Tri-Faith Initiative. Dr. Mohiuddin answered other parts of the question, but did not respond to the request for the names of any supporting Muslim organizations.

Conclusion

The unanimous silence when asked about what Muslim organizations/mosques in Nebraska are supporting the Tri-Faith Initiative is telling. The answer appears to be simple: there are no Muslim organizations/mosques in Nebraska supporting the Tri-Faith Initiative. There appears to be only a few, individual Muslims involved in the Tri-Faith venture. Why?

The answer lies in the fact that verses in the Koran and teachings of Muhammad prohibit Muslim participation in ventures like the Tri-Faith Initiative. In his recent presentation on Islam, Dr. Mohiuddin advised a group of non-Muslims that a good translation of the Koran was *The Meaning of the Glorious Koran* by Marmaduke Pickthall, a Muslim convert. So consider the following three verses from Pickthall's translation:

> *O ye who believe! Take not the Jews and the Christians for friends. They are friends one to another. He among you who taketh them for friends is (one) of them. Lo! Allah guideth not wrongdoing folk.* (5:51)

> *Thou wilt find the most vehement of mankind in hostility to those who believe (to be) the Jews and the idolaters.* (5:82)

> *Lo! those* [sic] *who disbelieve, among the People of the Scripture* [Jews and Christians] *and the idolaters, will abide in fire* [sic] *of hell. They are the worst of created beings.* (98:6)

These three Koran verses in particular, and the many other verses with similar messages, appear to be ignored by Dr. Mohiuddin and the few Muslims actively promoting the Tri-Faith Initiative. In contrast, it appears that the greater Muslim community in Nebraska is paying attention to

187

these three verses and the many others that prohibit Muslims from participating in a venture like the Tri-Faith Initiative.

Consequently, the Tri-Faith Initiative appears to be standing mainly on two crutches: Jews and Christians. Bi-Faith Initiative anyone?

Fantasy Islam in Israel

Verily, you will find the strongest among men in enmity to the believers (Muslims) the Jews...

Koran, 5:82

Narrated Abu Hurairah: Allah's Messenger said, "The Hour will not be established until you fight against the Jews, and the stone behind which a Jew will be hiding will say, 'O Muslim! There is a Jew hiding behind me, so kill him.'"

Sahih Al-Bukhari, Vol. 4, Book 56, No. 2926, p. 113

26

Jewish-Muslim coexistence through the Koran?[263]

In the January 7, 2016 edition of *Arutz Sheva*, Rebecca Abrahamson wrote an op-ed piece about Dr. Omer Salem, an Egyptian Muslim sheikh who was determined to pursue peace between Jews and Muslims. The basis for this peace was to be "scripture," and Salem was encouraging Jews "to deepen their attachment to the Torah and mitzvot." But to have any prospect for achieving such peace, more is required.

Jews are People of the Book

According to Abrahamson, Salem believed that

> *The closer Jews are to their book, he insists, the more they will be viewed as Ahlul Kitab – people of the book – by Muslims, and the more they will earn respect in the Muslim world.*

But if the basis for this peace is to be "scripture," then we must also take into account what Islamic scripture has to say; for that we must look to the Koran and the *hadiths*, the teachings and example of Muhammad.

Here is some of what the Koran has to say about the People of the Book: Many of the People of the Book have enmity and hatred toward Muslims

---

[263]   This appeared in *Arutz Sheva 7* on January 13, 2016 with the title "Jewish-Muslim coexistence through the Koran? Wishful thinking": http://www.israelnationalnews.com/Articles/Article.aspx/18229.

(2:109); the People of the Book mix truth with falsehood and conceal the truth (3:71); the People of the Book know that Islam is the true faith but they reject it anyway and hinder those seeking to follow Islam (3:98-99); Allah commands the People of the Book to believe in Islam and Muhammad, or he will "efface faces and turn them hindwards" (4:47); Muslims are commanded to fight the People of the Book until those People pay the *jizyah*, "with willing submission and feel themselves subdued" (9:29); and, if the People of the Book don't believe in Islam, then they are among the worst of creatures and they will abide in the Fires of Hell (98:6).

If Muslims truly believe that the Koran consists of the Words of Allah, then there is no support in the Koran for claiming that Jews will earn respect in the Muslim world by being viewed as People of the Book. And there are additional Koranic verses that also undermine the idea of Jews earning the respect of Muslims: the Jews are among the worst enemies of the Muslims (5:82); Muslims are forbidden from being friends with Jews (especially 5:51, and, e.g., 3:28, 5:57, and 60:13); and Allah curses the Jews (9:30).

Muslims and Jews are "Coreligionists"

According to Abrahamson, Salem claims Muslims and Jews are "coreligionists," and he uses two Koran verses to support this claim: 49:13 and 5:48.

Here is the portion of 49:13 quoted in the article:

> *O Mankind! We created you from a male and female, and made you into peoples and tribes so that you might come to know each other.*

It sounds like Allah is stating that all people are equal and calling for them to get along and get to know each other. However, the verse continues with this:

*Verily, the most honourable of you with Allah is that who
has At-Taqwa.*

At-Taqwa is acting in obedience to the commands of Allah and following
the teachings of Muhammad. So although this verse appears to begin with
the idea of equality among people, it ends by stating that the most
honorable among people are those who are devout Muslims.

According to Abrahamson, Salem regarded 5:48

> *as invoking multi-covenantism – Jewish law for the Jews,
> Islamic law for the Muslims - a teaching demanding more
> than mere tolerance, but actual acceptance of the other
> faith community.*

Here is how that verse was quoted:

> *To each among you (Muslims and Jews) have We
> prescribed a law and an open way. If Allah had so willed,
> He would have made you a single people, but (His plan is)
> to test you in what He hath given you: so strive as in a
> race in all virtues.*

The problem with how this verse was quoted is that it leaves out the first
half of the verse. In the first half we find that Allah has sent the Koran to
Muhammad, and Allah commands Muhammad to

> *judge among them by what Allah has revealed, and follow
> not their vain desires, diverging away from the truth that
> has come to you.*

For centuries authoritative Koran commentators have explained that this
verse meant that Muhammad was to judge matters by the Koran, in which

192

the truth is found, and which had abrogated the "vain desires" of the Jews and Christians as found in their respective scriptures.[264]

Unfortunately, Salem appears to be selecting only portions of verses and is engaging in his own personal interpretation of the Koran; and his interpretation is at odds with those of authoritative Koran commentators over the centuries. He is also ignoring a warning from Muhammad:

> *Muhammad bin Jarir reported that Ibn 'Abbas said that the Prophet said, 'Whoever explains the Qur'an with his opinion or with what he has no knowledge of, then let him assume his seat in the Fire.'[265]*

And with his claim that Jews and Muslims are "coreligionists," Salem is ignoring the clear message of 3:85 in the Koran:

> *And whoever seeks a religion other than Islam, it will never be accepted of him, and in the Hereafter he will be one of the losers.*

Greater *Jihad* versus Lesser *Jihad*

Dr. Salem emphasized the importance of *jihad al nafs*, the inner battle to make one's own self better, and claimed that this was a higher form of *jihad* than "*jihad al sayeef* - the struggle of the sword." Salem invited Muslims to favor this "higher and more difficult path." Unfortunately for Salem's claim, the idea that the "greater *jihad*" is an inner struggle, and fighting with the sword is the "lesser *jihad*" has no basis in Islamic Doctrine. That Muhammad supposedly made such a distinction between *jihads* is based largely on weak or fabricated *hadiths* and later commentary

---

[264]   E.g. *Tafsir Al-Jalalayn*, p. 254; *Tafsir Ibn Kathir*, Vol. 3, pp. 195-202; *Tafsir Ahsanul-Bayan*, Vol. 1, pp. 613-614; and *Tafsir As-Sa'di*, Vol. 1, pp. 509-511.

[265]   *Tafsir Ibn Kathir*, Vol. 1, pp. 32-33.

inserted into *Reliance of the Traveller*, a Shafi'i manual of Sharia Law, which has erroneously been considered part of the original manual. I cover this in more detail on pp. 115-123 of my book *Islam According to Muhammad, Not Your Neighbor*.

A History of Prospering Side by Side

Dr. Salem insisted "that both Jews and Muslims can prosper side by side," and he stated that, "Our ancestors prospered in parallel." Dr. Salem is ignoring the facts that his prophet Muhammad drove the Jewish tribes out of Medina, supervised the beheading of 600-900 captured Jewish males (combatants and non-combatants), and had this to say:

> *Narrated Abu Hurairah: Allah's Messenger said, "The Hour will not be established until you fight against the Jews, and the stone behind which a Jew will be hiding will say, 'O Muslim! There is a Jew hiding behind me, so kill him.'"*[266]

Here are some additional comments Muhammad made about the Jews:

> *It was narrated from 'Amr bin Shu'aib, from his father, from his grandfather, that the Messenger of Allah ruled that the blood money for the People of the Book is half of that of the blood money for the Muslims, and they are the Jews and Christians.*[267]

> *Abu Huraira reported that Allah's Messenger (may peace be upon him) had said: Do not greet the Jews and the Christians before they greet you and when you meet any*

---

[266]   *Sahih Al-Bukhari*, Vol. 4, Book 56, No. 2926, p. 113.

[267]   *Sunan Ibn Majah*, Vol. 3, No. 2644, p. 521.

one of them on the roads force him to go to the narrowest part of it.[268]

Abu Burda reported on the authority of his father that Allah's Apostle (may peace be upon him) said: No Muslim would die but Allah would admit instead of him a Jew or a Christian in Hell-Fire.[269]

And on his deathbed Muhammad gave one last command:

It has been narrated by 'Umar b. Al-Khattab that he heard the Messenger of Allah (may peace be upon him) saying: I will expel the Jews and Christians from the Arabian Peninsula and will not leave any but Muslims.[270]

In spite of Dr. Salem's belief, his prophet Muhammad certainly did not believe that Jews and Muslims could "prosper side by side."

Conclusion

One has to appreciate Dr. Salem's desire for peace between Jews and Muslims. Unfortunately, with his primary focus currently being on encouraging Jews to deepen their attachment to their own scriptures, the prospects for success are minimal. To improve these prospects will require Salem to also turn a focus on the commands of Allah and the teachings of Muhammad that directly counter his peace efforts. Salem will have to decide if these commands and teachings are still relevant and applicable to today. He will then likely find that encouraging Jews to deepen their attachment to their own scriptures has been the easiest part of his quest.

---

[268]   *Sahih Muslim*, Vol. 6, No. 2167, p. 439.

[269]   *Sahih Muslim*, Vol. 8, No. 2767R1, p. 269.

[270]   *Sahih Muslim*, Vol. 5, No. 1767, p. 189.

27

Real Islam is not based on personal interpretations[271]

I would like to thank Dr. Salem for taking the time to respond to my article. He and I are in agreement about the importance of improving relations between Jews and Muslims; our disagreement is over the efficacy and nature of his approach. But his response has appeared to raise more questions than it answered. The focus of my article is on addressing those questions.

Dr. Salem wrote that the Koran he used for his response was 'Abdullah Yusuf 'Ali's translation: *The Meaning of the Holy Qur'an* (Amana Publications, 2009). For this article I use an edition of that same Koran translation printed by Amana Publications in 2004.

To understand the meaning of the Koran verses examined, I use English translations of the following Koran commentaries (*tafsirs*): *Tafsir Ibn Kathir*, *Tafsir Al-Jalalayn*, *Tafsir Ahsanul-Bayan*, *Tafsir As-Sa'di*.

So let's begin.

God or Allah?

Dr. Salem uses the words God and Allah interchangeably when writing about Muslims and Jews. This is because he apparently believes that

---

[271]   This appeared in *Arutz Sheva 7* on February 8, 2016:
http://www.israelnationalnews.com/Articles/Article.aspx/18369.

Muslim and Jews all believe in the same God, of which Allah is just another name. But what does the Muslim god Allah say about this in the Koran?

To set the stage, Allah states that the only religion acceptable to him is Islam (e.g., 3:19 and 3:85). And Allah states that Islam is to be made superior over all other religions, even if the non-Muslims don't like it (e.g., 9:33, 48:28, and 61:9).

Allah states that he is angry with the Jews (1:7) and he curses them (9:30). Allah states that the Jews are among the worst of creatures who "will abide in the fire of Hell" (98:6), while Muslims are the best of creatures (3:110 and 98:7). He forbids Muslims from being friends with Jews (5:51). Instead, Allah commands Muslims to fight the Jews until the Jews pay the *jizyah* (protection tax) with willing submission and feeling themselves subdued (9:29). And Allah specifically states that the Jews are among the worst enemies of Islam (5:82).

How could one expect Jews to believe in and worship a God who hates and curses them, orders Muslims to fight them, and condemns them to Hell simply because they are not Muslims? In response, Dr. Salem talks about "God-fearing Jews" and "atheist Jews," and he believes that such Koran verses are directed only toward the "atheist Jews."

It is easy to understand why Jews would fear the god found in the Koran. But this is not what Dr. Salem means when he talks about "God-fearing Jews." In his view, these "God-fearing Jews" will earn the respect of the Muslim world.

So what does Dr. Salem mean when he talks about "God-fearing Jews"?

Who are the "God-fearing Jews"?

Dr. Salem wrote:

According to the Qur'an, People of the Book are not all the same, among them are the believer and the disbeliever.

According to Salem, the "believer" is the "God-Fearing Jew," and the "disbeliever" is the "atheist Jew." He wrote that

there is support, in the Qur'an, for claiming that God-fearing Jews are considered people of the Book and will earn respect in the Muslim world by being viewed as People of the Book.

And throughout his article he provided the following Koran verses to support this distinction between "atheist Jews" and "God-fearing Jews," and the purported Muslim acceptance of the "God-fearing" Jews: 2:62 (listed in the article as 2:69), 3:113, 7:159, 13:36, and 34:6. Let's see what our *tafsirs* have to say about these verses and whether or not they support Dr. Salem's claims.

Chapter 2, Verse 62

Those who believe (in the Qur'an), and those who follow the Jewish (scriptures), and the Christians and the Sabians – Any who believe in Allah and the Last Day, and work righteousness, shall have their reward with their Lord; on them shall be no fear, nor shall they grieve.

The *Tafsir Ahsanul-Bayan* provides a pertinent commentary:

Some modernists advance this verse as proof that all the religions, despite their apparent diversity in beliefs and rites of worship, are in essence one, and that it is not essential to believe in the prophetic mission of Muhammad and that deliverance depends on faithfully following one's

198

own religion and doing good works. *This is an absolutely erroneous idea.*[272]

The *Tafsir Ibn Kathir* provided a similar explanation:

> *...Allah does not accept any deed or work from anyone, unless it conforms to the Law of Muhammad that is, after Allah sent Muhammad. Before that, every person who followed the guidance of his own Prophet was on the correct path, following the correct guidance and was saved.*[273]

And Ibn Kathir was very specific about the change that had arrived with Muhammad:

> *When Allah sent Muhammad as the Last and Final Prophet and Messenger to all the Children of Adam, mankind was required to believe in him, obey him and refrain from what he prohibited them; those who do this are true believers.*[274]

So 2:62 pertained only to good deeds done before the advent of Islam. This verse actually means that, after the advent of Islam, *righteousness*

---

[272] *Tafsir Ahsanul-Bayan*, Vol. 1, p. 71.

[273] *Tafsir Ibn Kathir*, Vol. 1, p. 249. This ten volume collection

> *is the most popular interpretation of the Qur'an in the Arabic language, and the majority of the Muslims consider it to be the best source based on Qur'an and Sunnah.*

> *Tafsir Ibn Kathir*, Vol. 1, p. 5

[274] Ibid., p. 250.

199

will be accepted only if it conforms to the commands of Allah and the Law of Muhammad.

Chapter 3, Verse 113

This verse was cited throughout Dr. Salem's article:

> *Not all of them are alike: Of the People of the Book are a portion that stand (for the right); they rehearse the signs of Allah all night long, and they prostrate themselves in adoration.*

Let's start off with the editor's comments about this verse found in 'Ali's translation of *The Holy Qur'an*, the Koran used by Dr. Salem:

> *This verse, according to Commentators, refers to those People of the Book who eventually embraced Islam.*[275]

The *Tafsir As-Sa'di* explained what is meant by standing *for the right*:

> *Allah now says about the faithful, [they are the ones] that are upright, that is, this is the group that remains dedicated to Allah's ordained religion, obeys His commandments, and performs the devotions commanded from them.*[276]

The *Tafsir Ahsanul-Bayan* explained that this verse talked about "good" Jews who had converted to Islam and "who act by the *shari'ah* and follow the Messenger of Allah."[277]

---

[275]   *The Meaning of The Holy Qur'an*, trans. 'Abdullah Yusuf 'Ali (Beltsville, Maryland: 2004), p. 156. n. 437

[276]   *Tafsir As-Sa'di*, Vol. 1, p. 274.

[277]   *Tafsir Ahsanul-Bayan*, Vol. 1, p. 350.

The *Tafsir Al-Jalalayn* also explained that this verse referred to Jews who had converted to Islam and referred to them as "straight and holding firmly to the truth."[278]

The *Tafsir Ibn Kathir* explained that this verse was "revealed" about Jews who had embraced Islam, and

> *a party of the People of the Scripture stand for the right*
> *for they implement the Book of Allah, adhere to His Law*
> *and follow His Prophet Muhammad.*[279]

So that "portion" of the People of the Book who stand for the right are actually those Jews who converted to Islam.

Chapter 7, Verse 159

> *Of the people of Moses there is a section who guide and*
> *do justice in the light of truth.*

The *Tafsir As-Sa'di* explained that among the people of Moses, "Allah designated leaders within them who guide them according to His teachings."[280] Meaning they guide them according to Islamic Doctrine.

The *Tafsir Ahsanul-Bayan* stated that this verse referred to those Jews "who embraced Islam."[281]

The *Tafsir Ibn Kathir* stated that there were some Jews "who follow the truth and judge by it, just as He said in another *Ayah* [verse]," and Ibn

---

278   *Tafsir Al-Jalalayn*, p. 147.

279   *Tafsir Ibn Kathir*, Vol. 2, p. 246.

280   *Tafsir As-Sa'di*, Vol. 2, p. 66.

281   *Tafsir Ahsanul-Bayan*, Vol. 2, p. 234.

Kathir referred to 3:113.[282] So there are Jews who follow, and judge by Islam.

We can see that this verse is understood to mean that those *who guide and do justice in the light of the truth* are those Jews who believed in Allah and embraced Islam.

Chapter 13:36

> *Those to whom We have given the Book rejoice at what hath been revealed unto thee: but there are among the clans those who reject a part thereof. Say: "I am commanded to worship Allah, and not to join partners with Him. Unto Him do I call, and unto Him is my return."*

The *Tafsir Ahsanul-Bayan* explained that some commentators believed "the Book" pertained to the Koran and this verse referred to Muslims rejoicing over that; other commentators believed that "the Book" referred to the Torah and Bible and those rejoicing were Jews and Christians who had become Muslims.[283]

The *Tafsir Al-Jalalayn* explained this verse in terms of those Jews who had converted to Islam being the ones rejoicing.[284]

The *Tafsir As-Sa'di* explained that *those who reject a part thereof* are those who reject parts of the Koran "and do not attest it."[285]

---

[282]   *Tafsir Ibn Kathir*, Vol. 4, pp. 185-186.

[283]   *Tafsir Ahsanul-Bayan*, Vol. 3, p. 106.

[284]   *Tafsir Al-Jalalayn*, p. 532.

[285]   *Tafsir As-Sa'di*, Vol. 2, p. 362.

The *Tafsir Ibn Kathir* explained that "the Book" was the Koran, and *among the clans those who reject a part thereof* refers to Jews and Christian who reject "the truth" that was sent down to Muhammad.[286]

So we have another verse that is talking about Jews converting to Islam and rejoicing, while other Jews reject Islam.

Chapter 34:6

> *And those to whom knowledge has come see that the (Revelation) sent down to thee from thy Lord – that is the Truth, and that it guides to the Path of the Exalted (In Might), Worthy of all praise.*

The *Tafsir Al-Jalalayn* explained that this verse referred to People of the Book who had converted to Islam, and the Revelation that had been sent down to them was the Koran.[287]

The *Tafsir Ahsanul-Bayan* explained that the Truth was what Allah had revealed to Muhammad, and those receiving this knowledge were those among the People of the Book who had converted to Islam, and all Muslims in general.[288]

Dr. Salem has used these five Koran verses to support his claim that the Koran distinguishes between "atheist Jews" and "God-fearing Jews," with animosity in the Koran only toward the former. Based on these verses, it appears that the "atheist Jews" are those who do not believe in Islam or reject it; the "God-fearing Jews" are those who convert to Islam. This throws a new light on Dr. Salem's statement:

---

[286]   *Tafsir Ibn Kathir*, Vol. 5, pp. 294-295.

[287]   *Tafsir Al-Jalalayn*, pp. 915-917.

[288]   *Tafsir Ahsanul-Bayan*, Vol. 4, p. 425.

According to the Qur'an, People of the Book are not all the same, among them are the believer and the disbeliever.

The word "believer" is commonly used in the Koran to refer to a Muslim; the word "disbeliever" is commonly used to refer to a non-Muslim. This explains why Dr. Salem claims that verses of the Koran that refer to Jews in negative ways are directed only at "atheist Jews" (his examples included 5:51, 5:82, and 9:29), and why he claims that the *hadiths* I cited that were hostile toward the Jews were directed only against "atheist Jews." "God-fearing Jews" are believers, those who have converted to Islam and thus earned the respect of the Muslim world; "atheist Jews" are those who are still Jews, or disbelievers, and, inter alia, among the worst enemies of Muslims (5:82).

Greater *Jihad* versus Lesser *Jihad*

In my article I stated that there is no basis in Islamic Doctrine for the claimed distinction that Muhammad supposedly made between a "greater *jihad*" (an inner struggle) and a "lesser *jihad*" (armed fighting in the cause of Allah). Dr. Salem disagreed and quoted Meccan verse 25:52:

Therefore listen not to the Unbelievers, but strive against them with the utmost strenuousness, with the (Quran).

Dr. Salem wrote:

It is clear from this Meccan verse that Allah is instructing the newly found Ummah to strive in the path of Allah, not by the sword, but by the Qur'an—that is Jihadul Nafs.

Dr. Salem is correct in the message of this verse. But the *Tafsir Ahsanul-Bayan* made a crucial observation about 25:52: This verse "was revealed in Mecca and Allah had not yet given the command to the Muslims to fight

204

the pagans."[289] This means that at that time in Mecca the only way the Muslims were allowed to "strive against" the non-Muslims was verbally and by teaching the verses that had been "revealed" to that date. It wasn't until around the Fall of 622 that Allah "revealed" verses to Muhammad that allowed the Muslims to engage in armed fighting against non-Muslims (e.g., 22:39). So up until that time the Muslims were simply not allowed by Allah to engage in armed combat. This changed with the "revelation" of verses such as 22:39.

The Doctrine of Abrogation is important to addressing this issue.[290] There is an important significance to where a verse or chapter was "revealed." While in Mecca, the religion of Islam was just starting and it was generally not well received. Perhaps as a result of this, the verses of the Koran "revealed" in Mecca were generally more peaceful and accommodating toward non-Muslims than the verses later "revealed" in Medina. The verses from Medina have a general tendency to be more belligerent and intolerant, and more inclined to make sharp differentiations between Muslims (believers) and non-Muslims (disbelievers).

This can lead to a conflict between the message of a Meccan verse and that of a Medinan verse addressing the same general topic. But how can there be such a conflict if the Koran is the infallible, eternal, "revealed" word of Allah? This was covered in Medinan verse 2:106 that introduced the concept of "abrogation":

> *None of Our revelations do We abrogate or cause to be forgotten, but we substitute something better or similar: Knowest thou not that Allah hath power over all things?*

Abrogation therefore means that if there is a conflict between the messages of two "revelations" in the Koran, then the most recent "revelation" is the

---

[289]   Ibid., p. 36.

[290]   Due to space constraints, this is only a general overview. For a more detailed look at the Doctrine of Abrogation, see *An Introduction to the Sciences of the Qur'an*, pp. 232-256.

one to be followed. Consequently, a "revelation" made in Medina would supersede a similar, earlier "revelation" made in Mecca if there was a conflict between the messages of the two.

Chapter 9 of the Koran was the last chapter to be "revealed," so Allah's commands found in the verses of that chapter are the final words in terms of the topics covered. So here is Allah's final command in terms of general armed fighting in His Cause, *jihad*:

> 9:5:   *But when the forbidden months are past, then fight and slay the Pagans wherever ye find them, and seize them, beleaguer them, and lie in wait for them in every stratagem (of war); but if they repent* [by accepting Islam], *and establish regular prayers and practice regular charity, then open the way for them: For Allah is Oft-Forgiving, Most Merciful.*

There are numerous peaceful-sounding verses in the Koran, such as 25:52. But they are mainly Meccan verses. So when there is a conflict between the message of a peaceful-sounding Meccan verse and that of a belligerent-sounding Medinan verse, the Meccan verse is abrogated. The Meccan verse is still in the Koran, because it consists of the words of Allah. But it is the Medinan verse that is carrying the doctrinal authority: 9:5 abrogated 25:52.

Chapter 9, Verse 29

In 9:29 Muslims are commanded to fight Jews and Christians until the Jews and Christians pay the *jizyah* (a protection tax):

> *Fight those who believe not in Allah nor the Last Day, nor hold that forbidden which hath been forbidden by Allah and His Messenger, nor acknowledge the Religion of Truth, from among the People of the Book, until they pay the Jizyah with willing submission, and feel themselves subdued.*

Dr. Salem wrote that this verse was directed only against the "atheist Jews." He said it was not directed toward the "God-fearing Jews." He concluded:

> *This verse proves my thesis that "Jews cleaving to the laws of Moses will be respected by Muslims" they* [sic] *will not have to pay Jizyah in a Muslim state.*"

So what do our *tafsirs* have to say about 9:29? In a paragraph titled *The Order to fight People of the Scriptures until They give the Jizyah*, Ibn Kathir explained the meaning of this verse:

> *Therefore, when People of the Scriptures disbelieved in Muhammad, they had no beneficial faith in any Messenger or what the Messengers brought. Rather, they followed their religions because this conformed with their ideas, lusts and the ways of their forefathers, not because they are Allah's Law and religion. Had they been true believers in their religions, that faith would have directed them to believe in Muhammad...Allah commanded His Messenger to fight the People of the Scriptures, Jews and Christians...*[291]

In a paragraph titled *Paying Jizyah is a Sign of Kufr* [disbelief] *and Disgrace*, Ibn Kathir explained that if the Jews and Christians chose not to embrace Islam, they would have to pay the *Jizyah* "in defeat and subservience," and feel "disgraced, humiliated, and belittled." [292]

This was affirmed in the *Tafsir Al-Jalalayn* when the *Jizyah* section of 9:29 was being discussed:

> *...until they pay the jizya with their own hands - meaning the Jews and the Christians who must pay it in submission*

---

[291]   *Tafsir Ibn Kathir*, Vol. 4, pp. 404-405.

[292]   Ibid., pp. 405-406

*or directly with their actual hands - in a state of complete
abasement - humble and subject to the judgements of
Islam.*[293]

The *Tafsir Al-Jalalayn* also pointed out that the Jews and Christians were
to be fought if they did not accept Muhammad and did not accept Islam as
their faith.[294]

This was also noted in the *Tafsir Ahsanul-Bayan*:

> *The command to fight the pagans was already given. Now
> Allah commands the believers to fight the Jews and
> Christians (if they do not accept Islam) until they pay the
> jizya and live under the rule of the Muslims.*[295]

The *Tafsir As-Sa'di* explained this verse:

> *The command to fight the disbelievers includes the Jews
> and Christians who do not believe in Allah... They assume
> that they have a religion, but their religion is not the true
> religion for it has been changed and modified, and is not
> the one that Allah had originally ordained. Or are they
> following a religion that now stands revoked, meaning, it
> was first ordained by Allah but has now been replaced
> with the one sent to Prophet Muhammad.*[296]

This tafsir expounded on the nature of the *jizyah*:

---

293   *Tafsir Al-Jalalayn*, pp. 404-406.

294   Ibid., p. 404.

295   *Tafsir Ahsanul-Bayan*, Vol. 2, pp. 345-346.

296   *Tafsir As-Sa'di*, Vol. 2, p. 137.

These people are to be fought against until they pay the jizyah, which is the payment made to the Muslims in exchange for the right to live in the Muslim land and for security of their life and wealth...When this becomes their condition that they agree to pay the jizyah to the Muslims, live under their rule, refrain from creating chaos and mayhem, and accept whatever terms and conditions the Muslims have applied on them, which indicates their submission and is an end to their self-rule...[297]

There is nothing in these *tafsirs* about differentiating between "atheist Jews" and "God-fearing Jews." And in fact, these *tafsirs* directly refute Dr. Salem's claim that 9:29 proves his "thesis" that "Jews cleaving to the laws of Moses will be respected by Muslims" and "they will not have to pay Jizyah in a Muslim state." Jews who do not accept Islam will be fought against until they pay the *Jizyah, with willing submission, and feel themselves subdued.*

98:6 - Among the worst of creatures

Dr. Salem wrote:

> *Dr. Kirby cited 98:6 saying that: "if the People of the Book don't believe in Islam, then they are among the worst of creatures and they will abide in the Fires of Hell." Again this is part of a verse that should be considered in context, it should be read with the verse before it and the verse after it as one unit to get to the intended meaning. Here is what the verse says:*
>
> *"Those who reject Truth, among the People of the Book and among the Polytheists, will be in Hell-Fire, to dwell therein. They are the worst of creatures."*

---

[297]   Ibid., p. 138.

Please note the conjunction "among." It is clear that the verse does not say that "all People of the Book will be in hell fire," it says that "Those who reject Truth, among the People of the Book... will be in Hell-Fire."

Dr. Salem is correct in terms of the wording of 98:6, but incorrect in terms of its meaning. The *Tafsir Ahsanul-Bayan* explains that the Truth this verse is talking about is the religion of Islam, the Koran, and Muhammad.[298]

And no devout Jew or Christian, by definition, accepts the religion of Islam as their faith, and therefore they will be consigned to Hell-Fire. This was reiterated by Dr. Salem's prophet Muhammad:

It is narrated on the authority of Abu Huraira that the Messenger of Allah (SAW) said: By Him in whose hand is the life of Muhammad, he who amongst the community of Jews or Christians hears about me but does not affirm his belief in that with which I have been sent and dies in this state (of disbelief), he shall be but one of the denizens of Hell-Fire.[299]

Now for comparison's sake, let's look at the following verse, 98:7:

Those who have faith and do righteous deeds – They are the best of creatures.

The *Tafsir Ahsanul-Bayan* explained that "those who have faith" believe "in the Oneness of Allah, and in His Messenger (Muhammad) including all obligations ordered by Islam."[300] In other words, they are the Muslims.

---

[298]   *Tafsir Ahsanul-Bayan*, Vol. 5, p. 742.

[299]   *Sahih Muslim*, Vol. 1, p. 103, No. 153.

[300]   *Tafsir Ahsanul-Bayan*, Vol. 5, p. 743.

210

Ibn Kathir pointed out that some Muslim scholars had used this verse

> *as a proof that the believers* [Muslims] *have a status among the creatures that is better than the angels. This is because Allah says, "They are the best of creatures."*[301]

To sum it up, Jews and Christians, who by definition do not adhere to the Religion of Islam, are among the worst of creatures; Muslims, by definition, are the best of creatures.

Conclusion

Dr. Salem's quest to improve relations between Jews and Muslims revolves around his distinction between "God-fearing Jews," who he claims will earn the respect of the Muslim world, and "atheist Jews," who will not. He claims there is support in the Koran for such a distinction, and we looked at five Koran verses he used to support this claim. What we found was that the distinction these verses made focused on those Jews who had converted to Islam and those Jews who had rejected Islam. These converts appear to be the "God-fearing Jews" Dr. Salem is talking about, who earn the respect of the Muslim world; those Jews who reject Islam and remained Jews appear to be the "atheist Jews" who, according to Dr. Salem, are the sole targets of the negative verses in the Koran about Jews.

Dr. Salem stated that his "interpretations" were supported by the four Koran commentaries (*tafsirs*) he had mentioned; but of his 25 endnotes, only five made any reference to these four *tafsirs*.
Dr. Salem stated that his "interpretations" were supported by his professors at Al-Azhar University; but he did not list any such professors in his article or indicate the extent of that support, and from whom, for any of his "interpretations."

---

[301] *Tafsir Ibn Kathir*, Vol. 10, p. 554. That Muslims have a higher status than angels was also noted in *Tafsir Ahsanul-Bayan*, Vol. 5, p. 743.

In his article he relied extensively on 3:113 of the Koran to show that the People of the Book were not all alike and to support his differentiation between "God-fearing Jews" and "atheist Jews." But in the *tafsirs* I use, and even in the translation of the Koran Dr. Salem used, we find that 3:113 was understood to refer to those Jews who had converted to Islam.

It would be very enlightening if perhaps Dr. Salem would devote an article just to his concept of "God-fearing Jews," defining his terms, presenting criteria for determining who is a "God-fearing Jew" and who is an "atheist Jew," presenting the supportive Koran verses with specifically referenced supportive *tafsirs* (with quotes translated into English when necessary), and commentary from identified professors who support his particular interpretations.

The quest for peaceful relations between Muslims and Jews is too important to leave unanswered questions, and perhaps some confusion, about the basis for that quest.

28

Fantasy Islam[302]

Fantasy Islam is a popular game among many non-Muslims and so-called "moderate" or "reformist" Muslims. And in his recent *Arutz Sheva 7* article ("A call for sanity: How the Quran-abiding Muslims view the Jews") Adnan Oktar shows a mastery of that game.[303]

Oktar was very critical of those who take Koran verses "out of context," and pointed out the fact that "in some cases one would need other verses to understand a verse." But in his article he often proceeded to do the first while ignoring the latter.

Jews according to the Quran

Oktar had a section of his article titled "Jews according to the Quran," and used some Koran verses to indicate the respect for Jews supposedly found in the Koran.

Oktar used a portion of 2:62 of the Koran to claim that Allah praises "righteous people among Jews and Christians." Here is the complete verse:

---

[302]   This appeared in *Arutz Sheva 7* on January 24, 2016: http://www.israelnationalnews.com/Articles/Article.aspx/18286.

[303]   Adnan Oktar, "A call for sanity: How the Quran-abiding Muslims view the Jews," *Arutz Sheva 7*, January 18, 2016; accessible at: http://www.israelnationalnews.com/Articles/Article.aspx/18253.

Verily, those who believe and those who are Jews and Christians, and Sabians, whoever believes in Allah and the Last Day and does righteous good deeds shall have their reward with their Lord, on them shall be no fear, nor shall they grieve.

But Oktar is taking this verse out of context and ignoring a related verse in the Koran. For centuries Muslim scholars have understood that in terms of non-Muslims this verse only pertained to good deeds done before the advent of Islam; after the advent of Islam, people needed to believe in Allah, the god of Islam, and Muhammad to receive their reward.[304]

And Oktar left out the fact that 2:62 had actually been abrogated by 3:85.[305] Here is 3:85:

And whosoever seeks a religion other than Islam, it will never be accepted of him, and in the Hereafter he will be one of the losers.

Oktar used another verse in the Koran to indicate that there are Jews that are considered to be righteous:

Those who have faith and those who are Jews and the Sabaeans and the Christians, all who have faith in God and the Last Day and act rightly will feel no fear and will know no sorrow. (Qur'an, 5:69)

But as with 2:62, Muslim scholars understand this verse to mean only that one need have no fear or sorrow as long as they believed in Allah and their

---

[304]   *Tafsir Al-Qurtubi*, p. 267; *Tafsir Ibn Kathir*, Vol. 1, p. 249; *Tafsir Al-Jalalayn*, p. 23; and *Tafsir Ahsanul-Bayan*, Vol. 1, pp. 71-72.

[305]   *Tafsir Al-Qurtubi*, p. 267; *Tafsir Ibn Kathir*, Vol. 1, pp. 248-249; *Tafsir Ahsanul-Bayan*, Vol. 1, p. 72; and *The Noble Qur'an*, p. 24, n. 2.

deeds conformed to "Muhammad's Law."[306] And 5:69 was also abrogated by 3:85.[307]

Oktar wrote that "our Lord draws attention to a distinguished people amongst the Jews," and then quoted the follow Koran verse:

> *Among the people of Moses there is a group who guide by the truth and act justly in accordance with it. (Qur'an, 7:159)*

But this verse is understood to mean that these *distinguished people amongst the Jews* are those Jews who believe in Allah, embrace Islam, and recite the verses of the Koran.[308] So how can they still be Jews?

As Oktar pointed out, context is important. So to provide some additional context, take into consideration what Muhammad himself had to say about the status of Jews and Christians who remained faithful to their religions after the advent of Islam:

> *It is narrated on the authority of Abu Huraira that the Messenger of Allah (SAW) said: By Him in whose hand is the life of Muhammad, he who amongst the community of Jews or Christians hears about me but does not affirm his belief in that with which I have been sent and dies in this state (of disbelief), he shall be but one of the denizens of Hell-Fire.[309]*

---

[306]   *Tafsir Ibn Kathir*, Vol. 3, p. 232; and *Tafsir As-Sa'di*, Vol. 1, pp. 522-523.

[307]   *The Noble Qur'an*, p. 169, n. 1.

[308]   *Tafsir Ibn Kathir*, Vol. 4, pp. 185-187; *Tafsir Ahsanul-Bayan*, Vol. 2, p. 234; *Tafsir As-Sa'di*, Vol. 2, p. 66.

[309]   *Sahih Muslim*, Vol. 1, No. 153, p. 103.

The Koran and Prophet Muhammad's loving embrace of the Jews

Oktar wrote that

> *As one reads the Quran in its entirety, it will become plainly clear that there is no adverse viewing of the Jews...Indeed, Prophet Mohammed was a great example with his loving, embracing attitude towards them...*

No "adverse viewing of the Jews" in the Koran? I don't know what Koran Oktar is using, but I use *The Noble Qur'an* by Darussalam Publishers. In this Koran we find such things as: Muslims are forbidden from being friends with Jews (5:51); the Jews are among the worst enemies of Muslims (5:82); Muslims are specifically commanded to fight Jews (9:29); Allah curses the Jews (9:30); and Jews are among the worst of creatures and will live in the Fires of Hell (98:6).

And here are some examples of Muhammad's "loving, embracing attitude" toward the Jews:

Muhammad drove the Jewish tribes out of Medina, supervised the beheading of 600-900 captured Jewish males (combatants and non-combatants), and had this to say:

> *Narrated Abu Hurairah: Allah's Messenger said, "The Hour will not be established until you fight against the Jews, and the stone behind which a Jew will be hiding will say, 'O Muslim! There is a Jew hiding behind me, so kill him.'"*[310]

Here are some additional comments Muhammad made about the Jews:

---

[310]   *Sahih Al-Bukhari*, Vol. 4, Book 56, No. 2926, p. 113.

216

It was narrated from 'Amr bin Shu'aib, from his father, from his grandfather, that the Messenger of Allah ruled that the blood money for the People of the Book is half of that of the blood money for the Muslims, and they are the Jews and Christians.[311]

Abu Huraira reported that Allah's Messenger (may peace be upon him) had said: Do not greet the Jews and the Christians before they greet you and when you meet any one of them on the roads force him to go to the narrowest part of it.[312]

Abu Burda reported on the authority of his father that Allah's Apostle (may peace be upon him) said: No Muslim would die but Allah would admit instead of him a Jew or a Christian in Hell-Fire.[313]

And on his deathbed Muhammad gave one last command:

It has been narrated by 'Umar b. Al-Khattab that he heard the Messenger of Allah (may peace be upon him) saying: I will expel the Jews and Christians from the Arabian Peninsula and will not leave any but Muslims.[314]

---

[311]   *Sunan Ibn Majah*, Vol. 3, No. 2644, p. 521.

[312]   *Sahih Muslim*, Vol. 6, No. 2167, p. 439.

[313]   *Sahih Muslim*, Vol. 8, No. 2767R1, p. 269.

[314]   *Sahih Muslim*, Vol. 5, No. 1767, p. 189.

Conclusion

"Quran-abiding Muslims" are required to follow the commands of Allah found in the verses of the Koran. And among those verses is one specifically commanding Muslims to follow the teachings and example of Muhammad (59:7). The commands of Allah and the teachings and example of Muhammad are rife with anger and hostility toward the Jews.

Nevertheless, the final paragraph of Oktar's article started out with these words:

> *We cannot allow ourselves to be swallowed by anger and hatred when our religion commands us the opposite.*

Only by being a Master of Fantasy Islam could Oktar cap off his article with those words.

29

Fantasy Islam comes to the Knesset[315]

Ms. Rebecca Abrahamson recently provided a brief report about the Knesset conference titled "Building a Culture of Peace in the Middle East and the Global Arena" (*OpEd: Putting UN resolutions to work*).[316] She noted that

> *Dr. Cihat Gündoğdu, goodwill ambassador from Turkey, brandished a new book called, "Bigotry, the Dark Danger" which goes right to the sources in rebutting those who manipulate the Qur'an and hadith, taking them out of context to malign Jews. "The Qur'an should be taken as a whole, as Muslims, we see this as our duty to clarify the message of Islam. Indeed there are Muslims speaking of hatred and endless death penalties, instead of the love and gratitude that Islam commands."*

Ms. Abrahamson provided a link to *Bigotry, the Dark Danger*,[317] so I downloaded it to see what kind of contribution it might make to building a culture of peace. The book was written by Adnan Oktar (aka Harun

---

[315]   This appeared in *Arutz Sheva 7* on February 17, 2016: http://www.israelnationalnews.com/Articles/Article.aspx/18413.

[316]   Rebecca Abrahamson, "Putting UN resolutions to work," *Arutz Sheva 7*, February 11, 2016; accessible at: http://www.israelnationalnews.com/Articles/Article.aspx/18389.

[317]   http://www.harunyahya.com/en/Books/191085/bigotry-the-dark-danger

Yahya), a prolific Turkish writer and publicist in the Muslim world, and the subject of one of my earlier *Artuz Sheva 7* articles, "Fantasy Islam."[318]

The premise of Oktar's book is that a "fanatical faith produced by peddlers of superstition has appeared in the name of Islam" (p. 16). He explained the source of this "fanatical faith":

> *The religion of the fanatics lies in traditions and*
> *superstition spread by word of mouth, but mainly in*
> *fabricated hadiths, which have been invented but*
> *presented as the words of our Prophet (pbuh).*   (p. 81)

Focusing on *Hadiths*

Hadiths are stories about the teachings and examples of Muhammad originally related by those who witnessed them. They were generally passed on orally for over 200 years after Muhammad died, and it was not until the 9th Century that they were collected in different written volumes. During that time period many *hadiths* had been fabricated for various reasons, and the Muslim scholars collecting the *hadiths* had to determine which *hadiths* were legitimate and which had been fabricated. Factors involved in making this determination included the reliability of individuals in the chain of narration, and praying over each *hadith*.

By around the end of the 9th Century there were six, multi-volume collections of what each of the six Muslim scholars considered to be legitimate *hadiths*; these collections are referred to as "The Sound Six," or "The Six Books of *Hadiths*." The most authoritative of these is considered to be *Sahih Al-Bukhari*; the second most authoritative is *Sahih Muslim*. For over a thousand years Muslim scholars, and Muslims seeking to understand their faith, have relied on these collections to help them understand the Koran and Islam. The English translations of these six collections total 39 volumes.

---

[318]   Stephen M. Kirby, "Fantasy Islam,"*Arutz Sheva 7*, January 24, 2016.

For Oktar, it was not enough that a *hadith* was included in "The Sound Six." He wrote on p. 81:

> ...*we need to look to the Qur'an to see whether a hadith really represents the words or actions of our Prophet (pbuh). If a hadith is in agreement with the Qur'an, then it is true. If a hadith that refers to the future has already come about, then it is also true. If, however, the hadith in question conflicts with the Qur'an, then there is no room for doubt; that hadith cannot be regarded as true.*

But as you read through Oktar's book, you find that for him to consider a *hadith* legitimate, it has to be not only in agreement with the Koran, but the subject matter of that *hadith* needs to be specifically mentioned in the Koran. Oktar wrote that, "none of the superstition we shall be examining here actually appears in the Qur'an" (p. 104), and

> *Our Prophet (pbuh) governed on the basis of the Qur'an and lived by the Qur'an alone. Our Prophet (pbuh) has absolutely no authority to make anything lawful or unlawful outside the Qur'an, and because of his prophethood and powerful fear of God, he would in any case never do such a thing.* (p. 102)

But there are things required of Muslims that are not specifically mentioned in the Koran. A prime example of this is what a Muslim is expected to do during each cycle of prayer. For that one must turn to the teachings and examples of Muhammad. Muhammad said,

> *offer your Salat (prayers) in the way you saw me offering my Salat (prayer).*[319]

And in terms of what is to be done during *Hajj*, Muslims are expected to following the teachings and examples of Muhammad (*Hajj Mabrur*),

---

[319]   *Sahih Al-Bukhari*, Vol. 8, Book 78, No. 6008, p. 35.

221

which is not in the Koran either. Adding in the procedures for ablution, again demonstrated by Muhammad and not in the Koran, we can see that there is a lot about Islam that is not in the Koran. That is why in the Koran Allah specifically commands Muslims to obey and follow the teachings and example of Muhammad:

> *He who obeys the Messenger (Muhammad), has indeed obeyed Allah...* (4:80)

> *Indeed in the Messenger of Allah (Muhammad) you have a good example to follow for him who hopes for (the Meeting with) Allah and the Last Day, and remembers Allah much.* (33:21)

> *...And whatsoever the Messenger (Muhammad) gives you, take it; and whatsoever he forbids you, abstain (from it). And fear Allah; verily, Allah is Severe in punishment.* (59:7)

The message of these three Koran verses, and of 59:7 in particular, was aptly summed up in the following authoritative *hadith* in which a lady, Umm Ya'qub, asked a Muslim man named 'Abdullah why he had cursed some women for doing certain things. 'Abdullah replied:

> *"Why should I not curse these whom Allah's Messenger has cursed and who are (cursed) in Allah's Book!" Umm Ya'qub said, "I have read the whole Qur'an, but I did not find in it what you say." He said, "Verily, if you have read it (i.e., the Qur'an), you have found it. Didn't you read: '...And whatsoever the Messenger (Muhammad) gives you take and whatsoever he forbids you, you abstain (from it)...[320]*

---

[320]   *Sahih Al-Bukhari*, Vol. 6, Book 65, No. 4886, pp. 340-341.

And Oktar's prophet Muhammad even said there was more to Islam than just the Koran:

> *Yahya related to me from Malik that he heard that the Messenger of Allah, may Allah bless him and grant him peace, said, "I have left two things with you. As long as you hold fast to them, you will not go astray. They are the Book of Allah and the sunna [sic] of His Prophet.*[321]

In spite of this, Oktar has decided that if the subject of a particular *hadith* is not specifically mentioned in the Koran, then that *hadith* is fabricated. This allows him in his book to dismiss the following authoritative *hadiths* regarding Jews:

1. *It was narrated from Sufyan: "Abdul-Malik bin 'Umair narrated to us; "Atiyyah Al-Qurazi narrated to me, he said: I was among the captives of Banu Quraizah, and they examined (us). Those whose pubes had started to grow were executed, and those whose pubes had not started to grow were not executed. I was among those whose pubes had not started to grow."*[322] (p. 365)

The above *hadith* is referring to the fact, reported in multiple Muslim sources, that after the Muslims defeated the Jewish Banu Quraizah tribe, Muhammad supervised the beheading of 600-900 captured Jewish males, combatants and non-combatants. The only prerequisite for execution was that they had reached puberty.

2. *Narrated Abu Musa: Allah's Messenger said: On the Day of Resurrection, my Ummah (nation) will be gathered into three*

---

[321]   *Al-Muwatta of Imam Malik ibn Anas*, 46.3. *Sunnah*: The Way of Muhammad, consisting of the examples, ways, and teachings of Muhammad that have become rules to be followed by Muslims. Sources for the *Sunnah* are *hadiths* and the *Sira*, the authoritative biography of Muhammad.

[322]   *Sunan Abu Dawud*, Vol. 5, No. 4404, p. 45. Oktar referred to this as *Hadith* No. 4390.

groups...Yet another sort will come bearing on their backs heaps
of sins like great mountains. Allah will ask the angels though He
knows best about them: Who are these people? They will reply:
They are humble slaves of yours. He will say: Unload the sins
from them and put the same over the Jews and Christians; then let
the humble slaves get into Paradise by virtue of My Mercy.[323]

        (p. 366)

3.   *It has been narrated by 'Umar b. Al-Khattab that he heard the*
     Messenger of Allah (may peace be upon him) saying: I will expel
     the Jews and Christians from the Arabian Peninsula and will not
     leave any but Muslims.[324]   (p. 370)

4.   *Abu Huraira reported that Allah's Messenger (may peace be upon*
     him) had said: Do not greet the Jews and the Christians before
     they greet you and when you meet any one of them on the roads
     force him to go to the narrowest part of it.[325]   (p. 373)

Even though the above *hadith* was reported in *Sahih Muslim*, Oktar has
decided it was fabricated. But it was also reported in two others of "The
Sound Six": *Sunan Abu Dawud*, Vol. 5, No. 5205, p. 458; and *Jami' At-
Tirmidhi*, where the Muslim scholar At-Tirmidhi wrote the following
explanation for this *hadith*:

> *"Do not precede the Jews and the Christians* [in
> greeting]*": Some of the people of knowledge said*
> *that it only means that it is disliked because it*
> *would be honoring them, and the Muslims were*

---

[323]   *110 Ahadith Qudsi: Sayings of the Prophet Having Allahs Statements*,
No. 8, titled *Superiority of the believers in the Oneness of Allah and the
punishment of Jews and Christians*, pp. 19-20.

[324]   *Sahih Muslim*, Vol. 5, No. 1767, p. 189.

[325]   *Sahih Muslim*, Vol. 6, No. 2167, p. 439. Oktar referred to this as *Hadith*
No. 5389.

only ordered to humiliate them. For this reason,
when one of them is met on the path, then the path
is not yielded for him, because doing so would
amount to honoring them.[326]

5. *Abu Huraira reported that Allah's Messenger (may peace be upon*
   him) had said: The last hour would not come unless the Muslims
   will fight against the Jews and the Muslims would kill them will
   [sic] the Jews would hide themselves behind a stone or a tree and
   a stone or a tree would say: Muslim, or the servant of Allah, there
   is a Jew behind me; come and kill him; but the tree Gharqad
   would not say, for it is the tree of the Jews.[327]   (p. 374)

In spite of Oktar's claim that the above *hadith* is fabricated, a variation of
it was also reported in *Sahih Al-Bukhari*:

> *Narrated Abu Hurairah: Allah's Messenger said, "The*
> *Hour will not be established until you fight against the*
> *Jews, and the stone behind which a Jew will be hiding will*
> *say, 'O Muslim! There is a Jew hiding behind me, so kill*
> *him.'"*[328]

Conclusion

According to Rebecca Abrahamson, Adnan Oktar's book *Bigotry, the
Dark Danger* appears to make a significant contribution to the idea of
"Building a Culture of Peace in the Middle East and the Global Arena."
This is because Oktar's book

---

[326]   *Jami' At-Tirmidhi*, Vol. 3, No. 1602, p. 365.

[327]   *Sahih Muslim*, Vol. 8, No. 2922, p. 349.

[328]   *Sahih Al-Bukhari*, Vol. 4, Book 56, No. 2926, p. 113.

*goes right to the sources in rebutting those who
manipulate the Qur'an and hadith, taking them out of
context to malign Jews.*

But in terms of the *hadiths*, we must remember that in his book Oktar is
the sole source for determining whether or not a *hadith* has been
fabricated. And as we have seen, his main criterion for making this
determination flies in the face of commands of Allah in the Koran,
statements of his prophet Mohammad, and general consensus among
Muslim scholars for over one thousand years. Nevertheless, there are
those who appear to view Oktar's book as a Muslim contribution to
building a culture of peace. Such is the ease, and the lure of playing
Fantasy Islam.

And how did Oktar address verses in the Koran that were supposedly
manipulated "to malign Jews"? A topic for another occasion.

30

Koran verses made for the Knesset[329]

Rebecca Abrahamson recently provided a brief report about the Knesset conference titled "Building a Culture of Peace in the Middle East and the Global Arena" (*OpEd: Putting UN resolutions to work*).[330] In this report she mentioned a book titled *Bigotry, the Dark Danger*, by Adnan Oktar, which had been presented at this conference, and which she believed would make a significant contribution to building this "Culture of Peace." Abrahamson wrote that this book

> *goes right to the sources in rebutting those who*
> *manipulate the Qur'an and hadith, taking them out of*
> *context to malign Jews.*

In my last article, titled *Fantasy Islam comes to the Knesset*,[331] I looked at how Oktar's book addressed *hadiths* supposedly fabricated to malign Jews; and we found that his main criterion for determining whether or not a fabrication had occurred flew in the face of commands of Allah in the Koran, of statements by his prophet Mohammad, and of a general consensus among Muslim scholars for over one thousand years. In this article, I look at how Oktar addressed Koran verses supposedly

---

[329]   This appeared in *Arutz Sheva 7* on March 3, 2016: http://www.israelnationalnews.com/Articles/Article.aspx/18497.

[330]   Rebecca Abrahamson, "Putting UN resolutions to work," *Arutz Sheva 7*, February 11, 2016.

[331]   Stephen M. Kirby, "Fantasy Islam comes to the Knesset," *Arutz Sheva 7*, February 17, 2016.

manipulated to malign Jews. As we shall see, there has been manipulation of Koran verses, but it has been done by Oktar.

Koran Verses Praise Jews and Christians?

Throughout his book Adnan Oktar repeatedly pointed out that the Koran praises Jews and Christians (the People of the Book). On pp. 380-381 Oktar presented Koran verses to support this claim: 2:62; 3:113-115; 3:199; 4:162; 5:69; 7:159; and 28:52-53. Let's look at these verses and ask two questions: Do these verses really praise Jews and Christians, and if so, why?

In a previous article I had written about Oktar,[332] I showed that the praise of Jews and Christians in 2:62 and 5:69 pertained only to good deeds done before the advent of Islam, and that after the advent of Islam the Jews and Christians were required to believe in Islam in order to be rewarded. In that same article I showed that, with regard to 7:159, those "who guide by the truth and act justly in accordance with it" are in fact those Jews who had converted to Islam. It is interesting to note that in *Bigotry, the Dark Danger*, Oktar referred to these converts mentioned in 7:159 as "righteous Jews" (p. 353).

In an earlier *Arutz Sheva 7* article,[333] I showed that in 3:113 the "community among the People of the Book who are upright" were in fact those Jews and Christians who had converted to Islam.

In his book Oktar listed 3:199 as praising the People of the Book. Here is that verse:

---

[332]   Stephen M. Kirby, "Fantasy Islam," *Arutz Sheva 7*, January 24, 2016.

[333]   Stephen M. Kirby, "Real Islam is not based on personal interpretations," *Arutz Sheva 7*, February 8, 2016.

*Among the people of the Book there are some who have
faith in God and in what has been sent down to you and
what was sent down to them, and who are humble before
God. They do not sell God's signs for a paltry price. Such
people will have their reward with their Lord. And God is
swift at reckoning.*

What do our authoritative Koran commentaries (*tafsirs*) have to say about
this verse? The *Tafsir Ibn Kathir* explains that this verse is about the Jews
and Christians who converted to Islam.[334] This same explanation is given
in the *Tafsir Al-Jalalayn*[335], *Tafsir Ahsanul-Bayan*[336], and the *Tafsir As-
Sa'di*[337].

Oktar also listed 4:162. Here is that verse:

*But those of them [the Jews] who are firmly rooted in
knowledge, and the believers, have faith in what has been
sent down to you and what was sent down before you:
those who perform their prayers and pay alms, and have
faith in God and the Last Day – We will pay such people
an immense wage.*

But as before, this verse is referring to Jews who converted to Islam.[338]

And here is 28:52-53:

---

[334]   *Tafsir Ibn Kathir*, Vol. 2, pp. 357-360.

[335]   *Tafsir Al-Jalalayn*, p. 172.

[336]   *Tafsir Ahsanul-Bayan*, Vol. 1, p. 413.

[337]   *Tafsir As-Sa'di*, Vol. 1, pp. 320-321.

[338]   *Tafsir Ibn Kathir*, Vol. 3, p. 46; *Tafsir Al-Jalalayn*, p. 228; *Tafsir
Ahsanul-Bayan*, Vol. 1, pp. 551-552; and *Tafsir As-Sa'di*, Vol. 1, p. 458.

Those We gave the Book before this have faith in it. When it is recited to them they say, "We have faith in it; it is the truth from our Lord. We were already Muslims before it came."

And once again, this verse refers to Jews and Christians who converted to Islam.[339]

The last of the verses that Oktar mentioned in this group as praising Jews in particular was 5:12:

God made a covenant with the tribe of Israel and We raised up twelve leaders from among them. God said, "I am with you. If you perform your prayers and pay alms, and have faith in My messengers and respect and support them, and make a generous loan to God, I will erase your wrong actions from you and admit you into Gardens with rivers flowing under them. Any of you who are irreligious after that have gone astray from the right way."

It appears that "God" has "made a covenant with the tribe of Israel" and will forgive them and admit them to Paradise. But that is only the first part of the story. The rest of the story is found in 5:13:

So, because of their breach of their covenant, We cursed them and made their hearts grow hard. They change the words from their (right) places and have abandoned a good part of the Message that was sent to them. And you will not cease to discover deceit in them, except a few of them. But forgive them and overlook (their misdeeds). Verily, Allah loves Al-Muhsinun (good doers).

---

[339]   *Tafsir Ibn Kathir*, Vol. 7, pp. 420-422; *Tafsir Al-Jalalayn*, p. 841; and *Tafsir Ahsanul-Bayan*, Vol. 4, pp. 205-206.

The rest of the story is that the tribe of Israel violated their covenant with "God" and tampered with the Torah. Consequently, "God" cursed them and made their hearts grow hard. And "God" proclaimed that, except for a few, deceit will always be found with the Jews. And who are those exceptional few? They are the Jews who converted to Islam.[340]

On p. 392 Oktar turned to 5:66 as an example of a Koran verse praising the Torah and the Bible:

> *If only they had implemented the Torah and the Gospel and what was sent down to them from their Lord, they would have been fed from above their heads and beneath their feet. Among them there is a moderate group but what most of them do is evil.*

Our *tafsirs* confirm that this is a criticism of Jews and Christians for not following the teachings in the Torah and the Bible. But what were those teachings that they ignored? Those teachings supposedly foretold the coming of Muhammad and the Koran. And, according to this verse, had the Jews and Christians followed those teachings, instead of altering their Books, those Christians and Jews would have believed in Muhammad and the Koran, and would have become Muslims. The fact that they did not become Muslims shows that they did not follow those supposed teachings of the Torah and the Bible. And the "moderate group" that doesn't do evil? They are the Jews and Christians who converted to Islam.[341]

So with these verses we find that the only way for Jews and Christians to earn praise in the Koran was by converting to Islam.

---

[340]   *Tafsir Ibn Kathir*, Vol. 3, pp. 126-130; *Tafsir Al-Jalalayn*, p. 241; *Tafsir Ahsanul-Bayan*, Vol. 1, pp. 580-582; and *Tafsir As-Sa'di*, Vol. 1, pp. 487-489.

[341]   *Tafsir Ibn Kathir*, Vol. 3, pp. 225-226; *Tafsir Al-Jalalayn*, p. 260; *Tafsir Ahsanul-Bayan*, Vol. 1, pp. 629-630; and *Tafsir As-Sa'di*, Vol. 1, p. 521.

Don't Take Jews and Christians as Friends

On p. 360 of *Bigotry, the Dark Danger* Oktar addresses 5:51 of the Koran:

> *O you who believe! Take not the Jews and the Christians*
> *as Auliya' (friends, protectors, helpers), they are but*
> *Auliya' of each other. And if any amongst you takes them*
> *as Auliya', then surely, he is one of them. Verily, Allah*
> *guides not those people who are the Zalimun (polytheists*
> *and wrongdoers and unjust).*

Oktar provides a unique explanation for this verse:

> *When we look at the original Arabic meaning we can*
> *easily see that the references to "friends" in this verse*
> *really means "rulers." What is forbidden for Muslims*
> *here is for them to come under the rule and management*
> *of Jews and Christians. (Prof. Dr. Bayraktar Bayraklı,*
> *Text of the Qur'an)*

So according to Oktar, this verse forbids Muslims from coming under the rule and management of Jews and Christians. But how has this verse been historically understood?

In a section titled *The Prohibition of Taking the Jews, Christians and Enemies of Islam as Friends*, Ibn Kathir explained this verse by pointing out that,

> *Allah forbids His believing servants from having Jews and*
> *Christians as friends, because they are the enemies of*
> *Islam and its people, may Allah curse them. Allah then*
> *states that they are friends of each other and He gives a*
> *warning threat to those who do this, And if any among you*
> *befriends them, then surely he is one of them.*[342]

---

[342]   *Tafsir Ibn Kathir*, Vol. 3, p. 204.

The *Tafsir Al-Jalalayn* explained that this verse meant Muslims were not to join Jews and Christians "in mutual friendship and love," or "in their unbelief."[343]

The *Tafsir as-Sa'di* explained this verse:

> *Allah, while describing to His believing servants the ignorant condition and unethical demeanor of the Jews and the Christians, orders them to not maintain alliance with them. This is because the Christians and the Jews aid one another and are united in their opposition of others. You should not make them your allies; rather, they are your enemies and they care not the least concerning your loss; they will leave no stone unturned to misguide you. Only a person who is like them will make alliance with them.*[344]

And here is how the *Tafsir Ahsanul-Bayan* explained 5:51:

> *The verse forbids Muslims to keep intimate relations with them and take them as protectors and helpers, because they are the enemies of Allah, the Muslims, and Islam. It should be noted that those who take them as protectors and helpers will be considered among them.*[345]

Whether *Auliya'* means friends, protectors, helpers, or rulers, Muslims are forbidden by Allah to have such relationships with Jews and Christians, because this verse is understood to mean that Allah has declared Jews and Christians to be the enemies of Muslims.

---

[343] *Tafsir Al-Jalalayn*, p. 256.

[344] *Tafsir as-Sa'di*, Vol. 1, p. 512.

[345] *Tafsir Ahsanul-Bayan*, Vol. 1, p. 616.

Harbingers of Muslim Relations with the People of the Book

Throughout his book Oktar repeatedly wrote about the peace, respect and love that "true Islam" would bring to relations between Muslims and the People of the Book. He quoted Koran verses and events from the life of Muḥammad that could provide the basis for that relationship. Let's look at a few of his examples.

On p. 381 Oktar displayed 5:82-85 of the Koran. For purposes of this article, we will focus on 5:82. Here is how Oktar started that verse out:

> ... *You will find the people most affectionate to those who have faith are those who say, "We are Christians."*

But here is how 5:82 really starts out:

> *Verily, you will find the strongest among men in enmity to the believers (Muslims) the Jews and those who are Al-Mushrikun, and you will find the nearest in love to the believers (Muslims) those who say: "We are Christians."*

If we are to believe Oktar then, the Koran is respecting and loving Jews by declaring that they are among the worst enemies of the Muslims.

On pp. 386-387 Oktar listed examples of Muhammad's relations with the People of the Book that should be considered as models for Muslims. Here are three of them:

> *One of the wives of our Prophet (pbuh) was Marya bint Sham'ûn (also known as Maryam al Qubtiyyah), a Coptic Christian from Egypt.*

But Marya was not even a wife of Muhammad. She was a Coptic Christian given as a slave to Muhammad. She bore Muhammad a son named Ibrahim, who died as a young child.

*Our mother Safiyya bint Huyayy, one of the wives of the
Prophet (pbuh), was the daughter of the chief of the
Jewish tribe Banu Nadir of Medina, Huyayy ibn Akhtab.*

Safiyya was among the captives taken when the Muslims conquered
Khaybar in May 628; her father was killed during the battle. Muhammad
bought her from another Muslim warrior for the price of seven slaves.
Muhammad married her after ordering the torture and beheading of her
husband, Kinanah b. al-Rabi'.

Oktar wrote that in 630 AD Muhammad "issued the following command
to envoys of the King of Himyar." Oktar then gave a partial quote from
the *Sira* (*The Life of Muhammad (Sirat Rasul Allah)*, written by Ibn Ishaq
and edited by Ibn Hisham); this partial quote stated that whoever wanted to
remain a Jew or a Christian should not be interfered with. But Oktar left
out some very important sentences that provided the real meaning of
Muhammad's command. Below is that quote and I have underlined the
portion left out by Oktar:

> *If a Jew or a Christian becomes a Muslim he is a believer
> with his rights and obligations. He who holds fast to his
> religion, Jew or Christian, is not to be turned from it. He
> must pay the poll tax* [Jizyah]*– for every adult, male or
> female, free or slave, one full dinar calculated on the
> valuation of Ma'afir or its equivalent in clothes. He who
> pays that to God's apostle has the guarantee of God and
> His apostle, and he who withholds it is the enemy of God
> and His apostle.*[346]

Oktar used these three examples, among others, to show how relations
should be between Muslims and the People of the Book. But in these
examples we find Christian and Jewish female slaves owned by
Muhammad, and Muhammad's command that Jews and Christians can

---

[346]   *The Life of Muhammad (Sirat Rasul Allah)*, p. 643.

hold fast to their faith only if they pay the *Jizyah*; otherwise they become the enemies of Allah and Muhammad.

Conclusion

There are two things in particular we learned in this article: 1) Koran verses that Oktar claimed indicated praise for Jews and Christians in general actually praised only Jews and Christians who had converted to Islam; and 2) Oktar's examples of ideal relations between Muslims and the People of the Book were examples of Jewish and Christian subservience to Muhammad and to Islam.

On p. 399 Oktar wrote:

> ...the world can never be without Islam. The peace and love for which the world longs can only come through Islam. We have the Qur'an, the true and immutable Book of Islam for that; the only thing needing to be done is to educate people with the Qur'an.

So we will end by educating people with the Koran. Here are two verses from Chapter 9 for consideration:

> Fight against those who believe not in Allah, nor in the Last Day, nor forbid that which has been forbidden by Allah and His Messenger (Muhammad), and those who acknowledge not the religion of truth (i.e. Islam) among the people of the Scripture (Jews and Christians), until they pay the Jizyah with willing submission, and feel themselves subdued.   (9:29)

9:29 is simply a codification of Muhammad's command to the King of Himyar.

> And the Jews say: 'Uzair (Ezra) is the son of Allah, and the Christians say: Messiah is the son of Allah. That is

236

their saying with their mouths, resembling the saying of those who disbelieved aforetime. Allah's curse be on them, how they are deluded away from the truth! (9:30)

9:30 states that Allah curses Jews and Christians.

The significance of these verses is twofold. They were among those "revealed" in late 630 AD and early 631 AD, and their message was directed toward all non-Muslims.[347] Chapter 9 of the Koran was the last chapter to be "revealed" to Muhammad, so the commands found in Chapter 9 were Allah's final, timeless instructions to Muslims on how to deal with non-Muslims.

The reality is that certain *hadiths* and Koran verses do malign Jews and Christians, except for when they are being manipulated for presentation at a Knesset conference.

---

[347]   *The Life of Muhammad (Sirat Rasul Allah)*, pp. 617-620; *Tafsir Ibn Kathir*, Vol. 4, pp. 370-376, and 404-410; *The History of al-Tabari: The Last Years of the Prophet*, pp. 77-79.

31

Muhammad's Islam or Adnan Oktar's?[348]

I appreciated Adnan Oktar responding to my first article about his book *Bigotry: The Dark Danger.*[349] As I had pointed out in that article, Mr. Oktar seemed to be playing Fantasy Islam:

> *Fantasy Islam: A game in which an audience of non-Muslims wish with all their hearts that Islam was a "Religion of Peace," and a Muslim strives to fulfill that wish by presenting a personal version of Islam that has little foundation in Islamic Doctrine.*

Unfortunately, in his response he continues to play that game and present his own version of Islam.

Differentiating Between Muslims and Islam

Mr. Oktar stated:

> *Stephen Kirby seems oddly intent on convincing himself and anyone he can find that Muslims cannot love Jews and that peace between these two faiths is impossible. It*

---

[348] This appeared in *Arutz Sheva 7* on March 14, 2016 with the title "Should peace efforts be based on Muhammad's Islam or Adnan Oktar's?": http://www.israelnationalnews.com/Articles/Article.aspx/18551.

[349] Kirby, "Fantasy Islam comes to the Knesset."

seems that clear facts and evidence don't have any effect on the way his mind works.

Mr. Oktar conflated Muslims and Jews with their respective religions. Muslims and Jews come in all degrees of devotion and adherence to their respective religions; some are very devout while others are only nominal in their faiths. Some are even Muslim/Jewish-in-name-only and have nothing to do with their faiths. So I would never claim, or try to convince anyone that Muslims cannot love Jews. It is up to the individual Muslim.

But Islam is the "faith" of Muslims. Clear facts and evidence found in the Koran show us that Allah says the Jews are among the worst enemies of the Muslims (5:82) and he forbids Muslims from being friends with Jews (5:51). Allah curses Jews (9:30), commands Muslims to fight them (9:29), and says that the Jews are among the worst of creatures (98:6).

Clear evidence and facts show us that individual Muslims are perfectly free to love Jews, but it is Islam that prohibits it.

"Fake" *Hadiths*

On p. 81 of his book *Bigotry: The Dark Danger*, Mr. Oktar stated that the

> *religion of the fanatics lies in traditions and superstition spread by word of mouth, but mainly in fabricated hadiths, which have been invented but presented as the words of our Prophet (pbuh).*

And in his book he listed many *hadiths* that he considered to be fabricated.

In his recent article,[350] he stated that my "one supposed weapon against Islam" consisted of *hadiths* which he claims are "fake." But the examples

---

[350]   Adnan Oktar, "Why try to show that Muslims hate Jews?" *Arutz Sheva 7*, March 3, 2016; accessible at:
http://www.israelnationalnews.com/Articles/Article.aspx/18498.

of "fake" hadiths from his book that I used in my article are actual *hadiths* largely found in sources that are listed among "the traditional Sunni Islamic Canon" by the Royal Islamic Strategic Studies Centre (RISSC)[351]. If Mr. Oktar really thinks these particular *hadiths* are "fake," then he needs to take the matter up with the folks at the Centre.

Only the Koran

In his article Mr. Oktar wrote:

> *In another attempt to make the hadiths look credible, he [Kirby] says that not everything is explained in the Qur'an. He is once again wrong as God says that the Qur'an is sufficient and Muslims will be responsible only for the Qur'an:*

He then lists three verses to support his claim that Muslims are responsible only to the Koran: 12:111, 16:89, and 7:52.

It is interesting that he chose to use the last half of 16:89:

> *We have revealed the Book (Qur'an) to you explaining clearly everything, and a guidance and mercy and good news for those who submit. (Qur'an, 16/89)*

The 14th Century *Tafsir Ibn Kathir*, listed among the RISSC's traditional Sunni Islamic Canon, explained this verse:

> *Al-Awza'i said: "And We have revealed the Book (the Qur'an) as an explanation of everything," meaning, with the Sunnah.[352]*

---

[351]   *The Muslim 500: The World's 500 Most Influential Muslims, 2016*, The Royal Islamic Strategic Studies Centre, Amman, Jordan, p. 24.

[352]   *Tafsir Ibn Kathir*, Vol. 5, p. 511.

The *Sunnah* is the Way of Muhammad, consisting of the examples, ways, and teachings of Muhammad that have become rules to be followed by Muslims. The authoritative *hadith* collections listed by RISSC are a major source for the *Sunnah*.

The 20th Century *Tafsir Ahsanul-Bayan* provided a similar explanation:

> *Moreover, it* [the Koran] *contains the Law, that is, what is permissible and what is forbidden, the injunctions and the interdictions, and all that which relates to man's temporal and spiritual life. All these details are to be found **in the Qur'an and hadeeths*** [my emphasis].[353]

So here we have two Koran commentaries stating that in order for "everything" to be understood, one must consult both the Koran and the *Sunnah*.

And as I noted in an earlier article,[354] Allah specifically commands Muslims to obey and follow the *Sunnah*:

> *He who obeys the Messenger (Muhammad), has indeed obeyed Allah...* (4:80)

> *Indeed in the Messenger of Allah (Muhammad) you have a good example to follow for him who hopes for (the Meeting with) Allah and the Last Day, and remembers Allah much.* (33:21)

> *...And whatsoever the Messenger (Muhammad) gives you, take it; and whatsoever he forbids you, abstain (from it). And fear Allah; verily, Allah is Severe in punishment.* (59:7)

---

[353] *Tafsir Ahsanul-Bayan*, Vol. 3, p. 236.

[354] Kirby, "Fantasy Islam Comes to the Knesset."

In that same article I also pointed out that even Oktar's prophet Muhammad said there was more to Islam than just the Koran:

> *Yahya related to me from Malik that he heard that the Messenger of Allah, may Allah bless him and grant him peace, said, "I have left two things with you. As long as you hold fast to them, you will not go astray. They are the Book of Allah and the sunna [sic] of His Prophet.*[355]

This *hadith* is found in *Al-Muwatta of Imam Malik ibn Anas*, also listed among "the traditional Sunni Islamic Canon" by RISSC.

Mr. Oktar wrote that I had claimed that

> *ablution, pilgrimage or prayer are not explained in the Qur'an, demonstrating a lack of knowledge* [on my part] *about the Holy Book of the Muslims.*

Mr. Oktar then listed verses of the Koran that explained and confirmed "those practices."

Here is what I had actually written:[356]

> *But there are things required of Muslims that are not specifically mentioned in the Koran. A prime example of this is what a Muslim is expected to do during each cycle of prayer. For that one must turn to the teachings and examples of Muhammad. Muhammad said,*
>
> > *offer your Salat (prayers) in the way you saw me offering my Salat (prayer).*[357]

---

[355] *Al-Muwatta of Imam Malik ibn Anas*, 46.3.

[356] Kirby, "Fantasy Islam Comes to the Knesset."

[357] *Sahih Al-Bukhari*, Vol. 8, Book 78, No. 6008, p. 35.

*And in terms of what is to be done during Hajj, Muslims
are expected to following [sic] the teachings and examples
of Muhammad (Hajj Mabrur), which is not in the Koran
either. Adding in the procedures for ablution, again
demonstrated by Muhammad and not in the Koran, we can
see that there is a lot about Islam that is not in the Koran.*

With regard to prayer, the Koran certainly does list verses dealing with
prayer. But as I had pointed out, there are details about the cycles of
prayer that are not in the Koran. For example, a *rak'ah* is the basic cycle
of prayer and includes standing, bowing, and prostration. The Koran does
not specify when or how often these are to take place during the prayer;
the *Sunnah* does.

With regard to the *Hajj*, there are numerous verses in the Koran about it.
But the Koran does not explain a number of things, including: 1) The
miqats, the places at which pilgrims assume a state of physical and
spiritual purification to begin the Hajj; 2) *Hajj* is required only once in a
lifetime; and 3) The garments worn by pilgrims. The *Sunnah* explains
these things and more. It was well summed up in an article about
Muhammad's Farewell Pilgrimage:

*The Muslims learned the rituals of the hajj from the
Prophet (peace be upon him) when he said: "Take your
rituals from me." His hajj was full of laws pertaining to
the Shari'ah, especially matters pertaining to the hajj, and
general advice and laws which were mentioned in the
Sermon of Arafat. For this reason, the scholars showed
great interest in the farewell pilgrimage and derived many
laws from it, dealing with the rituals of hajj and other
matters...*[358]

---

[358] Dr. Akram Diya Al Umari and Muhammad Zeeno, "Prophet's Farewell
Pilgrimage," *Perform Hajj, Muslim's Pilgrimage to Mecca*; accessible at:
http://www.performhajj.com/prophets_farewell_pilgrimage.php.

With regard to ablution, the Koran does mention it in 4:43 and 5:6. But the Koran does not go into details such as rinsing out one's mouth and how to clean one's nose; the *Sunnah* does.

So in spite of Mr. Oktar's claim, the Koran itself states that Muslims are expected to follow the *Sunnah*, which is found largely in the authoritative *hadith* collections from which I have quoted. And we have some examples of where the *Sunnah* is the only source for certain information.

Hadiths have "to be in compliance" with the Koran

Mr. Oktar has repeatedly stated that for a *hadith* to be genuine it has to be "in compliance" with the Koran. I have already pointed out that *hadiths* he considers "fake" have actually come from works considered to be a part of "the traditional Sunni Islamic Canon." Here I will show that the five *hadiths* I used in my previous article are in compliance with the message of the Koran; each *hadith* is followed by some Koran verses showing that compliance.[359]

This first *hadith* is referring to the fact, reported in multiple Muslim sources, that after the Muslims defeated the Jewish Banu Quraizah tribe, Muhammad supervised the beheading of 600-900 captured Jewish males, combatants and non-combatants. The only prerequisite for execution was that they had reached puberty.

1. *It was narrated from Sufyan: "Abdul-Malik bin 'Umair narrated to us; "Atiyyah Al-Qurazi narrated to me, he said: I was among the captives of Banu Quraizah, and they examined (us). Those whose pubes had started to grow were executed, and those whose*

---

359   Kirby, "Fantasy Islam Comes to the Knesset."

244

pubes had not started to grow were not executed. I was among those whose pubes had not started to grow. "[360]

4:101 – The disbelievers (non-Muslims) are ever to you open enemies.
5:82 – Jews are among the worst enemies of the Muslims.
8:57 – If you gain mastery over them, punish them severely in order to disperse those behind them.
8:67 – It is not for a Prophet to have prisoners until he has made a great slaughter in the land.
9:30 – Allah curses Jews.
9:123 – Fight disbelievers and let them find harshness in you. Also 9:14, 9:73, 48:29, and 66:9.
98:6 – Jews are among the worst of creatures and will abide in Hell.

2. *Narrated Abu Musa: Allah's Messenger said: On the Day of Resurrection, my Ummah (nation) will be gathered into three groups...Yet another sort will come bearing on their backs heaps of sins like great mountains. Allah will ask the angels though He knows best about them: Who are these people? They will reply: They are humble slaves of yours. He will say: Unload the sins from them and put the same over the Jews and Christians; then let the humble slaves get into Paradise by virtue of My Mercy.*[361]

3:85 – The only religion acceptable to Allah is Islam.
9:28 – Non-Muslims are impure.
9:30 – Allah curses Jews and Christians.

---

[360]   *Sunan Abu Dawud*, Vol. 5, No. 4404, p. 45. Oktar referred to this as *Hadith* No. 4390.

[361]   *110 Ahadith Qudsi: Sayings of the Prophet Having Allahs Statements*, No. 8, titled *Superiority of the believers in the Oneness of Allah and the punishment of Jews and Christians*, pp. 19-20.

9:33 and 48:28 – Islam is to be made superior over all
other religions.
98:6 – Jews and Christians are among the worst of
creatures and will abide in Hell.

3.   *It has been narrated by 'Umar b. Al-Khattab that he heard the*
     Messenger of Allah (may peace be upon him) saying: I will expel
     the Jews and Christians from the Arabian Peninsula and will not
     leave any but Muslims.[362]

     3:85 – The only religion acceptable to Allah is Islam.
     9:33 and 48:28 – Islam is to be made superior over all
     other religions.

4.   *Abu Huraira reported that Allah's Messenger (may peace be upon*
     him) had said: Do not greet the Jews and the Christians before
     they greet you and when you meet any one of them on the roads
     force him to go to the narrowest part of it.[363]

     5:51 – Allah forbids Muslims from being friends with
     Jews and Christians.
     5:82 – Jews are among the worst enemies of the
     Muslims.
     9:30 – Allah curses Jews and Christians.
     98:6 – Jews and Christians are among the worst of
     creatures and will abide in Hell.

5.   *Abu Huraira reported that Allah's Messenger (may peace be upon*
     him) had said: The last hour would not come unless the Muslims

---

[362]   *Sahih Muslim*, Vol. 5, No. 1767, p. 189.

[363]   *Sahih Muslim*, Vol. 6, No. 2167, p. 439. Oktar referred to this as *Hadith*
No. 5389.

will fight against the Jews and the Muslims would kill them will [sic] *the Jews would hide themselves behind a stone or a tree and a stone or a tree would say: Muslim, or the servant of Allah, there is a Jew behind me; come and kill him; but the tree Gharqad would not say, for it is the tree of the Jews.*[364]

4:101 – The disbelievers (non-Muslims) are ever to you open enemies.
5:82 – Jews are among the worst enemies of the Muslims.
8:57 – If you gain mastery over them, punish them severely in order to disperse those behind them.
8:67 – It is not for a Prophet to have prisoners until he has made a great slaughter in the land.
9:30 – Allah curses Jews.
9:123 – Fight disbelievers and let them find harshness in you. Also 9:14, 9:73, 48:29, and 66:9.
98:6 – Jews are among the worst of creatures and will abide in Hell.

So we can see that not only are these *hadiths* from authoritative sources, but they are also in compliance with the message of the Koran.

Conclusion

Mr. Oktar and I appear to have a common interest in there being peace between Jews and Muslims. Our major difference is that I think efforts to achieve such peace need to be based on the Islam of Muhammad; Mr. Oktar appears to think it can be based on his own version of Islam.

And until such time as Mr. Oktar gets his obvious differences over authenticity issues worked out with the folks at the Royal Islamic Strategic Studies Centre, I'll continue to rely on the Centre, not Mr. Oktar, for authoritative sources.

---

[364] *Sahih Muslim*, Vol. 8, No. 2922, p. 349.

32

Is Islam senselessly targeting Muslims?[365]

I appreciated reading Rebecca Abrahamson's recent article titled: *A Muslim Counter Narrative.*[366] She started her article off with the words, "In the shadow of the terror attacks increasingly aimed at Muslims," and then proceeded to list three recent attacks in which Muslims were killed by "suicide" bombers: the March 27th Easter Sunday attack in Lahore, Pakistan, targeting Christians; the March 26th attack on soccer fans in Iskandariya, Iraq; and the March 16th attack on a Nigerian mosque.

Abrahamson concluded this introductory section by writing:

> But aren't Christians *"People of the Book"*, and who says that soccer is haram (forbidden) and what objection was there to a mosque? No one is safe.

According to Abrahamson, there seems to be a senselessly violent version of Islam out there that is now consuming even Muslims.

But she notes that "some Muslims are speaking out," and the rest of her article focused on Javed Ahmad Ghamidi, "a Muslim theologian who, at

---

[365]   This appeared in *Arutz Sheva 7* on April 15, 2016:
http://www.israelnationalnews.com/Articles/Article.aspx/18717.

[366]   Rebecca Abrahamson, "A Muslim Counter Narrative," *Arutz Sheva 7*, April 1, 2016; accessible at:
http://www.israelnationalnews.com/Articles/Article.aspx/18649.

personal self-sacrifice, is spreading the word that there can be a peaceful Islam."

Is there really a senselessly violent version of Islam? Aren't People of the Book supposed to be protected under Islam? Is soccer now *haram* and any mosque subject to attack? Is no one really safe? Can the ideas of Javed Ahmad Ghamidi help address this seemingly senseless violence that is apparently now directed against other Muslims? To answer those questions, let's look at each of these attacks in the order listed by Abrahamson.

As a framework for examining these attacks, we will rely on an insightful article about ISIS (the Islamic State) by Raymond Ibrahim: *But ISIS Kills More Muslims than Non-Muslims!*[367] In this article, Ibrahim makes two observations that we will use as our framework:

> Observation No. 1: ISIS does not consider its victims to be Muslim. ISIS is a Sunni Muslim organization and views all non-Sunni Muslims (e.g. Shias) as false Muslims.

> Observation No. 2: If fellow Sunnis are accidently killed by ISIS, those Sunni victims are considered martyrs, destined to enter Islam's paradise.

The Easter Sunday Attack, Lahore, Pakistan

As the *BBC News* explained, on March 27th

> *The area around Gulshan-i-Iqbal park was more crowded than usual, as members of Lahore's minority Christian*

---

[367] Raymond Ibrahim, "But ISIS Kills More Muslims Than Non-Muslims," *FrontPage Mag*, December 18, 2015; accessible at: http://www.frontpagemag.com/fpm/261156/isis-kills-more-muslims-non-muslims-raymond-ibrahim.

community had gathered to celebrate Easter at a funfair there.[368]

Dur_ng the festivity, a lone "suicide" bomber joined the crowd and blew himself up, killing over 70 people and injuring hundreds.

The Taliban-related group Jamaat-ul-Ahrar (JA) took credit for sending the lone "suicide" bomber, Salahuddin Khorasani, in amongst the crowd. A spokesman for JA later stated:

> *"Members of the Christian community who were celebrating Easter today were our prime target...We didn't want to kill women and children. Our targets were male members of the Christian community."*[369]

It was also reported that a JA spokesman stated:

> *"We claim responsibility for the attack on Christians as they were celebrating Easter...It was part of our annual martyrdom attacks we have started this year."*[370]

So the intended targets of this attack were Christians, not Muslims.

---

[368]   "Lahore attack: Pakistan 'detains 200' after Easter blast," *BBC News*, March 29, 2016. Accessed at: http://www.bbc.com/news/world-asia-35916578.

[369]   "Lahore Bombing: Suicide Attack Kills 72 in Park on Easter Sunday," *NBC News*, March 28, 2016. Accessed at: http://www.nbcnews.com/news/world/lahore-bombing-suicide-attack-kills-72-park-easter-sunday-n546231.

[370]   "Carnage as 29 children bombed in Pakistan - death toll rises to 72," *Independent.ie*, March 29, 2016. Accessed at: http://www.independent.ie/world-news/asia-pacific/carnage-as-29-children-bombed-in-pakistan-death-toll-rises-to-72-34579847.html.

But Christians and Jews are the People of the Book mentioned in the Koran. Doesn't this automatically mean then that Muslims are supposed to respect and protect Christians? On the contrary, as I pointed out in a previous article:

> *Here is some of what the Koran has to say about the People of the Book: Many of the People of the Book have enmity and hatred toward Muslims (2:109); the People of the Book mix truth with falsehood and conceal the truth (3:71); the People of the Book know that Islam is the true faith but they reject it anyway and hinder those seeking to follow Islam (3:98-99); Allah commands the People of the Book to believe in Islam and Muhammad, or he will "efface faces and turn them hindwards" (4:47); Muslims are commanded to fight the People of the Book until those People pay the jizyah, "with willing submission and feel themselves subdued" (9:29); and, if the People of the Book don't believe in Islam, then they are among the worst of creatures and they will abide in the Fires of Hell (98:6).[371]*

So we find no indication that the designation "People of the Book" guarantees any respect from, or protection by Muslims.

In addition, in the Koran Allah states that he curses Christians (9:30), that the only religion acceptable to him is Islam (3:85), and Islam is to be superior over all other religions (9:33 and 48:28).

But what about Javed Ahmad Ghamidi and his "peaceful" approach to Islam? Abrahamson pointed out that Ghamidi condemns "suicide" bombings and the intentional killing of civilians. But what Abrahamson did not point out was that Ghamidi stated that there were certain areas of

---

[371]   Stephen M. Kirby, "Jewish-Muslim coexistence through the Koran? Wishful thinking," *Artuz Sheva 7*, January 13, 2016.

the Middle East where the People of the Book should not be allowed. In a 2013 interview Ghamidi stated:

> *You must keep two things in mind, i.e. Allah has preserved two places, Canaan in Palestine and the land of the Arabs for the preaching of His Messengers since the time of Abraham (sws). Worshipping idols in these places is completely forbidden. No other religion except Islam can be propagated in these places. It is just the same as declaring the whole area as a mosque. It means that no one has the right to enter this territory.*[372]

Modern day Israel, along with Christian holy sites such as Bethlehem, are located in "Canaan in Palestine," so according to Ghamidi, Jews and Christians have no right to be there. We can presume that JA feels the same way about Christians in Pakistan.

But perhaps Ghamidi has his own, more inclusive version of Islam that could include Jews and Christians? No. Ghamidi wrote that Islam, "the only true religion in God's sight," consisted of the following five things:

> *1. Bearing witness that there is no god besides Allah and Muhammad (sws) is His Messenger*
> *2. Offering the prayer*
> *3. Paying zakah*
> *4. Keeping the fasts of Ramadan*
> *5. Offering the hajj of the Baytullah* [the Ka'bah in Mecca][373]

---

[372]   *An Interview of Javed Ahmad Ghamidi with the Indian Media*, September 27, 2013. Accessed at: http://www.almawridindia.org/article-categories/islam/11-an-interview-of-javed-ahmad-ghamidi-with-the-indian-media.

[373]   Javed Ahmad Ghamidi, *Islam: A Comprehensive Introduction, An English Rendering of Mizan by Shehzad Saleem*, (Lahore, Pakistan: Al-Mawrid, A Foundation for Islamic Research and Education, 2009), p. 75. Accessed at: http://muqweb.yolasite.com/resources/Islam%20A%20comprehensive%20introduction%20-%20Javaid%20Ahmed%20Ghamidi.pdf.

You won't find many practicing Jews and Christians believing that Muhammad is the final prophet whose example must be followed and who spoke for Allah, or who feel it necessary to make *hajj* to Mecca at least once in their lifetime. So even though Ghamidi might condemn the Easter Day attack, he nevertheless stated that there were areas of the Middle East in which Jews and Christians should be prohibited. In this he is simply following the command of his prophet Muhammad:

> *It has been narrated by 'Umar b. Al-Khattab that he heard the Messenger of Allah (may peace be upon him) saying: I will expel the Jews and Christians from the Arabian Peninsula and will not leave any but Muslims.*[374]

So we can see that the Easter Day attack was not senseless violence, but rather supported by Islamic Doctrine. With regard to the Muslims killed during this attack, their death was incidental and they can be considered as martyrs (Observation No. 2). In terms of a solution coming from Ghamidi, he believes that Jews and Christians should not be in Canaan or the "land of the Arabs," while JA apparently believes that Christians should not be in Pakistan. In this respect, Ghamidi and JA differ only in terms of location.

Attack in an Iraqi Soccer Stadium

On March 26th a "suicide" bomber blew himself up inside a soccer stadium in Iskandariya, Iraq, killing at least 30 and wounding many more in the crowd, apparently all Muslim. Abrahamson asked if soccer was now *haram* (forbidden)?

In reality, this act of terrorism had nothing to do with the game of soccer; it was just that the playing of the game provided a venue in which a terrorist attack could take place.

---

[374]   *Sahih Muslim*, Vol. 5, No. 1767, p. 189.

ISIS claimed credit for this attack. By why would ISIS be intentionally killing fellow Muslims? The answer is, because ISIS did not consider them to be fellow Muslims. As an *Al Jazeera* news report pointed out: "Iskandariya is a Shia town."[375] And as we saw with Observation No. 1, ISIS does not consider Shias to be fellow Muslims. Rather ISIS literature is rife with statements that Shias are apostates and/or infidels and should be killed. And such an idea is supported by commands of Allah in the Koran which order Muslims to fight and kill infidels (e.g. 9:5 and 9:123).

Add in the fact that Iraqi military forces had been recapturing territory from ISIS and it was thus important for ISIS to strike back, and we have two adequate explanations for why ISIS attacked soccer fans in Iskandariya.

But what does Ghamidi have to say about Shias? His views were described in a 2012 article titled "Javed Ahmed Ghamidi's views about Shias and Sufi Sunnis":

> [Ghamidi] *does not treat Shias or Sufis as infidels. He treats them as deviant sects of Islam who can be treated as Kafir (infidel) only when a State (Pakistan or Saudi Arabia) formally apostates them (just as the State of Pakistan did in the case of Ahmadis). What is unmistakable in his ideology is the fact that he remains inspired by a Salafist-Deobandi ideology which is borderline Nasibi. Nasibi is a term used for those people who despise the Ahl-e-Bait (family) and Aal (progeny) of the Prophet Muhammad...Ghamidi has a subtle anti-Shia and anti-Sufi tone to his talks.* [376]

---

[375]   "Suicide bomber kills dozens at football stadium in Iraq," Al Jazeera, March 26, 2016. Accessed at: http://www.aljazeera.com/news/2016/03/suicide-attack-kills-dozens-football-stadium-iraq-160325181900028.html.

[376]   "Javed Ahmed Ghamidi's views about Shias and Sufi Sunnis," *World Shia Forum*, September 27, 2012. Accessed at: https://worldshiaforum.wordpress.com/2012/09/27/javed-ahmed-ghamidis-views-about-shias-and-sufi-sunnis-by-abdullah-rahim/.

Iskandariya is a Shia town, and Ghamidi considers Shias to be a "deviant sect" which can be declared as apostates by a "State." ISIS, the Islamic State, has declared the new Caliphate, an Islamic state, so would Ghamidi join ISIS in declaring Shias to be infidels and apostates?

So this was not a senseless attack on Muslims because soccer was being played. Rather it was an attack on apostates/infidels (Observation No. 1) supported by Islamic Doctrine; any Sunnis accidentally killed would be considered martyrs (Observation No. 2). In terms of a solution from Ghamidi, there appears to be nothing of significance: he believes the Shias belong to a deviant sect of Islam that can be declared an apostasy.

Attack on a Nigerian mosque

On March 16th, during early morning prayers, two female "suicide" bombers blew themselves up at a mosque in Umarari, Nigeria. One bomber went inside before blowing herself up, while the second bomber waited outside for people rushing out after the first bomb blast. At least 24 Muslims were killed and 18 wounded. It was the second attack on this same mosque in five months; in October 2015 two "suicide" bombers struck that mosque, killing six people. With regard to this March incident, Abrahamson had asked, "What objection was there to a mosque."

In March 2015 the terrorist group Boko Haram had pledged its allegiance to ISIS. Boko Haram was later linked to the October 2015 attack,[377] and to the March 16th attack.[378] What was Boko Haram's "objection" to the mosque?

---

[377]   "Maiduguri hit again as army warns on Boko Haram," *The Guardian*, October 16, 2015. Accessed at: http://guardian.ng/news/maiduguri-hit-again-as-army-warns-on-boko-haram/.

[378]   Statement by Nigerian Army Chief of Staff Tukur Buratai on March 17, 2016 - http://nigeria.watsupafrica.com/news/national-security-umarari-mulai-attacks-linked-to-boko-haram/. Also see "Curbing Boko Haram's Attacks on Soft Targets," *This Day*, March 19, 2016. Accessed at:

There are two interesting facts that explain Boko Haram's "objection." The first involves the immediate condemnation of the March attack by the Iranian government:

> *Iranian Foreign Ministry Spokesman Hossein Jaberi Ansari on Thursday strongly denounced Wednesday's terrorist attack on a mosque in Nigeria's Maiduguri, which killed more than 20 innocent people.*[379]

This Iranian condemnation is a good indication that the Umarari mosque was Shia. Boko Haram's specific attitude toward Shias is found in a November 2015 statement from Boko Haram after it had attacked a Shia procession:

> *By the permission of Allah, these attacks of ours against Shi'a polytheists will continue until we cleanse the earth of their filth.*[380]

As with the attack in the soccer stadium, this was an attack on apostates/infidels (Observation No. 1), and it was supported by Islamic Doctrine.

There was also a strategic element to this attack on the mosque: it was reported to be a command center in the Nigerian army's battle against Boko Haram:

---

http://www.thisdaylive.com/index.php/2016/03/19/curbing-boko-harams-attacks-on-soft-targets/.

[379]   "Iran Condemns Deadly Terrorist Attack in Nigerian Mosque," *AhlulBayt (a.s.) News Agency*, March 17, 2016. Accessed at: http://en.abna24.com/service/iran/archive/2016/03/17/741667/story.html.

[380]   "'We would cleanse the earth of their Filth,' Boko Haram claims responsibility for attack on Shia Muslims," *Olisa.tv*, November 29, 2015. Accessed at: http://www.olisa.tv/2015/11/29/we-would-cleanse-the-earth-of-their-filth-boko-haram-claims-responsibility-for-attack-on-shia-muslims/.

According to the coordinator of the local civilian self-defense Vigilante Group, Abba Aji, the mosque in Umarari served as a military command center in the Nigerian army's war against the Boko Haram terrorist group.[381]

So we can see that this attack on the mosque was not a senseless act of violence, and, as indicated in the previous section, Ghamidi would contribute nothing of significance in terms of addressing it.

The "Support" Ghamidi has in the Muslim World

According to Abrahamson, one could get an idea of the kind of support Ghamidi has in the Muslim world by looking at his 2015 Australian tour, which was "a great success." In that tour he spoke in seven venues "with audiences ranging from one hundred to four hundred participants."

In the first place, since Muslims make up only about 2.2% of the Australian population of about 23,783,500, it is hard to consider Australia as part of the Muslim world. Let's then look at the attendance figures. To keep the math simple, let's assume there were 400 participants at each event. This means there were 2,800 total participants. The Muslim population of Australia is about 523,237. So assuming that each of these participants was Muslim, that means that only .005 percent of Australia's Muslims attended. In reality, we know the overall attendance figures were not even this high, and from reading about Ghamidi's presentations, we find that the audiences were not even exclusively Muslims.

Since Abrahamson wrote that this Australian tour was an indication of the support Ghamidi has in the Muslim world, it would appear that Ghamidi has little support in the Muslim world.

---

[381]   "Iran denounces deadly bombings at local mosque in Nigeria," *PressTV*, March 17, 2016. Accessed at: http://presstv.com/Detail/2016/03/17/456286/Iran-Jaberi-Ansari-Nigeria-Boko-Haram-Maiduguri/.

Conclusion

Rebecca Abrahamson started her recent article with examples of what she considered to be a senselessly violent version of Islam that was now consuming even Muslims. The antidote for this was to be found in Muslims like Javed Ahmad Ghamidi who advocate for a "peaceful Islam."

However, we have seen that this supposed senseless violence is actually supported by Islamic Doctrine. And we have seen that there are aspects of Ghamidi's "peaceful Islam" that, although perhaps not directly supporting this violence, do not necessarily rule it out completely. On the other hand, this view of a "peaceful Islam" might be irrelevant because, based on Abrahamson's standard for judging support, Ghamidi appears to have little support for his opinions even in the Muslim world.

But This isn't Islam!

*How can you use the term radical without
first identifying the norm? Normative Islam
is based on the unabrogated commands of
Allah in the Koran, and the examples and
teachings of Muhammad (the Sunnah). If the
Koran and the Sunnah support a Muslim's
actions, that Muslim is not radical, he is
devout.*

Stephen M. Kirby

Charlie Hebdo was Attacked by Islam, Not Islamism[382]

Charlie Hebdo is a French satirical magazine with a strong record of satirizing many religious figures, and for years Islam's prophet Muhammad has been included among the recipients of the satirical cartoons. For the folks working there, death threats from people claiming to be Muslims were not unusual, and a firebomb destroyed its old offices in November 2011, the day after the magazine had announced that it had selected Muhammad as its editor-in-chief.

On January 7, 2015 two gunmen, brothers Said and Cherif Kouachi, went into the magazine's offices and gunned down eleven people, including a police officer. The gunmen then killed another police officer outside the offices. It seemed that within minutes of the massacre, pundits and members of the media went into overdrive trying to keep Islam out of the picture; we were assured that the "religion of peace" had nothing to do with this. This was in spite of the facts that the two gunmen were Muslims yelling *Allahu Akbar*, and were heard shouting in French, "We have killed Charlie Hebdo. We have avenged the Prophet Mohammad."[383]

---

[382] This appeared in *FrontPage Mag* on January 14, 2015 (the footnotes were left out of the published article): http://www.frontpagemag.com/2015/dr-stephen-m-kirby/charlie-hebdo-was-attacked-by-islam-not-islamism.

[383] "Police hunt three Frenchmen after 12 killed in Paris attack," *Reuters*, January 7, 2015, accessed at: http://www.reuters.com/article/2015/01/07/us-france-shooting-idUSKBN0KG0Y120150107.

The disturbing reality is that Islam had everything to do with it. Satirizing and drawing pictures of Muhammad goes against 33:57 of the Koran, which states that those who "annoy" Muhammad would be cursed by Allah:

> *Verily, those who annoy Allah and His Messenger, Allah has cursed them in this world and in the Hereafter, and has prepared for them a humiliating torment.*

The authoritative Muslim scholar Ibn Kathir explained this verse:

> *Here, Allah warns and threatens those who annoy Him by going against His commands and doing that which He has forbidden, and who persist in doing so, and those who annoy His Messenger by accusing him of having faults or shortcomings - Allah forbid. 'Ikrimah said that the Ayah [verse]: Verily, those who annoy Allah and His Messenger, <u>was revealed concerning those who make pictures or images</u> [my emphasis]...The Ayah appears to be general in meaning and to apply to all those who annoy him [Muhammad] in any way, because whoever annoys him annoys Allah, just as whoever obeys him obeys Allah.*[384]

So the satirical cartoons were not only "annoying" Muhammad, they were also "annoying" Allah. This was sheer blasphemy! What were the two brothers to do?

Said and Cherif apparently looked to the teachings and examples of Muhammad. Muhammad had personally ordered the killing of four specific individuals whose only crime was that they had criticized him and/or Islam ('Asma' Bint Marwan, Abu 'Afak, Ka'b bin Al-Ashraf, and Abu Rafi'). And Muhammad had even given retroactive approval to the separate killings by Muslims of three individuals who had criticized him and/or Islam. That the brothers had learned from Muhammad's example

---

[384]   *Tafsir Ibn Kathir*, Vol. 8, pp. 42-43.

was shown in Cherif's January 9th statement to Igor Sahiri, a journalist for France's BFMTV:

> *We defend the prophet. If someone offends the prophet then there is no problem, we can kill him.*[385]

So the Muslim brothers were simply following the commands of Allah in the Koran, and the teachings and examples of Muhammad when they committed the massacre.

Some have claimed that Islam had nothing to do with the massacre because the gunmen also killed two Muslims. The first was Moustapha Ourrad, a copy editor for the magazine. However, Ourrad's involvement in satirizing and creating pictures of Muhammad meant that he was going against the commands of Allah and the teachings of Muhammad; Ourrad had therefore left Islam and was an apostate. Islamic doctrine commands that apostates be killed. And this is even assuming the gunmen knew Ourrad was a Muslim, for which there is no evidence. The second Muslim killed by the gunmen was a police officer named Ahmed Merabet. He was executed outside the office building. However, there is no evidence that he had identified himself as a Muslim to the gunmen. So the claim that the gunmen knowingly shot two Muslims is baseless.

The Islamic teachings about being killed as a martyr and being rewarded in paradise for doing so were influential on the two gunmen. On January 9th, after they were surrounded by French security forces, the brothers reportedly said they wanted "to die as martyrs."[386] In fact, a few years earlier, in December 2007, Cherif had stated in a court deposition that

---

[385]   Emmanuelle Saliba, "Paris Killer Cherif Kouachi Gave Interview to TV Channel Before He Died," *NBC News*, January 9, 2015; accessed at: http://www.nbcnews.com/storyline/paris-magazine-attack/paris-killer-cherif-kouachi-gave-interview-tv-channel-he-died-n283206.

[386]   Lori Hinnant and Elaine Ganley, "French security forces kill gunmen, end terror rampage," *Associated Press*, January 9, 2015; accessed at: https://www.adn.com/nation-world/article/french-police-official-charlie-hebdo-suspects-dead-hostage-freed/2015/01/09/.

"the wise leaders in Islam told him and his friends that if they die as martyrs in jihad they would go to heaven" and "that martyrs would be greeted by more than 60 virgins in a big palace in heaven."[387]

These "wise leaders in Islam" had it right. Islamic doctrine teaches that the only guaranteed way for a Muslim to get into paradise is to die as a martyr fighting in in the cause of Allah (*jihad*); this is based on 9:111 of the Koran:

Verily, Allah has purchased of the believers their lives and their properties for (the price) that theirs shall be Paradise. They fight in Allah's Cause, so they kill (others) and are killed...

But Cherif potentially shortchanged himself in the number of virgins, because Muhammad had promised 72 virgins to the Muslim who died fighting in Allah's Cause:

Al-Miqdam bin Ma'diykarib narrated that the Messenger of Allah said: "There are six things with Allah for the martyr: He is forgiven with the first flow of blood (he suffers), he is shown his place in Paradise, he is protected from punishment in the grave, secured from the greatest terror, the crown of dignity is placed upon his head - and its gems are better than the world and what is in it - he is married to seventy-two wives among Al-Huril-'Ayn of Paradise, and he may intercede for seventy of his close relatives."[388]

---

[387]   Scott Bronstein, "Terror suspect Cherif Kouachi: 'I was ready to go and die in battle', " *CNN Investigations*, January 9, 2015; accessed at: http://www.cnn.com/2015/01/09/europe/cherif-kouachi-court-documents/.

[388]   *Jami' At-Tirmidhi*, Vol. 3, No. 1663, p. 410. The *Al-Huril-'Ayn* (*Houris, Hur*) are the very fair female virgins of Paradise.

The massacre at the *Charlie Hebdo* offices was not committed by *Islamists* following a belief system called *Islamism*; the massacre was carried out by two Muslim brothers who were following the teachings and examples of Muhammad, and the commands of Allah found in the Koran. Islam killed *Charlie Hebdo* and avenged Muhammad.

34

Islam and Burning People Alive[389]

In December 2014, Lt. Muath al-Kaseasbeh, a 26 year old Jordanian Air Force pilot, was flying his F-16 in Syria in support of a U.S.-led coalition raid on the Islamic State (IS). During this mission his plane crashed near Raqqa, and he was captured by IS fighters. On February 3, 2015, Lt. al-Kaseasbeh was burned alive by IS. An IS-released video of the burning was titled *Healing the Believers Chests*, an apparent reference to 9:14 of the Koran.

Outrage was immediate, along with the claims that Islam not only prohibited Muslims from killing fellow Muslims, but also prohibited the burning of captives. As seems to have become usual in matters involving violence done in the name of Islam, there is more to this story.

Lt. al-Kaseasbeh was a Muslim fighting for the King of Jordan, in coalition with non-Muslim governments, against the Islamic Caliphate of IS. This combination would allow IS to declare their captured pilot a

---

[389]   This appeared in *FrontPage Mag* on February 5, 2015: http://www.frontpagemag.com/2015/dr-stephen-m-kirby/islam-and-burning-people-alive/.

One week after this article was published an article titled "The Burning of the Murtadd Pilot" appeared in Issue 7 of *Dabiq*, the Islamic State's magazine. This article explained the Islamic Doctrinal basis for the burning alive of "the Jordanian crusader pilot." A copy of Issue 7 of *Dabiq* can be accessed at: http://jihadology.net/2015/02/12/al-%E1%B8%A5ayat-media-center-presents-a-new-issue-of-the-islamic-states-magazine-dabiq-7/.

Hypocrite (*Munafiq*), someone whose external appearance was that of a Muslim, but who, by fighting for a secular government in coalition with non-Muslims against the new Caliphate, was actually showing his inner disbelief in Islam.

Here are some of the things the Koran says about Hypocrites: Allah has cursed them and prepared the fires of Hell for them (e.g., 4:145, 9:68, 9:73, and 48:6); and Allah commanded Muhammad to "strive hard against" and "be harsh" to the Hypocrites (9:73).

So IS was not killing a fellow Muslim; they were killing a Hypocrite who was already cursed by Allah and condemned to Hell, and against whom Allah had commanded Muslims to be harsh.

But doesn't Islam prohibit burning people alive? To answer this question, we need to first look at Muhammad, who spoke for Allah (4:80) and is considered the standard of perfect conduct for Muslims (33:21). Muhammad had no qualms about burning people.

In December 627 Muhammad led an attack against the Al-Mustalaq tribe. Because that tribe fought back, Muhammad ordered their fortifications to be set on fire, even though the Muslims knew there were women and children inside.

Around June 628, when Kinanah bin al-Rabi of the Jewish Bani al-Nadir tribe would not reveal where his conquered tribe's treasures were hidden, Muhammad ordered one of his soldiers, "Torture him until you extract what he has," so a fire was built on Kinanah's chest until Kinanah nearly died.

In October 630 there was some resistance among the Muslims (Hypocrites) toward a military expedition Muhammad was planning against the Byzantines at Tabuk. Muhammad heard that these Hypocrites were gathered in a particular house, so he ordered that the house be burned down on top of them. The Hypocrites managed to escape from the flames.

In June 632, after Muhammad's death, an attack on Ubna that he had earlier ordered took place. The leader of the Muslim force said,

> ... *the Messenger of God commanded me and this was his last command to me: ...to raid them, without inviting them* [to Islam], *and to destroy and burn.*[390]

And Muhammad even considered burning down Muslims' houses around them to compel their attendance at congregational prayers:

> *It was narrated that Abu Hurairah said: "The Messenger of Allah said: 'I was thinking of commanding that the call to prayer be given, then I would tell a man to lead the people in prayer, then I would go out with some other men carrying bundles of wood, and go to people who do not attend the prayer, and burn their houses down around them.'"*[391]

So Muhammad's statements and actions show that during his lifetime it was permissible for Muslims to burn people alive. This was continued after Muhammad's death.

After Muhammad died there were many Arab tribes that left Islam. This resulted in the Wars of Apostasy (*Riddah* Wars) under Abu Bakr, the first of the four "Rightly Guided" Caliphs (so named because they are believed to have held the most firmly to the teachings of Muhammad). The commander of each army that Abu Bakr sent out had a letter to be read to the tribe before it was attacked. The letter explained that if the tribe did not return to Islam, the army commander

---

[390]   Muhammad b. 'Umar al-Waqidi, *The Life of Muhammad: Al-Waqidi's Kitab al-Maghazi*, trans. Rizwi Faizer, Amal Ismail, and AbdulKader Tayob, ed. Rizwi Faizer (London and New York: Routledge, 2013), p. 549.

[391]   *Sunan Ibn Majah*, Vol. 1, No. 791, pp. 513-514.

*will not spare any one of them he can gain mastery over,
[but may] burn them with fire, slaughter them by any
means...*[392]

Abu Bakr even set the example when a captive who had fought against the Muslims was brought to him. Abu Bakr

*ordered a fire to be kindled with much firewood in the
prayer yard (musalla) of Medina and threw him, with
arms and legs bound, into it.*[393]

The commander of one of the Muslim armies was Khalid bin al-Walid. Here is a command that Abu Bakr gave to Khalid:

...kill them by every means, by fire or whatever else.[394]

And Abu Bakr gave Khalid a specific command when he sent him against the Bani Hanifah in Al-Yamamah:

*Kill their wounded, seek out those of them who flee, put
the captives among them to the sword and strike terror
among them by killing and burn them by fire. And I warn
you against contradicting my orders. Peace (be upon
you).*[395]

---

[392] Abu Ja'far Muhammad b. Jarir al-Tabari, *The History of al-Tabari: The Conquest of Arabia*, Vol. X, trans. and annotated Fred M. Donner (Albany, New York: State University of New York Press, 1993), p. 57.

[393] Ibid., p. 80.

[394] Ibid., p. 100.

[395] Muhammad ibn 'Abdul Wahhab at-Tamimi, *Abridged Biography of Prophet Muhammad*, ed. 'Abdur-Rahman bin Nasir Al-Barrak, 'Abdul 'Azeez bin 'Abdullah Ar-Rajihi, and Muhammad Al-'Ali Al-Barrak (Riyadh, Kingdom of Saudi Arabia: Darussalam, 2003), p. 345.

Khalid took Abu Bakr's admonitions to heart and was known for burning many captives alive. Abu Bakr's response was,

I shall not sheathe a sword that Allah had unsheathed against the 'unbelievers.[396]

The burning continued, as Ali, the fourth "Rightly Guided" Caliph (656-661), ordered people to be burned alive for being hypocrites.

So we can see that the burning-to-death of the captured pilot can be fully supported by Islamic doctrine, and it even falls under Allah's admonition found in 8:57 of the Koran:

So if you gain the mastery over them in war, punish them severely in order to disperse those who are behind them, so that they may learn a lesson.

---

[396]   Ahmad ibn Yahya ibn Jabir al-Baladhuri, *The Origins of the Islamic State, Being a Translation from the Arabic, Accompanied with Annotations, Geographic and Historic Notes of the Kitab Fituh Al-Buldan of Al-Imam Abu-L Abbas Ahmad Ibn-Jabir Al-Baladhuri*, trans. Philip Khuri Hitti (1916; rpt. Lexington, Kentucky: Ulan Press, 2014), p. 148.